C000227095

Narrowing the Attainment Gap

OTHER TITLES FROM BLOOMSBURY EDUCATION

Leading from the Edge: A School Leader's Guide to Recognising and Overcoming Stress by James Hilton

Creating Tomorrow's Schools Today by Richard Gerver

The A-Z of School Improvement by Tim Brighouse and David Woods

8 Qualities of Successful School Leaders by Jeremy Sutcliffe

The Reality of School Leadership: Coping with the Challenges, Reaping the Rewards by Richard Parker

Achievement for All: Raising Aspirations, Access and Achievement by Sonia Blandford and Catherine Knowles

Narrowing the Attainment Gap

A handbook for schools

Daniel Sobel

BLOOMSBURY
LONDON • OXFORD • NEW YORK • NEW DELHI • SYDNEY

Bloomsbury Education
An imprint of Bloomsbury Publishing Plc

50 Bedford Square
London
WC1B 3DP
UK

1385 Broadway
New York
NY 10018
USA

www.bloomsbury.com

BLOOMSBURY and the Diana logo are trademarks of Bloomsbury Publishing Plc

First published 2018

Copyright © Daniel Sobel, 2018

Daniel Sobel has asserted his right under the Copyright, Designs and Patents Act, 1988, to be identified as Author of this work.

Every reasonable effort has been made to trace copyright holders of material reproduced in this book, but if any have been inadvertently overlooked the publishers would be glad to hear from them.

All rights reserved.

No part of this publication may be reproduced or transmitted in any form or by any means, electronic or mechanical, including photocopying, recording, or any information storage or retrieval system, without prior permission in writing from the publishers.

No responsibility for loss caused to any individual or organisation acting on or refraining from action as a result of the material in this publication can be accepted by Bloomsbury or the author.

A catalogue record for this book is available from the British Library.

ISBN: PB: 978-1-4729-4637-9
ePub: 978-1-4729-4635-5
ePDF: 978-1-4729-4636-2

2 4 6 8 10 9 7 5 3 1

Typeset by Newgen Knowledge Works Pvt. Ltd., Chennai, India
Printed and bound in the UK by CPI Group (UK) Ltd, Croydon CR0 4YY

This book is produced using paper that is made from wood grown in managed, sustainable forests. It is natural, renewable and recyclable. The logging and manufacturing processes conform to the environmental regulations of the country of origin.

To find out more about our authors and books visit www.bloomsbury.com. Here you will find extracts, author interviews, details of forthcoming events and the option to sign up for our newsletters.

Contents

Acknowledgements

This book is a labour of my genuine, deeply felt belief in the power of education, and my hope that I may be able to contribute to its evolution. My experience of school was a largely unhappy one, during which I was left to flounder and experience failure. The aim of my work is to help future students to encounter something vastly more positive, within a system where the attainment gap will one day disappear.

I would first like to thank those people who encouraged me to build a career in education and later to pen a book. The encouragement of David and Renée Mirwis inspired me to complete my MA in Education Psychology through their unconditional belief in me. My three closest friends – Danny Shine, Danny Newman and Chananel Rosen – have shown me endless support and love, and the mentorship and guidance of Richard Street has been invaluable. I am grateful to the team at Bloomsbury, particularly my editors Hannah Marston and Miriam Davey, for their expertise in navigating me along the path of becoming an author.

Secondly, I want to express my thanks to the team at Inclusion Expert for providing me with the time and space to write; my gratitude in particular goes to Sharon Finn, Renate Pruessman, Jude Farshi and Jill O'Connell. The editorial skills of Mossy Wittenberg are matchless, and have been integral to our team from the first day that our company was launched; Mossy is one of the 'gifted and talented' students with whom I have been fortunate to work, and is one of several whose careers I follow with considerable pride.

Finally, I thank and dedicate this book to my family: my wonderful wife, Deborah, who is both my most ardent supporter and fiercest critic, who speaks and demands truth, and choreographs the stage upon which we act; and my two young boys, Boaz and Toby, for inspiring me to achieve great things and to seek to make the world a fairer place in which they will grow up.

Introduction

The purpose and structure of the book

The attainment gap is one of the most insidious social injustices in the developed world, responsible for concreting the growing inequality of our societies. Schools everywhere are obliged to tackle it, if not officially by their national or local government, then morally. In England, from 2010 to the present, the Department for Education has expressed this obligation in policy form in the **pupil premium**[1] grant. The grant allocates funding to schools on the basis of the number of their pupils deemed to come from disadvantaged backgrounds, and asks schools to demonstrate how the money is helping to close the gap.

But seven years on from the introduction of this policy, and despite the reams of academic research conducted all around the world on the attainment gap, there is still a limited amount of practical guidance out there for school leaders on how to actually respond.

This book aims to guide schools through the practical steps they can take to narrow their gap in a cost-effective and sustainable way. It will, I hope, offer insights to anyone working on attainment or broader inclusion issues; but its primary intended audience is senior school leaders and leaders of groups of schools, such as heads of education at local authorities in the UK, superintendents in the US, CEOs of **multi-academy trusts** and leaders of teaching school alliances. It will be equally useful for governors, who often know very little about the causes and impact of the gap, and policy mandarins removed from real practice. I had one final specific role in mind when writing: the pupil premium reviewer or consultant. In England, a school can be asked to undergo a pupil premium review by the local authority or national inspectorate, and I have seen far too many of these done with little sophistication and minimal impact.

Whilst the book is rooted in my experience of working in the education sector in the UK, the problems I describe are sadly far from UK-specific. My solutions and resources are, with a little adaptation, applicable everywhere.

The book is divided into three sections. Chapters 1, 2 and 3 explore the attainment gap issue – its causes, manifestations and the obstacles schools most often encounter when they try to tackle it. Chapter 1 focuses on academic research; Chapters 2 and 3 draw on a combination of research and my and my team's combined experience. Chapters 4 to 7 are more consistently hands-on, bringing together guidance and resources for responding to

[1]Terms in bold are defined in the glossary at the end of the book.

the attainment gap in a given setting. Chapter 8, finally, contains instructions for carrying out an attainment review and the book ends with a summary and some concluding thoughts.

About me

I came out of my schooling with no A levels and read my first book aged 18. Gradually, from that point on, I fell in love with reading and study in general, and managed to get myself onto a master's course in education psychology at the Institute of Education, University of London. I went on to take four postgraduate courses in psychology and education and eventually ran out of money in the middle of doctoral training, at which point I decided to teach full time.

I fairly quickly became a **SENCO** (special educational needs coordinator) and was dismayed by how much of the job was pointless paperwork and meetings that took up time whilst students continued to struggle. An 'I'll do it my way' attitude kicked in and I started reinventing the paperwork and the meetings to better support my students. Over time, I was asked to support other schools, to write about my work for the education press, and eventually to consult for the Department for Education, the European Union and governments abroad.

When this became too much to combine with being a senior leader in a school, I left and, somewhat hesitantly, became a full-time consultant. I formed Inclusion Expert, a small firm – a one-man band at first – focused on providing targeted training, consultancy and resources for schools across all areas of inclusion. Over the last few years, we have grown rapidly to encompass a team of highly experienced expert practitioners, who together have supported about one thousand schools in the UK and abroad.

We carry out attainment gap and special needs reviews; we train school leaders and teachers; and we lead workshops in person and online. But for us, the real change comes only in the implementation of our recommendations and systems by the school itself. It is the goal of my team to work with each school to make it an Inclusion Expert in its own right. If eventually our company becomes superfluous to the needs of most schools, I'll be thrilled.

I have drawn on these macro themes throughout the book. A lot of other educational consultants and leaders home in on the traditional curriculum-based functions and their mechanics. In the special needs arena, this translates into emphasising knowledge of autism, dyslexia and other **special educational needs**, and in the classroom, this discussion ends up focusing on assessment, progress indicators and so on.

The Inclusion Expert approach is predicated on three key assumptions:

1. **The key barriers to inclusion are time, money and attitudes** – not the SENCO's knowledge of the various special educational needs he or she may encounter. We believe that differentiation and personalised learning should ultimately save a teacher

time and save the school scarce funds. Once teachers and senior leaders witness this, hearts and minds are won over, the whole system becomes efficient and wide reaching, and effective inclusion can begin. Our method is to reduce a school's paperwork by an average of three quarters; this sounds astonishing, but what is left is all that is needed.

2. **Inclusion and the attainment gap are mostly to do with soft data.** Hard data is useful for absolute measurement; that's it. The route to success is through soft data: it tells us the real motivations and barriers for a student; it highlights the quality of engagement of the student in any lesson or intervention; and it guides the teacher to directly meet the specific needs of the student. A focus on soft data often entails a mental shift for school leaders who may be rooted in hard data, but through this shift a school can begin to best improve its inclusion approach.

3. **Two fundamental challenges underlie all inclusion issues**. Having visited hundreds of schools, I know that there are only ever two main themes that crop up time and again: classroom teaching and whole-school systems. Outstanding teaching can halve a school's attainment gap. Inclusion Expert's approach to whole-school systems is to focus on how to assess need, strategically deploy staff and resources, and evaluate and demonstrate impact. When these two themes are addressed together, and through planning that is bespoke to each school's unique setting and context, the results are transformational.

In writing this book, I have drawn on several Inclusion Expert resources, including the Pupil Premium Handbook (which we launched at the House of Commons, and which guides schools in spending their funding) and the research behind my regular articles for *Headteacher Update*, *SecEd* and *The Guardian*. By far the most important resources, however, are the inspirational teachers, leaders and students with whom I've had, and hope to long continue to have, the fantastic privilege of working.

PART 1

Issues

1 What is the attainment gap?

Many thousands of pages of research have been produced over the decades, by academics all over the world, to explain what the attainment gap is and the contexts in which it most commonly occurs. The question I try to answer in this chapter is, of all that information, what is most practically useful for a school leader? I have put together a summary of key themes, referenced thought-provoking research and indicated suggested key takeaway points throughout. You could share this chapter with your senior leadership team and governors to introduce them to the key themes and issues behind this challenging global issue, and to contextualise the approach you end up taking in your school.

Two students, two paths

Imagine two students, identical twins, who are separated at birth and adopted into different homes. The first child, Jane, is adopted into an average middle-class family. She grows up in financial and personal stability. Her adopted parents are married and stay so; she lives in a fairly wealthy area and within the catchment area of an **Ofsted** 'outstanding' state school. She does well at this school and goes on to a good university.

The second child, Samantha, is adopted into a slightly lower-income family that rapidly runs into difficulties. Her adoptive father loses his job and her new parents divorce when she is still young. Samantha stays with her adoptive mother, but in straitened circumstances. They do not live inside the catchment area of any good schools. Matters are made worse when her mother's drinking becomes problematic and a series of violent boyfriends appear on the scene, who are abusive to both mother and daughter. Samantha begins to use drugs at a relatively young age and comes to the attention of social services. Eventually her situation becomes so bad that she is taken into care.

Throughout all this, Samantha has continued to perform well at school. Like her long-lost sister Jane, she's bright. As her situation deteriorates, however, her attendance record becomes increasingly spotty, and eventually she performs poorly in her **GCSEs**, largely because she simply hasn't spent enough time in school. Her path in life, going forward, is difficult.

Key in this hypothetical is that the girls are identical twins, sharing their heredity and pre-natal environment. Any differences between them, therefore, represent the true causal effects of differences in the worlds that they grow up in: their families, housing, schools, lifestyle, peers, teachers and so on.

There should be no doubt that the differences in educational achievement that exist between individuals and groups do not entirely result from underlying differences in natural gifts. From studying twins like Jane and Samantha, researchers have found that the environment continues to exert strong effects on educational achievement at GCSE and beyond (Shakeshaft et al., 2013).

Key takeaway

There are large differences in individual outcomes, even between individuals starting from the same point. These differences are closely tied to family socio-economic status and quality of schooling.

The hypothetical scenario is realistic in noting that despite the difficult circumstances of her childhood, Samantha is bright and does well at school when she attends. This reflects research showing that general cognitive capacity is one of the most developmentally robust traits. The same twin-based research that shows strong environmental effects on educational achievement shows very small environmental effects on general cognitive capacity (Rijsdijk et al., 2002).

Education, however, is not one long test of general cognitive ability. Doing well in school requires not just the right sort of intelligence (which is narrowly defined in our current education system), but also the right sort of personality. Good students tend to be conscientious and open to new intellectual experiences (Noftle and Robins, 2007). It also really helps to have not only good teachers but good peers too: hard-working fellow students who serve as friendly competition and a source of inspiration (and who, on a very basic level, don't disrupt the lessons; Hoxby, 2000). In all these areas, disadvantaged students, on average, tend to lose out. Consider these statistics:

- In 2014, just 34 per cent of pupils eligible for **free school meals** (FSM) achieved the benchmark five A*–C GCSEs (including English and maths), compared to 61 per cent of all other pupils (Department for Education, 2015).
- Just 12 per cent of children looked after by local authorities in England (**'looked after children'**) achieved this benchmark (Department for Education, 2014a).

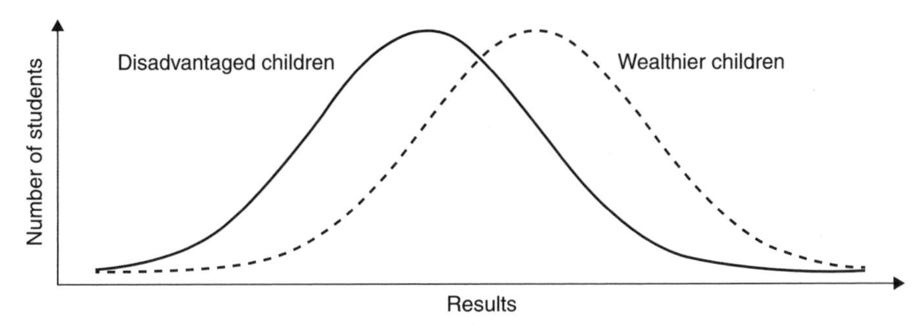

Figure 1.1: Disadvantaged versus wealthier children: average results

However, the word 'average' here is crucial and needs careful unpacking. Many children from poor families thrive in education and in the world beyond the classroom. British psychologist Sir Cyril Burt once made the (uncontroversial) observation that the working class is the nation's largest pool of talent: it is by far the largest class, and while income and educational success are correlated, the correlation is not very tight.

Nevertheless, taken as a group, wealthier children do better at school. Figure 1.1, though it is not plotted with actual data, is a useful way of visualising what this means in practice. It shows two overlapping normal distributions, or 'bell curves', which is the typical distribution of test scores on most standardised tests. The first bell curve graphs the results of disadvantaged children; the second of wealthier children.

Clearly the distributions overlap quite substantially. Many children from the first (less wealthy) group outperform the average of the second (wealthier) group. Both groups have children at the very top and bottom of the distribution of achievement. Nevertheless, there are more children from the disadvantaged group at the bottom of the distribution, and fewer children from this group at the top. The result is an average difference, as shown on the graph by the separation of the two peaks of the curves. It needs to be understood that when we talk about the attainment gap and its causes, we are talking about average differences, not individual students. As will be seen later, in the discussion of ethnicity, some subgroups of students from low-income families substantially outperform national achievement averages.

Key takeaway

Averages are not the same as individuals. Just because children on FSM do worse as a cohort does not mean we should necessarily expect any individual FSM child to perform worse than the average. This has wide-reaching significance for educational policy and whole-school planning. No FSM student can be assumed to be the same. General characteristics are useful but can't be translated directly into day-to-day planning about real students.

To return to Jane and Samantha, we have a broad general idea of why Samantha runs into difficulties: her challenging family situation. Of course, the reasons will be different for every student; when we talk about causes of the attainment gap, it is again important to stress that we do so in general terms. Specific things may or may not apply to individuals; just because a student has a difficult home life, for example, they won't necessarily underperform at school.

Schools also have very different intakes, depending on the local context. They may have an unusually high number of looked after children, or have a large number of students from a low-performing ethnic minority, or be situated in a town where multi-generational cycles of unemployment are common and aspirations are low. This book places a great emphasis on understanding the attainment gap in the context of a school embedded in a community, and coming up with community-focused solutions that make sense in that context.

Nonetheless, it is still useful to zoom out and take a high-level view for a moment. Big data and large-scale quantitative research can only ever tell us so much, and it's critical to interpret the findings of national-level data in local contexts. But the data contains plenty of useful lessons nonetheless, and can serve as a valuable check on our intuitions and a helpful point of reference.

Illusions of wealth

One of the most startling findings of the academic literature is that in developed nations, the attainment gap between the more and less well-off is *not* primarily caused by differences in family wealth and income. This is especially true in nations with extensive welfare states (the US is something of an exception to the rule).

This may sound surprising, but to put it in terms of our identical twins: if we were to give Samantha an extra five thousand pounds a year, would her problems be solved? There is no particular reason to think so. Her chaotic home life would still remain chaotic, and her emotional state would still prevent her from doing as well as she should. In fact, the money might make things worse: as many children of the ultra wealthy might tell us, sometimes all money does is enable people to indulge destructive impulses more fully. This logic is not wholly convincing, I know, but it's worth exploring the research more fully.

It is widely agreed that the randomised controlled trial (RCT) offers the optimal method for establishing causal inference in nearly all situations. The ideal trial for our research question would probably involve a large number of disadvantaged children, to whose parents we randomly allocate various sums of money. Some of these sums would be extremely large. We would then track the children for many years, studying their progress in school and in life. Sadly, such a trial would be both unethical and impossibly expensive. We must instead rely on natural experiments that approximate the conditions of this hypothetical trial.

Lottery winners are randomly picked out from the population of lottery players. Lottery wins allocate varying sums of money, some of which are very large, to adults, plenty of whom have young children at the time of the win. The outcomes of these children can be compared to the outcomes of the children of unsuccessful lottery players. Given a sufficiently large sample of lottery winners, therefore, a natural experiment based around a lottery approximates the ideal RCT very closely.

The Swedish state collects extensive data on its citizens and holds this data in a central repository, available to researchers. Very recently, one team of researchers used this registry data to ask the following question: 'What are the causal effects of sudden wealth on lottery winners and their families?' As part of this broad question, they investigated the effects of lottery wins on the educational outcomes of the children of the winners. They found that even very large increases in wealth had no effects on the educational outcomes of the children (nor, incidentally, did they find any significant effects of wealth on child health outcomes; Cesarini et al., 2016).

Key takeaway

In developed nations, raw differences in income do not seem to be key factors driving the attainment gap. The gap is more likely explained by other background differences between families. This turns the broad assumptions about FSM on their heads. It also suggests that school leaders could think with more nuance about a more sophisticated reason for the gap in their community other than the simple lack of income.

This study is not an outlier and generally fits quite well with the broader literature. When researchers make a genuine attempt to get beyond correlations and uncover causal relationships, similar results are found. It may seem strange that family wealth and child educational attainment should be more or less uncorrelated, but the data, on the whole, suggests that the true causal effect of the former variable (wealth) on the latter (attainment) is either very small or zero.

But outside of RCTs or natural experiments that approximate them closely, it is generally very hard to know if X causes Y, or if a hidden third variable, Z, is the true cause of Y – especially if Z is closely correlated with X. The potential pitfalls are sketched out in Figure 1.2.

The ability of the child's parents (which the child inherits) has a strong effect on the child's educational achievement and a modest effect on the family's wealth. But while family wealth and child educational achievement are correlated (and indeed in this model the parents' education has more of an effect on family wealth than their base ability does), there is no true causal effect of family wealth on child educational achievement.

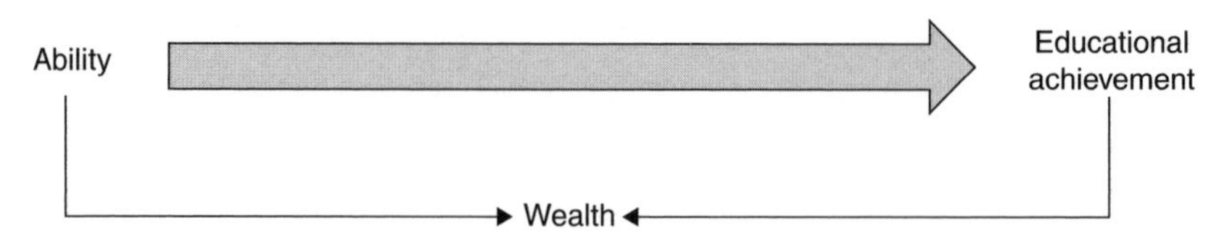

Figure 1.2: Pitfalls of mapping wealth against achievement

Therefore, a great deal of research energy has gone into the possible true causes of the observed correlations between family wealth and child educational performance. The social science literature abounds with hypotheses and data relating to these mysterious third factors. Suggested third factors include well-known variables such as early-life language exposure, and others that are rather less well known (for example, exposure to traces of lead). Researchers have also looked at the causal role of schools, both teachers and pupils, and other possible factors such as genetics, differences in parental involvement, shadow schooling (tutoring), excessive television viewing, and even knowledge loss over the long summer holidays. I will review some of this literature, focusing in particular on the research that has looked at the effects of schools.

Schools

To start with, the effect of schools on the attainment gap needs breaking down. Schools are composed of teachers and pupils, and all schools have better and worse teachers and more and less challenging groups of students. As such, the 'school effect' can be partly framed as the average of what goes on in its individual classrooms. Only *partly* though, because there are important whole-school variables that are not simply classroom effects – the most obvious being the school's overall level of funding.

Another unexpected variable is the long summer holiday. Knowledge decay over the holidays affects all students, but the effect on low-income students is considerably larger. Even worse, the negative effects are cumulative across the years. This problem does not seem to be easily fixed simply by moving to a 'year-round education' model of shorter but more frequent holidays. The real problem appears to be differential access during holidays to books, museums, and other intellectually and culturally stimulating material (Alexander et al., 2007). Funding and holiday time are not the only important school-level variables. Whole-school policies matter as well, most notably the degree of setting and streaming. It remains an awkward fact that disadvantaged pupils have a tendency to drift into the bottom sets and stay there (Hallam and Parsons, 2013). In such sets, they are generally assigned the least experienced or lowest-quality teachers in the school. Teachers in **comprehensive schools** in the UK tend to be 'anti-grammar', viewing **grammar schools** (publicly funded secondary schools to which pupils are admitted on the basis of ability) as perpetuating a form of educational apartheid. There's plenty of evidence to support them in this view. It is regrettable, therefore, that they do not view excessive setting policies in the same way, because the effects are much the same.

In almost any secondary school, some degree of setting and streaming is inevitable (even though it is contrary to my beliefs). The problems start when such policies become extremely inflexible. They contribute towards pupil mindsets that are generally disenchanted and limited in aspiration. The endemic 'target grades' culture in many schools only makes the problem worse. Despite a fairly robust academic literature outlining the problems and lack of genuine countervailing benefits, extremely rigid setting policies persist in many schools.

Key takeaway

Rigorous setting and streaming policies tend to hurt disadvantaged pupils and should be avoided – especially at younger ages when attitudes to learning and educational aspiration are more likely to be embedded.

A set of little-appreciated technical issues further compounds the problems of setting. In many secondary schools, setting is based on the results of tests taken fairly early on in the child's school career. These tests are invariably administered in classroom environments that are often far from ideal testing conditions. Even reliable standardised cognitive ability tests (e.g. the **CATs** in the UK) may be unreliable in practice if testing conditions are suboptimal. As a result, the rate of children put into the wrong set is higher than teachers think. To complicate things further, cognitive ability does not develop in a wholly linear fashion. Just as children go through physical growth spurts, they also go through mental growth spurts, especially before adolescence (Jensen, 1980). Testing a child at the peak of a mental spurt, or just before a spurt begins, can give a misleading impression of where the child is likely to end up in the distribution of ability. This should be a compelling reason, at the very least, not to assign children to sets based purely on a single test or set of tests administered at one time. Multiple tests spaced out over a few months are recommended, and even then it is important to set flexibly.

Up a level of detail, after the school-level variables affecting the attainment gap, there are the issues within any single classroom. Schools can be remarkably siloed environments. More often than not when I'm called as an expert witness in exclusion tribunals, the student in question has a few classes in which he or she learns and behaves well. But best practice and insights into what works for individual students are not shared between school staff, so even outstanding teaching doesn't narrow the overall gap.

On the flipside, students tend to bring the assumptions and bad behaviours from classrooms in which they have been mismanaged to the rest of their lessons. This amplifies the problem for good teachers.

Clearly, good teachers are not sufficient to help close the attainment gap if other important classroom-level factors are missing. Schools need not just to hire the right teachers but to work across the board. Pushes to improve behaviour should be school wide. Persistently disruptive students can be spread out, if necessary. And schools can consider putting in place additional pastoral support to help students with personal barriers to accessing the curriculum.

Key takeaway

Surrounding a disadvantaged child exclusively with peers who are themselves disadvantaged will often have negative effects – some people refer to these as 'sink-sets'. Peers matter in the classroom, not just teachers.

It's also important not to consider teacher quality as a fixed entity. Some teachers may have a style that interacts better with certain types of children than with others; one teacher might achieve unusually good results with difficult low-achieving classes while others may excel in particular at, for example, teaching **gifted and talented** cohorts. Getting the right teachers matched to the right classes is vital, and it is not necessarily true that the 'best' teachers do best with children on the wrong side of the attainment gap. There is, for instance, growing evidence that students from ethnic backgrounds that are traditionally low achieving do slightly better when matched with a teacher of the same ethnic background (Dee, 2004).

It's important to remember in the course of this discussion that a large part of the attainment gap is in place before children ever arrive at school. And although the attainment gap grows over time throughout schooling, this does not necessarily mean that schools themselves are doing something wrong. As the material to be learned becomes harder and harder, pre-existing gaps are drawn ever more sharply into focus.

This may sound counter-intuitive but it makes sense. Many of you reading this will have excelled at one small set of subjects while at school and done quite well in others. Perhaps you did very well in English and quite well in maths. At GCSE, even though you had to work harder in maths, you still did well, perhaps even as well as your more mathematically gifted classmates. At A level, however, the material to be learned would have been much harder and the effects of natural mathematical talent would have been brought to the fore. At this stage, you would have struggled (and perhaps, sensibly, decided not to take A level maths but concentrate efforts on subjects that complemented your talents in English).

A similar process may be at work when the attainment gap grows over time. Good teaching in the early years and throughout primary school may contribute to a smaller gap, and it's easier for the positive, beneficial, equalising effects of many schools to actually have an impact, because the material being taught really is something that almost every child can learn. At higher levels, however, it is simply not the case that every child can master calculus or write a persuasive analysis of *Hamlet*. Those pre-existing factors that hold students back start to rear their heads again, and schools naturally struggle to cope.

Though earlier I outlined how schools can unwittingly contribute to magnifying the attainment gap, it's important also to understand the ways in which the school environment, especially the primary school environment, is naturally egalitarian. Children from families where linguistic deprivation is the norm find at school an atmosphere where they are exposed to good-quality English spoken by native English speakers. All else being equal, such children often catch up with their peers throughout **Key Stages** 1 and 2. Many schools have good behaviour policies that are well enforced – far better behaviour policies than exist in the family home of many youngsters from disadvantaged backgrounds. The FSM programme generally, though not universally, ensures that children who wouldn't get a decent meal at home can have one at school. As discussed above, the research on knowledge decay over the holidays indicates that far greater gaps grow when students spend a lot of time *outside* of school. While schools do contribute to the growth of the gap, if schools did not exist, the gap would be far, far larger. This does not mean that schools can't do a better job when it comes to preventing the growth of the gap – they can and must – but their present contribution deserves to be evaluated fairly.

Key takeaway

It is important to keep in mind the things schools get right. To a considerable degree, they compensate for pre-existing inequalities, and are especially effective at doing so at younger ages.

Differences in teacher quality are also fairly small and simply do not contribute to a large part of the variance in student achievement. In a recent massive experiment in Ecuador, students were assigned randomly to teachers upon entering kindergarten, and given an extraordinarily excellent battery of cognitive and behavioural tests at the beginning and end of each year (Araujo et al., 2016). This version of an RCT presents a rare opportunity to obtain clean estimates of the magnitude of teacher effects, which were, as ever, fairly modest. For every standard deviation increase in teacher quality, student achievement rose by about a tenth of a standard deviation. Similar estimates are reported in the US (Chamberlain, 2013).

In summary, both structural- and classroom-level features of the educational system contribute to the growth of the attainment gap during the years of schooling, though not all of this growth is caused by the system. Schools can and do contribute to the attainment gap, but in the absence of schools, the gap would be far larger. Rigorous, inflexible setting and streaming policies are likely to be major culprits, as are persistent problems with the most experienced and highest-quality teachers being assigned to the students that need their input the least.

Attainment gap cohorts

Ethnicity

An especially salient factor in discussions of the attainment gap is ethnicity. As the UK has become increasingly multicultural, it has become clearer and clearer that attainment gaps are not just a function of family socio-economic status. Ethnicity matters. Some ethnic groups consistently outperform others, and in many cases these relationships persist even after rigorous statistical controls for other factors. Educational and labour market outcomes are correlated, and so children from certain ethnic groups are much more likely to be eligible for the pupil premium.

Economic disadvantage, however, may interact with ethnicity in complicated ways. There is, for example, evidence that some ethnic groups conventionally viewed as disadvantaged may be more likely to use private tutors and other forms of shadow schooling, especially in cultures with strong educational traditions (Kirby, 2016). Many immigrant parents may have arrived in this country with very little, but have high ability and a strong work ethic, which they transmit to their children. This book has a strong focus on the importance of local context. In many schools I have worked with, the ethnic backgrounds of their intake were an enormously important part of that context.

Measuring ethnic differences in achievement is a complicated business in the UK. Ethnic gaps seem to be suspiciously sensitive to the type of test used, and can close very rapidly at times when scores across the board are also rising quickly. Grade inflation, it seems, artificially shrinks the gaps in the short term.

Nonetheless, some facts are clear. Chinese and Indian pupils substantially outperform white British pupils at GCSE, even when pupils from these ethnic groups on FSM are compared to the white British average. This is a clear example of how the predictive power of ethnicity can at times trump that of economic disadvantage. Bangladeshi pupils now also tend to do somewhat better than white British children, but Pakistani and black Caribbean children do somewhat worse (Strand, 2015). Black African children perform very similarly to white British children, but there is vast variation: Igbo children perform very well, but African children who speak Portuguese have a GCSE pass rate below half the national average (Mcinerney, 2016).

It is often reported that the achievement of 'white working class' children is especially poor. This needs some unpacking. The group who self-identify as 'working class' is much bigger than the group eligible for FSM. It is true that white British pupils on FSM do worse at GCSE than children on FSM from most other ethnic groups. It is not clear how this statistic should be interpreted. There are obvious reasons why FSM eligibility might be a particularly poor indicator of educational disadvantage for the children of immigrants. Amena might be a Syrian refugee, but if her parents are a doctor and a lawyer, it's hardly surprising if she excels in school.

Key takeaway

Ethnicity is relevant to the attainment gap, and it is important for school leaders to understand the contexts of different ethnic groups in their school and local area. But differences in attainment between ethnic groups are unpredictable and hard to measure.

Finally, I'll focus in on ethnic differences in **Programme for International Student Assessment (PISA)** results. The PISA dataset has a number of advantages. It is administered by an external body and hence not subject to the grade inflation that makes trends in GCSE data so hard to interpret. It is low stakes for pupils and schools alike and hence is not systematically cheated, gamed or tutored for. The major downside is that only a random selection of the nation's pupils sits the test, and consequently sample sizes for some ethnic groups are too small for useful analysis. Nonetheless, it is notable that in PISA, white pupils in England do between 25 and 40 points better than their black and Asian schoolmates (equivalent to roughly an additional year of schooling). This white–Asian difference is very strikingly different to that found at GCSE, where Asian pupils do better on average. There is no noticeable white working class underperformance relative to other ethnic groups in PISA; if anything, quite the opposite (Jerrim and Shure, 2016).

Gender

Another factor that attracts much comment in the press is gender. Boys consistently underperform girls in modern educational systems, especially in non-mathematical subjects. It must be stressed that the gap at GCSE between boys and girls is trivial compared to the differences between FSM and non-FSM or special educational needs (SEN) and non-SEN. Nevertheless, the gap exists and it matters; in magnitude it is quite comparable to some much-discussed ethnic gaps. It remains largely unexplained, especially since research shows no difference between genders in average intelligence (Johnson et al., 2008).

Again, the gender gaps differ substantially between GCSE and PISA results. In GCSE science, girls generally outperform boys; in PISA, the opposite is typically found (though in the 2015 wave, boys and girls did equally well). In GCSE maths, girls slightly outperform boys, but in PISA boys do better. In PISA reading and GCSE English language, the female advantage is consistent and fairly sizable, though only of average size compared to other countries (Jerrim and Shure, 2016). Between 2004 and 2013 the gender gap in GCSE performance grew slightly while many ethnic gaps shrunk, so that by 2013 the overall female advantage was very similar to the white British advantage over black Caribbean pupils (Strand, 2015).

English as an additional language

Children with English as an additional language (EAL) represent another challenge of inclusion for many schools, especially urban primary schools. I single out primary schools here because it is not clear whether or not EAL children do worse at GCSE than pupils with English as a first language (FLE). It is, however, very clear that EAL children do worse at primary level, and in particular at Key Stage 1, after which they begin to catch up. Notably, EAL students do only very slightly worse than FLE pupils at GCSE, with 54.6 per cent achieving the five A*–C benchmark versus 57.5 per cent (Department for Education, 2015).

Special educational needs (SEN)

One of the largest attainment gaps, perhaps unsurprisingly, exists between children with a statement of SEN and those without. Only around eight per cent of children with an **Education, Health and Care Plan (EHCP)** achieve the five A*–C GCSE benchmark. The figures for children with SEN but no EHCP needs are generally less severe, with around 20 to 25 per cent achieving the GCSE benchmark. It is noteworthy that even children with visual impairments underachieve at GCSE (with 44 per cent achieving the benchmark). This is probably an indicator of the effects of an unresponsive education system, since the vast majority of this group probably have typical cognitive ability.

Looked after children

The results of looked after children are undoubtedly the most desperate failing of the UK education system, and, not unlike our first-world counterparts, of our society as a whole. The figures are so dire that the phrase 'looked after children' has an air of cruel irony to it. Just 12 per cent of looked after children achieved the main GCSE benchmark in 2014 (Department for Education, 2014a). Looked after children are twice as likely as the general population to be permanently excluded and five times as likely to experience a fixed-term exclusion. At primary school the numbers are equally bleak; just 52 per cent of looked after children achieve Level 4 in reading, writing and mathematics, as compared to 80 per cent of other children (Department for Education 2016b).

There are a number of reasons for this. Many looked after children also have a special educational need. At Key Stage 2, nearly 60 per cent of looked after children have a special need. The remaining 40 per cent of looked after children who do not have a special need actually do okay at Key Stage 2; 82 per cent hit the Level 4 benchmark compared to 90 per cent of all children without a special need. At GCSE, however, the picture is bleaker: just 32 per cent of looked after children without a special need hit the five A*–C GCSE benchmark, compared to 64 per cent of all other children without a special need. It is clear, therefore, that the SEN overlap accounts for a considerable amount of this attainment gap – but not all of it (Department for Education, 2016b).

The academic literature makes it clear that we should not attribute the low achievement of looked after children primarily to the failings of the care system itself (which are manifest). Looked after children often suffer from compounded disadvantages: poor schools, adverse family backgrounds including histories of maltreatment, low levels of parental education and even low birth weight. When looked after children are compared to children with similar background characteristics, their educational progress and achievement is often worse – but not very much worse (O'Higgins et al., 2015). In this regard, they are not radically different from many other students who, for a wide variety of overlapping reasons, have come to believe educational failure as their inevitable lot in life.

This should make us realise that we need not abandon looked after students to their fate, no more than we would any other group of disadvantaged students. They are not doomed to failure simply because they are in the care system. The care system does not create insurmountable difficulties; it just adds another layer.

Hard and soft data

Before concluding, I want to spend a few pages on the distinction between hard and soft data. This is integral to my approach to narrowing the gap and will be referenced throughout the book, particularly in Chapter 5, which looks in depth at capturing and making the most of data.

Hard data is best thought of as the typical numbers that senior school leaders are used to working with via **RAISEonline** (replaced in 2017 by the Department for Education's snappily named ASP, or 'Analyse School Performance service'). This includes exam results, absence rates, predicted grades, value added, and so forth. Soft data is the stuff that also matters but is not so easily quantified (though perhaps it could be): the ambitions and particular talents of individual pupils, pupil *X*'s bond with teacher *Y*, and the economic and social circumstances of the local community.

But just because a school will (and arguably should) be judged on its results as evaluated by hard data, this does not mean that hard data can or should be used to drive change within the school. If this book contains one core idea, it is a plea to senior school leaders to abandon the idea that hard data is anything more than somewhat descriptive of reality. It is very rare that strong prescriptions for what a school *should* do can be gleaned solely from its hard data. One of the fundamental and consistent bases of my consulting work is that

I encourage schools to get away from a preoccupation with crude hard data, and adopt a soft-data-led framework for narrowing the attainment gap.

Part of the reason for this is that schools do not often realise the limitations of the hard data available to them, which are severe. To explain these limitations will require a brief detour into psychometrics and classical test theory, which I will attempt to illustrate from the ground up.

Imagine that you wished to test a class's knowledge of Norman English history. How would you go about doing so? One thing you would almost certainly *not* do is simply ask one multiple-choice question (such as, 'In which year did the Battle of Hastings occur?') and leave it at that. Why not? The answer is that such a testing method would be very unreliable and would have low validity. Some children would simply guess the right answer. For others, although they might know that 1066 is the correct answer, this might be almost the only thing they do know about Norman English history. Others might have a generally good knowledge of the history of the period, but in fact get this question wrong because they were not paying attention or are unusually bad at dates. Others still will in fact know the right answer and get it wrong due to a simple slip of the pen.

From this straightforward example, we can come to understand the complex idea of measurement error a little more clearly. In fact, we can never perfectly measure the thing we want to measure, which is the amount of knowledge of a particular period of English history possessed by each child in the class.

This gap of understanding can be larger or smaller depending on the quality of the measurements we use. We can make a better test of Norman history by adding many more questions that all partially overlap. We would probably add a question asking not just when the Battle of Hastings took place, but who was the victor. And of course, we would also ask questions about other aspects of the period, not just the famous battle. To average out factors specific to the day of testing (perhaps half the class has a bad cold and can't concentrate), we would administer the test on multiple occasions. We would administer the test in strict exam conditions to prevent any cheating. The test would be piloted and thoroughly validated, probably by an external provider. One of the most obvious errors is in the very nature of a test, which for many children gives rise to anxiety or other non-normal response behaviours. What tests can end up assessing is how well students perform in a test environment, rather than knowledge-acquisition ability. Nearly all exams test the same problem of language acquisition and recall again and again but with different applications and subjects. This specific skill test is not necessarily reflective of either the depth of the grasp of a subject or how engaged and comprehending the student has been, and limits the variety of 'knowledge' to being able to memorise merely for the procedure of the examination. I, like most other teachers, forgot half the knowledge I gained at school not very long after gaining it. The value of testing short-term memory management is in itself a major topic of exploration, but one beyond the scope of this book.

Already we can see most tests used in schools fall far short of being ideal, and subsequently a fairly large amount of measurement error is usually present. This remains true for national tests, such as the Key Stage 2 SATs, which are designed to figure out whether or not a child has achieved some minimum baseline, and are not instruments designed for good individual-level prediction, even when 'fine grades' are available.

The problems of measurement error in tests are compounded when our variable of interest is a measure of progress. When we calculate a pupil's progress between Key Stage 2 and GCSE, we are incorporating test data from both Key Stage 2 SATs and GCSE exams into the final progress score. The result is that progress scores are doubly problematic, because they rely on measurement error from both tests, rather than just one. One final – and very important – issue is sample size. Many school cohorts are not large, especially in primary schools. As a result, measurement error remains, which in larger samples would be averaged out. In practical terms, this means your average school can expect a great deal of yearly fluctuation in both raw results and progress scores. This is even more true when focusing on the results of a sub-sample of the overall cohort, such as children on pupil premium. This fluctuation should not necessarily be attributed to any changes in the school environment. Much of it is probably just random noise.

There is no good solution to these problems. We can only be aware of the illusions of precision inherent to many forms of hard data. It is because of these issues that this book advocates a soft-data-led approach to narrowing the attainment gap. Hard data cannot always tell us what *is*, and even when it can, it can rarely tell us much about what ought to be done.

The virtue of a soft-data framework is that it allows for a genuinely personalised approach, in a way that hard data does not. A soft-data approach begins with knowing your students. That sounds banal but it isn't. Knowing your students does not simply consist of looking at a pupil's Key Stage 2 results and noticing that they did slightly worse in maths than English (in reality, this may simply have been due to luck). A soft-data approach to closing the attainment begins and ends with the people who know the children best, namely their teachers and teaching assistants (TAs). When asked, they will routinely be able to identify issues that RAISEonline cannot. From this initial process, interventions can be properly planned and justified to external stakeholders, including parents, governors and Ofsted. (Examples are given in later chapters.)

A secondary virtue of this soft-data approach to intervention is that it points away from 'intervention' as a word solely associated with a big push to prepare students for exams (often in year 6 and year 10). Too often schools operate on autopilot except when the sword of Damocles starts to hover over their heads in the form of SATs or GCSEs. In reality, 'intervention' should simply mean 'extra support for those who need it', and this support should be provided on an ongoing basis in all year groups, to whoever needs it. Furthermore, 'interventions' should not be viewed as something that takes place exclusively outside the classroom. Too often existing models of intervention take the most disadvantaged students away from the people best qualified to help them – the classroom teachers. Sensible interventions are instead often interwoven with the flow of everyday classroom life. Again, case studies will be presented in later chapters.

Lastly, a soft-data approach should extend not only to the planning of interventions but partly also to their evaluation. Schools are not places where pupils are trained for exams, though exams do matter. They are forming grounds for character, and a place of preparation for partaking in wider society. Consequently, engagement and positivity are valuable in their own right, and not just because they may (or may not) improve results later on. The individual and society both suffer when a person becomes entirely alienated from learning. Improving the intangibles, such as students' sense of belonging, can help to improve behaviour and reduce problems such as teacher turnover. This may or may not have an effect on exam results but it's important nonetheless.

Key takeaway

Hard data like test results is limited in a variety of ways. Hard data can reveal the existence of a problem but rarely points to the best solution. Schools should assign soft data at least the same significance as hard data, and should use it to guide both specific interventions and their overall response to the attainment gap issue.

To bring all of this back to Jane and Samantha, the hard data would tell us that there was indeed a gap in attainment between the two. But this is obvious. We wouldn't learn much about how to go about tackling the problem. Looking at the soft data – at Jane and Samantha as individuals – we would see quite quickly that what Samantha needs is not extra maths classes but a programme of pastoral support.

Jane and Samantha's story engages us in what they really need. Hard data can eclipse our seeing them as individuals – young, vulnerable ones. When we think of the attainment gap, our mind is in the hard data that is staring up at us from the page of numbers and figures that show us what many schools around the first world are also facing – that we have somehow failed a significant cohort. If there is one thing you take away from this book, I hope it's this: as long as you see the attainment gap in statistical terms, in a column relative to another statistic in a different column that shows a mathematical gap, then you will not be seeing people. We protect our teachers from seeing 'children' by calling them 'students' and emphasising professional conduct, and I would never disagree with the need for this professional distance. However, I would add to this the importance of thinking about students as people with their own stories, personal barriers and motivations.

The real problem is how to enable large school environments to grasp, track and make the most of the soft data without becoming quickly overwhelmed. This very problem is what my team and I have sought to tackle. For all the theories in books in the world, you could not manage the specific cases of Jane and Samantha and 200 others when you are dealing with over 100 emails, taking 20 phone calls, teaching three lessons, conducting seven meetings and sorting out 12 crises in any given day as well. When I think of the attainment gap, I think of the gap between what schools are having to cope with on a daily basis and how that is a barrier to all forms of inclusion. We want the teacher to personalise their learning to meet the needs of every individual student but the real challenge is to enable them to do that when they are teaching a couple of hundred students a week and are already working until 11pm at night and at weekends. I believe that all forms of inclusion can only work when it saves time and money to include Jane and Samantha. The moment it takes longer and costs more, you have lost the school because there is simply no room to move in terms of time or budget. For me, this is the fundamental departure from the realm of the theory in this chapter, to the realm of practice in the rest of this book. Jane and Samantha are narratives and it is precisely through this prism that we can understand what they need and how best to make them prosper in a school environment, and the trick is to accomplish that in less time than it would take to not do it at all.

As a caveat to all this – although I argue for a soft-data-led framework for intervention, I don't advocate ignoring hard data. One especially vital area of hard data that is often curiously neglected is financial information. It is all too easy to regard 'what we have always done' as fixed and inevitable spending, when this should not be the case. In reality, what could you spend on *X* new intervention if you cut back on *Y* old spending that has proved to be ineffective? While every school is different, one of the most common issues that I and my team encounter is an over-provision of badly trained TAs, when the school would do far better, and spend the same or less, by halving the number of TAs but making sure those they do employ are trained properly. More on this in Chapter 3.

The attainment gap as a function of the market state

The stubborn persistence of the attainment gap, across time and nations, presents a fundamental moral difficulty for modern societies. By and large, the developed world aspires towards meritocratic ideals, and their states are what philosopher Philip Bobbitt has termed *market states* (Bobbitt, 2008). Unlike the nation states that preceded them, market states do not seek to maximise the welfare of the individual but to provide the opportunity for each individual to maximise their own welfare. In essence, equality of opportunity, not equality of outcome, is the goal.

How then can a market state accept an attainment gap? How can it square its promise of equality of opportunity with a game of education that seems to be rigged in favour of the privileged before it even begins? Simply put, it can't. The gap has been a significant concern of policymakers for decades, and renewed focus on the issue led to the introduction of the pupil premium. So, the state turns to you and me, to teachers, to fix the problem. Perhaps it places too heavy a burden on our shoulders, and perhaps the problem can never be entirely solved. But we have to do our best, and it's very clear to me from my work with more than 800 schools in the UK, Europe and around the world, that we can do better than we are doing today.

Some obvious solutions to the gap must be ruled out. One straightforward solution would be (and I say this only partly tongue-in-cheek) to decrease the performance of the advantaged. In a modern economy reliant on high-performing individuals working well in cognitively demanding professions, this would be a disaster. We have learned from PISA that Wales is one of the countries where socio-economic status is least predictive of educational success. The country as a whole, however, performs very badly. Its educational equity is not driven by high performance amongst the disadvantaged, but by unusually poor performance amongst the privileged (Jerrim, 2016). This is a national crisis, not a solution.

The second pitfall we must avoid is an overly narrow conception of the attainment gap. The educational divide between rich and poor is only a small part of a wider gulf in health outcomes, labour market success, marriage and divorce rates, welfare dependency – basically, in all domains of human success. I do not believe that the ultimate goal of education is test scores or even the success of our economy, but to produce people who can competently and confidently find their place in the world: people who have aspirations, whatever those are, and have the tools to achieve them.

This book is founded on stories and experiences from my work as a teacher and consultant. Not all these stories relate to narrowing the attainment gap as we conventionally understand it, though many do. Plenty are about finding ways for children to flourish in school in a deeper sense. I am convinced that this matters, perhaps because I myself did not flourish at school, and only found a purpose in life later, after spending much of my adolescence and twenties adrift. This book is underpinned by a holistic vision of education for which I make no apologies.

Stories are all very well, but the core of this book is strategy. Here I do not simply mean *tactics*, i.e. quick and easy fixes for working with children from disadvantaged backgrounds. By 'strategy' I mean a broader approach that encompasses both tactics and *vision*. In my work as a consultant, I have often found that many schools not only have no tactics for dealing successfully with the attainment gap, but do not even have a vision of what success would look like. Of course, no one vision can suffice because the context of schools varies enormously. No school can succeed if divorced from the local community from which it draws its pupils, parents and many of its staff. A school's guiding vision for what success looks like can therefore only be drawn from the community. Having reviewed the academic literature in this chapter, in the following chapter I will focus in on some of the more specific factors that contribute to the gap, including community and home life, as well as self-esteem, aspiration and SEN.

2 Why is there an attainment gap?

Chapter 1 looked at the context, scale and significance of the attainment gap within the UK and around the world. This chapter takes a closer look at some of the key factors that contribute to that gap. These include home life, community, self-esteem, aspiration and SEN.

In the course of my work, I encounter plenty of scepticism among headteachers about academic research. They take the view, and I'm inclined to agree, that statistics and theories are of limited use when you're facing up to yet another stressful senior leadership meeting. So, while Chapter 1 was conceptual, setting the scene with policy and quantitative studies, from here on in the book will be as hands-on as possible, drawing on the work that my team and I have done with more than 800 schools in the UK, Europe and around the world.

In this chapter, I aim to unpack the issue of why there is an attainment gap by looking at each of the following in turn:

Of course, each of these is a huge topic in its own right. I'll suggest a few out-of-the-box solutions along the way, but the point is to shine some light on the key factors that keep both individual students and whole schools performing below the level of their peers.

Parents, home life and economic deprivation

It's a point I'll make several times, but in my experience the schools that succeed in narrowing the gap are those that recognise the deeply compound nature of the issue. Having this more nuanced outlook allows leaders to see below the surface and respond intelligently to the unique challenges of both their school and individual students. In essence, it's the difference between automatically shunting a student who's behind in English along to extra lunchtime classes, and recognising that, in fact, he's behind because

English is his second language, or because English is a late morning lesson and he doesn't get breakfast at home, or because his parents struggled with English when they were at school and have told him the subject is a waste of time.

Students in the UK spend just over 15 per cent of their time in school. Even if these hours of the day were a level playing field (which they aren't, with a 2010 study suggesting that teachers try harder for better-off children), the huge impact of parents, home life and economic context on attainment would hardly be surprising (De Fraja et al., 2010).

There is a range of factors at play here, from aspiration, to the ability or willingness of parents to assist with learning outside of school, to challenges as basic as hunger or access to medical care. I will outline the most significant of these and go into detail on those that I encounter most often, or that have the greatest negative effect. Along the way, I will suggest some simple steps schools can take in response.

Pre-school and preparation

In a now infamous study from the 1990s, researchers Betty Hart and Todd Risley from the University of Kansas found that North American children from 'professional' backgrounds encountered, by age four, approximately 32 million more words than children from 'welfare' backgrounds (these categories are ill-defined in the study, but appear to denote children whose parents have jobs with above-average remuneration versus children whose families are dependent on state welfare). Hart and Risley also found a significant gap in breadth and complexity of vocabulary. They argued that this explained the limited success of Head Start, a well-funded programme aimed at increasing the attainment of children from economically disadvantaged families. In their view, the programme wasn't getting hold of students early enough (Hart and Risley, 1995).

The media buzz around the '30 million words' idea led to it being oversimplified: there are also big gaps between different groups from the same economic background, and there isn't a perfect correlation between the number of words children hear and how well they do in school. But Hart and Risley's point is still important. It's a headline-friendly way to draw attention to the fact that learning doesn't start when children begin school. There are a host of things from birth onwards that have a real effect on attainment: not just how many words children hear but whether or not there are books in their home, how often they're read to, whether or not their parents or carers facilitate pre-school learning, the amount of time they spend in stimulating environments, and so on.

Finally, there's the question of which language is spoken at home: particularly in inner-city areas, students from poorer backgrounds are less likely to have English as their mother tongue. Learning a second language, of course, makes starting school even more difficult. But on top of that, parents and carers who don't speak English well are less able to help out with homework or to engage with the school, and students may have to play translator.

There was one school I visited out of sheer interest because they are supposed to be one of the top state schools in the country. I was surprised to find a very average, 'adequate' school system that in no way was innovative, special or different from just another average school. What was different was almost their entire cohort of parents were older, postgraduates, high-achievers and, frankly, pushy. So, by the time their children started at the age of four, most of them could already read, and the parents were obsessing about which private school their child could win a scholarship to. These students arrive at school for a very mediocre level of teaching, which, in the end, has little impact on all of the culture capital, aspirations and daily involvement of these pushy parents. One could be mistaken for inferring that teachers therefore don't do anything. This would be a misinterpretation here; the value of this point is to think about the sheer impact of the parents and home situation.

Key takeaway

Students from low-income backgrounds are less likely to have access to quality early childhood education. This means that by the time they start school, they are already behind some of their peers and might be lacking basic skills like counting and letter recognition.

Nutrition

Students from poorer backgrounds, or who receive less attention in the home, are more likely to come to school hungry. Hunger is a major barrier to engaging effectively in a lesson. Another issue is diet: students who eat more sugary food are likely to find it harder than their peers to keep up their concentration levels.

Schools can combat these issues by providing breakfast in addition to FSM, and by offering guidance on healthy eating. One school that has done this with great success is Richmond Hill in Leeds, which I look at in more detail on page 33.

Medical care

Students from poorer backgrounds may not go to the doctor as often as they should. Problems that could be easily solved – bad eyesight or hearing, or even an excruciating and persistent toothache – hang around and have a serious impact on learning. More complex difficulties such as mental health problems are also left to develop and may get worse.

High mobility

Parents from poorer backgrounds are, obviously, far less likely to own their own home. Complex local authority housing arrangements or difficult landlords mean that students from these backgrounds tend to move from place to place more frequently than wealthier peers.

Each time students move school they have to adapt to the new environment and peer group. Their teachers have to get to know them and their level of ability. In addition, even if they follow the same curriculum, different schools might vary material or teach it in different orders. Students have to race to catch up, or find themselves bored as they are taught over again material they covered in their last school. If they move regularly, students are likely to end up missing entire concepts, which could hold them back significantly further down the line.

These issues are often even more acute for students with SEN.

Dysfunctional families

Families of low-income children are more likely to be exposed to a myriad of issues that make their home a chaotic rather than calm environment. This puts additional strain on the children who may be handling adult problems and makes it difficult for them to concentrate. In addition, children may have little space to do homework, gain no help with it and, if anything, may have their efforts or plans usurped by more urgent family crises.

One student I knew was desperate to fit in and make her fifth school placement work this time. However, for three weeks she did not produce any homework and came late a number of times. It became quickly apparent that her 'new start' was just going the way of her previous school. When I did a home visit, I found a mum who was quite spaced-out. She told me that her neighbours in the next-door bedsit apartment made a lot of noise until the early hours of the morning; they couldn't sleep and there seemed to be nowhere for this girl to do any homework.

Giving this student exclusions would be tantamount to punishing her for things out of her control and this clearly would only serve to make things worse for her. We arranged for her to be able to sleep in the nurse's room if she was too tired and for an older student to sit with her after school to help her with her work and to befriend her, whilst we supported the mother in dealing with social services to get a new housing placement.

Lack of enrichment

Low-income children often do not get the outside enrichment opportunities their peers have, such as music, dance, art or sports lessons and trips to museums, historical sites and other places. I like to ask teachers about this specific issue when I deliver workshops. We explore what the value of visiting a museum is. There isn't a definitive answer: one teacher said 'these are places that show that the world is bigger than the street or housing estate that they live on'. Another teacher said 'they allow the student to experience the curriculum and to see it in 3D'. These are interesting ideas – probably not things the teachers could measure or quantify, but things they feel inherently to be true.

An additional common viewpoint is that students who are regularly exposed to cultural experiences develop a sense of entitlement and belief that they will continue to encounter the world in vivid, rich experiences. One could argue that this lack of entitlement is part and parcel of the lack of aspiration and belief that life could be anything other than what they see around them – such as in an inner-city urban school, where younger students see older students falling into gangs and so on. Obviously I don't believe that taking students to art galleries is a solution to gang culture, but the point is to consider what 'a lack' causes relative to students on the other side of the attainment gap.

Low-quality housing

According to a report by housing and homelessness charity Shelter, students who grow up in low-quality housing are up to a quarter more likely to develop severe ill health and disability during childhood and early adulthood (Shelter, 2006). They face increased risk of asthma, meningitis and slow growth, which has been linked to coronary heart disease. The risk of mental health and behavioural problems is also exacerbated.

Low-quality housing is a prime example of how all the issues I am outlining tie into one another. Students growing up in low-quality housing may, as described above, also receive irregular medical attention, making the increased risk of poor health all the more concerning.

Communities

Communities can be challenging, not just for socio-economic reasons. Complacency and lack of aspiration can prove equally corrosive to schools. A common theme we have noticed is that dealing with the effect of social issues in an educational silo is doomed to failure because you cannot separate the student from the community. Schools that deal with a challenging community from an educational silo frequently become isolated, and this inevitably has a further negative impact on challenging behaviour and poor engagement by hard-to-reach parents.

Yet this is not the only way in which community relations can affect schools; I have also noticed a theme, especially in the more rural schools (of which there are 5,000 in England) where the complacency of the local community colludes with the school to perpetuate a lack of aspiration and general malaise. These 'comfy schools' often have no zest for academic aspiration because they take the attitude that no one is complaining and 'this is the way we have always done it' – a phrase that eliminates any chance of change.

Behavioural problems

'Behaviour problems are significantly more common among children from disadvantaged backgrounds – and are strongly apparent in the pre-school years', according to the preliminary findings of research that was carried out in 2010 by the University of Bristol and commissioned by The Sutton Trust.

The study of several thousand children had some depressing findings:

- A third of boys from the poorest 20 per cent of backgrounds had 'clinical-level symptoms' of behavioural problems by the age of three, compared with about a sixth of all other boys.
- By the age of seven, a fifth of the less well-off boys still had behavioural problems, versus a tenth of all other students.
- These inequalities widened in the decade before the study. In the 1990s, girls from disadvantaged backgrounds were twice as likely to exhibit behavioural problems as their wealthier classmates. Ten years later the figure was three and a half times more likely. This is largely because improvements in behavioural problems amongst the 80 per cent seemed not to make it to the poorest 20 per cent. (Sutton Trust, 2010)

Behavioural problems at nursery and primary age, as the study notes, are correlated with poor attainment later on, so it's important to intervene early. In nearly all cases where I have been an expert witness at a tribunal hearing about students who have been permanently excluded from school, there have been two key themes that I have noticed:

1. The issues emerged when the students were below the age of five.
2. The issues could easily have been prevented from spiralling out of control.

One student started hitting others aged five. The school despaired and eventually permanently excluded him at the age of six – a pattern that inevitably began to repeat on about a yearly basis. The boy's issues were centred around his autism, which had not been picked up by his schools or parents until he was almost ten. How to both recognise and include students with autistic traits is no mystery anymore and plenty of help and support is available, yet here, it was missed. This case, like most others that I have encountered, became so challenging because the adults around the child did not know how to respond effectively at the earliest age.

Neglect and abuse

A child's first few years of life have a disproportionate impact on brain development. An important aspect of this development is the child's relationship with his or her primary caregiver, be that mum, dad, another family member or a carer. In psychology, the study of these early relationships and their effect on development is the subject of attachment theory.

If a child is neglected, no close bond is formed with the primary caregiver. Psychologists would describe this as 'poor attachment'. It can have a significantly detrimental effect on the relationships a child forms throughout his or her life. If a baby is physically as well as psychologically neglected (if he or she is malnourished, for example) this can lead to worse long-term physical as well as mental health outcomes, and can also result in lowered brain function due to damage done to neural cells.

It is well established that neglect can lead to an increased risk of depression in later life as well as problems with memory and association forming. It has also been linked to panic disorder, post-traumatic stress disorder and attention deficit hyperactivity disorder.

Intervening early in poor attachment can change attachment patterns, reduce the harm to the child and improve outcomes for attachments in adulthood.

Conclusions

The chalk face is often not easy when dealing with disenfranchised and vulnerable children. We have to acknowledge that a potentially significant issue in the way of narrowing the gap is simply how hard it can be for teachers to face challenging, uninterested students every single day. The solution to the gap has to involve outstanding, quality-first teaching based on understanding students' needs and personalising approaches. The starting point here then is an investment in teachers as much as in the students. As a school leader, you cannot ignore this and you cannot impose strictness on teachers who have a tough time of it. You either support them really well or their students will have no chance of achieving. It is nearly always the case that in the schools my team and I visit we find a correlation between impoverishment and poor teaching. It becomes a vicious cycle: poor teaching leads to worse behaviour, which then leads to less motivated teachers, and so on.

One of my first questions when I consult with a school is: tell me about the school context. The response is nearly always generic and misses all that is unique to them. That uniqueness is their gateway to thinking about their setting and students differently. Can they think about their local context in a more in-depth way or differently? The starting point for any discussion about closing the attainment gap is the community because, simply put, it is a communal issue. Any given school faces a unique set of challenges on the issue of the attainment gap. This is obvious on the larger scale; inner-city schools, for example, have a very different set of problems to a rural school, or a school in an ex-industrial village with multiple generations of unemployment, or even a school in a small coastal town.

Lateness and absence

Lateness and absence are symptomatic of all attainment gaps. Obviously, however great your teaching, you can't do much for a child who isn't in school. Attendance is an obvious first problem to tackle for schools working on their attainment gap. This is one of those significantly large issues that require at least a book's worth of real exploration and cannot be dealt with sufficiently here. The correlation between these factors and the gap are quite widely assumed anyway as FSM students are twice as likely to be persistent absentees as similar pupils who are not eligible for FSM (Department for Children, Schools and Families, 2009).

According to data from the Department for Education:

- As overall levels of absence increase, the proportion of pupils achieving benchmarks at Key Stage 2 and GCSE decreases.
- Pupils who were persistently absent during the two years leading up to GCSE exams were, in 2009–10, about four times less likely to achieve the benchmark five A*–C grades including English and maths.
- Young people who were not persistently absent during the final year of compulsory education were about five times as likely as absentees to be studying for a degree by the age of 18, and three times as likely to go to a Russell Group university. (Department for Education, 2011)

Exercise for your senior leadership team

Step 1: Cross-reference the lateness and absence data with those students who form the attainment gap in your school.

Step 2: Speak to the students individually and find out exactly why they are late or absent.

Of course, this is more about opening that door to understanding the individual student and addressing their real needs. It has been popular to offer a 'breakfast club' (free breakfasts in school before classes begin) and I think these can be extremely valuable. But they are not for everyone. For example, I worked with one boy who suffered from self-mutism and avoided school because he was intimidated by it. Putting him in a breakfast club would not have been the solution. He loved one thing: table tennis. One of the staff also loved table tennis and so they played every day. He came to school and he practised talking about table tennis. Eventually, the teacher brought in a couple of other students to play and they became his first friends.

Step 3: Work through each student's barriers and motivations.

One student I interviewed in Manchester with a school leader didn't have much motivation and just shrugged his shoulders despondently when it came to thinking about what could motivate him not to be late. He did eventually share that his father had died. His dad loved Manchester City Football Club – and he would love to go to a match. Would he come to the school every day on time for six weeks if the school could arrange for him to go and see a match? The deal was made and the club donated the ticket.

Step 4: Bring some of the students together into the same planned intervention wherever this makes sense.

One school put on a street dance class for a cohort of 14-year-old girls who all loved hip-hop. They had the additional motivation of a performance at the end of the term if they turned up to the classes.

The (fairly simplistic) solutions offered here are based on two principles:

1. a more nuanced understanding of individual needs, barriers and motivations
2. a bespoke, home-made approach to support.

Hunger: a case study

Richmond Hill (named here with the school's permission) was not for the fainthearted headteacher, with every category of challenge on both the official and unofficial lists. The **Income Deprivation Affecting Children Index** places the school within the lowest two per cent; in Leeds, where it's based, Richmond Hill is ranked in the bottom 15 per cent in terms of deprivation. More than a third of pupils live in households that rank in the lowest three per cent of deprived households in the area.

From September 2014 to mid 2016, 153 children joined the school through the in-year admission process. Of these, 107 remain in school at the time of writing. 64 per cent of the new arrivals had some form of additional need: EAL, SEN, social, emotional and mental health needs or child protection issues. 11 children were admitted with significant behavioural needs.

Overall, 66 per cent of pupils at Richmond Hill are eligible for FSM and 48 different languages are spoken in school, with Portuguese the most widely spoken after English. 35 per cent of students have EAL. There are currently 60 pupils who receive intensive additional teaching because they are new to English, while a number have had no experience of schooling prior to admission.

Half of children are from an ethnic background other than white British. The most significant ethnic group after white British is black African children, followed by children of white Eastern European heritage. There are 25 children who are of Gypsy Roma Traveller heritage.

So, what would you do to narrow the gap in a school like this? I am not sure that the Department for Education or the larger academy chains really have the answer to this fundamental question. However, recently appointed head Nathan Atkinson seemingly wasn't put off. We met because the East Yorkshire Authority had asked me to look into how to increase learning outcomes for looked after children and Richmond Hill volunteered to be a guinea pig. I had an opportunity to spend some quality time with Nathan and the school and what I walked away with was that rare feeling that I had come across something genuinely and deeply inspiring.

Barriers to learning

Nathan identified the many barriers to learning that are caused by life in the local community. He and his team began with the obvious basics such as attendance and punctuality. One issue in particular began coming up again and again; Nathan wrote it in large capitals in his office as if gripped with mad inspiration: 'HUNGER'.

Speaking with students and their parents revealed that a high percentage of children attend school each day without having any food and often not even a drink. Subconscious neglect as well as general poverty are just two of many reasons for this desperate situation.

It is common knowledge that trying to teach students who are starving is ineffective. Hunger affects concentration, energy levels, attentiveness and emotional wellbeing. Prolonged exposure to a lack of food ultimately results in children working below age-related expectations. Throwing additional maths and literacy at this cohort would fall flat. Even one-to-one specialist teachers and any of the fancy computer programs available for schools could not overcome this significant barrier.

But providing children with food each morning would be costly, especially if kitchen staff had to be paid for additional hours each morning. Nathan got round this by intercepting large quantities of bread that had passed its sell-by date but not its use-by date. The school provides toast each morning to all pupils (600) using only this 'waste' bread.

Preparedness for learning

You might argue that the challenge to ensure that children arrive at school ready to learn could be considered a combined effort between home and school, with the emphasis on home. However, when schools are judged for their outcomes, the imperative has to shift towards increased effort from schools – *in loco parentis*.

Nathan had opened a Pandora's box. What other steps could the school take to maximise the pupils' wellbeing and preparedness for learning? The needs of the community are massive and he and his staff had decided to do all they could to reach out to them. They realised that if they could intercept bread then maybe this could be done with other foods too?

Perhaps through the medium of food, they could get the hardest-to-reach parents to engage with the school at last and possibly thaw their iced hearts towards education. If this was a movie rendition, there would be a montage at this point where you would see Nathan and his staff converting an empty learning space in the school to create a café, built to look and feel just like a high-street coffee shop.

The school worked in partnership with local supermarkets, caterers, independent traders and wholesalers who generate tons of waste food that predominantly ends up in the bin. They set up a weekly food shop and a wide variety of products have been distributed through this initiative, including fruit, vegetables, pastries, cakes, bread, cheese, cooking oil, and tinned and jarred products to name but a few.

This food was then made available to parents and members of the school and wider community on a 'pay-as-you-feel' basis, which ensured that the food was valued and that people had a sense of worth.

Parents who would normally avoid the school were now coming regularly. Parents started to talk to the staff over a coffee, sharing worries as well as laughter, and as a result of these interactions they developed an entire community's trust in the school, which was the biggest hurdle to developing a real shift in aspiration.

Nathan and his team have developed many other wonderful interventions that are entirely focused on bringing their families into the school and fostering a positive contact. Attendance has improved as a result of Nathan's work, with children keen to come to school and start their day with breakfast and a chat. Parents are more widely involved in school life too; at the most recent parent–teacher consultations, 90 per cent of families attended meetings, enabling them to share success stories as well as the next steps in learning required for their children.

When dealing with real impoverishment, you can't hope to narrow the gap without addressing preparedness for learning. As I said above, it takes more tenacity than any policy document or formal research can tell you.

Families on the move

There are a number of challenges associated with students whose families move around the country, or between countries, on a regular basis. This is particularly, though not exclusively, associated with children whose parents serve in the armed forces, students from Gypsy, Roma and Traveller (GRT) backgrounds, and new migrant families who are likely to be in temporary housing in different locations before being settled permanently.

There are some challenges common to all of these groups, including issues relating to a lack of consistency in tracking progress and gaps in curriculum knowledge, as well as problems with social integration arising from not being able to hold on to consistent relationships, and lack of willingness to invest in getting to know new routines and environments. The challenges in these two categories are listed below.

Tracking

- setting
- curriculum gaps
- lack of benchmarks for hard-data tracking
- failure to identify SEN, or lack of consistent provision for identified SEN
- complications with public exam schedules
- different approaches to the curriculum and assessment in different countries (e.g. within the UK, Scottish Highers versus A levels).

Social

- sense of loss at each move
- unwillingness to invest emotionally in the school and relationships with peers
- adaptive behaviours (e.g. overfriendliness or coldness).

Below I highlight some of the issues specific to the groups of children most likely to be from families who move around, but there's an important caveat to introduce first. This is that while we can pick out trends in these groups on a national scale, such trends won't necessarily apply in the context of your particular school. Hidden within the statistics, there are plenty of students who excel: in the UK, for example, there's traditionally a distrust of school in the Irish Traveller community, but there are of course plenty of individuals from Traveller backgrounds who do extremely well in school and progress to tertiary education. I advocate using labels only as a way of flagging the individuals who need greater attention given to what's going on for them personally. Interventions should be decided on the basis of the soft data that comes out of this individual attention.

Military families

Children of military or service families may frequently move house or have to take responsibility for the household at a young age ('adultifying' or 'young carer'). A sudden deployment from one country to another can impact on the way children develop and manage their relationships. Regular moves can lead to high levels of anxiety and stress, and their ability to engage with classroom learning may be disrupted especially when their parents are deployed to conflicts overseas. Children with additional or complex health needs may find continuity of care a problem. Children can also feel isolated or find it difficult to cope without the support of family or a friendship group. These phenomena are commonly experienced by children from all countries who have parents in military, ambassadorial or similar positions that require international movements. A colleague of mine became a psychologist having grown up the son of someone who worked for the Foreign Office. They moved countries every two years. The detriment to his friendships and personal development was significant. Now he spends his life helping others adjust to these trials.

New migrants

The most obvious problems experienced by new arrivals are language-based. However, there may be more extreme issues such as never having been to a European-style school, as in the case of a student who arrived to join a secondary school in England having only been in a madrasa in Yemen without any experience of the kind of numeracy and literacy or normative classroom practices that you can assume any student would gain from a school in Europe. You are required to make your school accessible using translation services, which in my experience are incredibly expensive and not really viable for schools. I would suggest drawing on local community experience, knowledge and translation help instead. I worked with a school in Sheffield that had a large number of Slovakian students, all from relatively recent migrant families. The school hired three Slovakian-speaking TAs, who not only helped with the obvious language barriers but also helped both the students and school acclimatise.

As a benchmark (and like with all of these issues, they do require much further investigation), the top area of concern should be social integration rather than language as children have their own speedy ways of picking up language. The biggest problems tend to emerge in children who are difficult to assess because of language barriers, which can mean SEN and home-life issues remain hidden for quite a while.

It is sometimes felt in the UK that Ofsted do not have accurate tools to judge schools with mobile pupil populations accurately and fairly. Certainly, mid-phase (mid-year) entry and exit of students skew data significantly and there are some schools that simply cannot get out of the eternal comings and goings of students because they are on the flight path to receive new arrivals. Their data has to be considered differently.

Key takeaway

The solutions to migration challenges are complex and varied, but here is a quick summary of some key steps:

- Get a robust and thorough procedure in place for initial assessments to rapidly identify what the new student knows, what they don't know, any gaps in their education and any SEN issues.
- Appoint a coach or a go-to person for emotional support.
- Support this new student's teachers with clear, concise advice that will be effective from the get-go.
- Ensure significant engagement with parents.
- Implement a socialisation programme for the student to bond with peers as quickly as possible.

Looked after children

There were around 70,500 looked after children in England in 2016, an increase of one per cent on the previous year and five per cent on 2012. About three quarters of looked after children live in foster homes (Department for Education, 2016a).

Anyone who has anything to do with the management of looked after children is fully aware of just how dire the statistics are. To repeat and add to some statistics quoted in Chapter 1:

- In 2016, only a quarter of looked after children reached expected levels in reading, writing and mathematics at Key Stage 2, compared to 54 per cent of all other children. Nearly 60 per cent had a special educational need identified by this stage (Department for Education, 2017a).
- Looked after children are twice as likely as the general population to be permanently excluded and five times as likely to experience a fixed-term exclusion (Department for Education, 2017a).
- Only six per cent of looked after children in England, and two per cent in Scotland, go on to university, compared to about 40 per cent of the general population (UCAS, 2014).
- As a group, looked after children have poorer employment prospects and health outcomes and are way over-represented in the homeless and prison populations.

Virtual Schools are an additional resource run by local councils to support all those involved in the education of looked after children. The structure of Virtual Schools often lends itself to focusing its liaison and training on a key person within an educational establishment: the Designated Teacher (DT). In all fairness, I don't know how **Virtual Heads** (individuals in charge of a virtual school) could do things any differently. But it leads teachers and others within the school to depend on trickle-down learning, which we can only assume really varies from school to school and has to be a contributing factor to the forever high numbers of exclusions. One has to question just how well the average teacher is really prepared to manage the wellbeing and attainment of looked after children and how well the governors, who ultimately ratify their permanent exclusions, really grasp both what is at stake and the causal relationships and dynamics at play. Predicating our upskilling and knowledge acquisition on the singled-out person per school is too precarious and variable. Let's consider what schools really need to learn and then how they could possibly go about it, and what our headteachers really need from our Virtual Heads.

I have written this section in consultation with Helen Worrall, a member of the Inclusion Expert team and one of the top school trainers on looked after children and related issues. Helen believes that some of the key difficulties that face a large proportion of our looked after learners and that greatly impact upon their wellbeing and achievement arise from the impact of their often disrupted and sometimes negative early experiences. Attachment theory, discussed above, is something that you study at every level of any type of psychology course nowadays; it is no longer niche or obscure. But attachment difficulties and how they impact upon the wellbeing and learning of the children in educational settings has not been a regular part of teacher training courses. I reckon most teachers have come across it but probably couldn't tell you what the signs are in their classroom or, most importantly, what they can do about them.

Helen has given us some examples of what children experiencing attachment difficulties may mean for your classroom teachers. She says that in every school there may be a child or young person who:

- Is so alert and hypervigilant to everything around her that she does not hear the teacher's instructions and then does not know what to do when she starts her task.
- Finds it unbearable to be wrong or make mistakes – this tends to be especially obvious with answers in maths or spelling.
- Finds relationships with adults difficult and sometimes frightening, and so finds it very hard to ask for or accept any help.
- Appears to be happy, attentive and cooperative in class but produces the bare minimum of work or shows that he or she has misunderstood the instructions.
- Explodes with anger when even small things go wrong – even the most kindly phrased constructive criticism.
- Regularly steals items from peers, from small trivial items such as pencils to (more seriously) food from lunch boxes.
- Continually interrupts teachers by asking lots of questions and making statements, often 'silly' ones.
- Has very low self-esteem and believes him or herself to be rubbish at everything, to the extent of not trying no matter the positive encouragement from teachers.
- Often looks sad, sullen and sulky but has no words to describe how he or she is feeling and denies that anything is wrong.
- Seems not to be making any progress despite being apparently positively behaved in school.
- Tells constant and fantastical lies with seemingly no idea that they are unreal. Lies are especially prevalent when he or she has done something wrong, taking the form of total denial of any knowledge of what has happened.
- Does not respond to any form of behaviour management strategy, appearing not to care or to be unable to improve.
- Is a school refuser or truants from lessons.
- Regularly has extreme behaviour difficulties at home after school, even though at school behaviour appears to be positive.

All of the above, and many other difficulties that may be apparent in our classrooms, are common features of a student who may be experiencing attachment difficulties. These students are common in their mistrust of adults in school to know what they need to keep them safe, and their enormous anxiety to gain a feeling of safety. Most of the behaviours that we see are in fact manifestations of their attempts to feel safe, rather than a desire to challenge and annoy teachers.

Students with attachment difficulties also expect to be 'bad' people or not to be good at things and therefore may struggle to take risks in school. Often they will be hypersensitive to things that appear to evidence their deeply negative self-image, and so blow up when even small things go wrong. Outbursts are also linked to the experience of high levels of shame, which stimulate the sympathetic nervous system and cause a fight/flight/freeze reaction. Students feel exposed and want to hide or react with rage, while also feeling profoundly alienated from others. They may not be able to think or talk clearly and may be consumed with self-loathing, which is made worse because they are unable to be rid of themselves.

Frustratingly for teachers, these features mean that students with attachment difficulties may not respond to many of the typical behaviour management strategies. Often, bad behaviours escalate to the point where teachers feel there is no alternative but to move students on to another school or pupil referral unit, or to exclude them. Teachers themselves, sadly, are often made to feel ineffective and take the bad behaviour personally.

So what do we need to do?

In Helen's experience, prioritising the emotional and attachment needs of our most vulnerable learners is the key to their academic success in terms of progress and attainment. She recommends that:

- All teachers, and ideally all staff working with young people, need effective training, especially in recognising and knowing how to respond to common attachment behaviours. It is ideal if the trainer delivering the training has had experience of applying attachment knowledge to school life. If it is impossible to train the whole staff due to time, staffing or budgetary restrictions, the person attending training must be given appropriate tools to effectively disseminate the training to the remainder of the staff.
- Training is regularly reinforced with ongoing coaching and support.
- Real time and effort are afforded to prioritise the emotional wellbeing of these children – to support and coach the individual student, helping them to build secure attachments with one or a small number of staff so that they can then support them to feel safe across their experience at school. This enables the student to access the learning opportunities that school offers.
- Flexibility is provided within behaviour policies to effectively support the needs of young people with attachment difficulties. This is highly important but also tricky, because what we need to do to support these young people effectively can also appear to be counter-intuitive to those not aware of the impact of attachment difficulties.

- We recognise that particular times of the school day and calendar are especially difficult for young people with these difficulties, for example transitions and school transfers. This can be mitigated by creating an effective transition pack that follows the student wherever they go, in order to minimise disturbance to their learning.
- Governors become knowledgeable about the challenges facing our looked after learners, especially the impact of attachment difficulties. This is especially important when schools and governors are considering exclusion. Exclusion, rather than teaching a child that he or she needs to change their behaviour, can actually provide proof to the child that the school cannot keep them safe and teachers cannot be trusted as they send them away and break relationships. This leaves children in a highly anxious state upon their return and means that they are far more likely to repeat the behaviours that may have led to the exclusion initially.

Special educational needs (SEN)

Let's home in on an essential ingredient in the above subtopics that impacts the gap: the extent to which we can personalise learning to the needs of the individual, to address their motivations from a whole-school and pastoral perspective but also to address their learning needs. It is easy to talk about and hard to actually deliver in reality. A clear way of seeing this is the specific case of ADHD, which teachers often get really stuck on.

Best practice in inclusion involves identifying the exact nature of difficulties experienced by pupils. It is all too easy to react to the behaviour of students at face value, or to make assumptions attached to specific diagnoses or labels. Sometimes known labels are a shortcut to appropriate differentiation, but in the case of ADHD, a child's difficulties can simply look like bad behaviour. Perhaps this explains the number of excluded students who are diagnosed or present with ADHD behaviours.

There is much to say about the pitfalls in the resources and training currently available for teachers and TAs. ADHD is not high enough on the continuing professional development (CPD) agenda, so staff simply lack the skills to manage these behaviours. In addition to that, headteachers with whom I work often describe the struggle to 'change hearts and minds' when it comes to including students with behaviours that can be so frustrating in the classroom.

I discussed the issue of staff attitudes towards ADHD with Ann Freeman, author of *Help Me Understand ADHD*, in a series of conversations that led to this section of the book. We felt it would be useful for teachers and TAs to learn more about the impact that the condition can have on a child.

While I talk about ADHD students throughout, it is important to bear in mind that, because the degrees of hyperactivity or disruptive behaviour are not easily apparent, many young people are undiagnosed. Differentiating for the range of needs in a typical classroom is difficult enough as it is, and a student who can't sit still and distracts others from the get-go is a huge additional challenge. I hear teachers describe students who experience hyperactivity as 'infuriating' and other words to that effect, in a tone that conveys all the frustration they feel. I can empathise, as I'm sure anyone who has taught a variety of students can. We can quickly jump the chasm from all-inclusive, haloed armchair pedagogue to exasperated teacher who deals harshly with or excludes the vulnerable, needy child who is making the lesson unbearable for everyone involved.

But the desire to blame ADHD students, to kick them out of the lesson to get rid of the problem, comes from seeing only the tip of the iceberg – the behaviours associated with ADHD – and not the mass under the water: the individual struggling with the impact of their difficulties. ADHD is a condition, not an illness; it is a neurobiological disorder that the person will have to manage for the rest of their lives. With age, some of the symptoms improve, but the condition can be painful for the young person, who is probably just as frustrated by it as their teachers are.

Key takeaway

There is a temptation with ADHD, more than with most other SEN, to blame the child for their behaviour. This is unfair and counterproductive. Like most SEN, ADHD can manifest in a variety of ways, and responses should be tailored to the individual.

A student with typical ADHD will frequently experience being told off, being told to do better and be better. They will sit countless times in an exclusion of some sort thinking about how bad they are and how they aren't like the other kids in their class. The accretion of these experiences leads the student to a hatred of school and a disregard for rules that don't seem to apply to them.

Cut to their secondary school geography teacher who is known for being strict: the student is told to sit still at the threat of being excluded yet again. This time, the student knows that they are at the end of their Pastoral Support Plan and could be permanently excluded, or worse, sent to another school in a managed move to fail again. Anyone who has sat on tribunal appeal panels for exclusion will have seen numerous iterations of this story.

Common to many ADHD students, too, is a low sense of self-worth resulting from negative responses from peers and adults. The sometimes cocky 'I don't care' attitude that an ADHD student might present is often a defence mechanism against this. ADHD students are just as hurt by being told off, and by the dislike of peers and adults, as anyone else. It is hardly surprising then that ADHD can evolve into other mental health problems such as depression.

Another obstacle for many ADHD students is poor motivation for school work. They come to feel that there is no point bothering because they can't succeed. The combination of all these challenges creates a negative spiral, which leads to students getting passed around from school to school in managed moves, each another nail in the coffin of their motivation, or even out of the education system to NEET (not in education, employment or training).

Approaches to support pupils

It is incredibly hard, but possible, for a school to contain and eventually nurture a student who has been rejected by a few schools already. With the right approach and intervention, ADHD students will offer a huge amount despite their difficulties. The following paragraphs detail techniques you can try with students who present hyperactivity.

Two umbrella points are, first, that in general, motivation through understanding, praise, encouragement and patience is key to success. Second, it is helpful if the class teacher can involve parents as well as the student when planning coping strategies. This lays the groundwork for continuity and teamwork and sends the message to the young person that adults are listening to and looking out for them, helping their motivation.

Another idea is to discuss with the young person the three behaviours that are causing the most difficulties in the classroom. Write them down on laminated card, with a copy for the teacher and another for the student. Encourage the student to look at their card before each lesson. Surreptitiously show the card to the student, highlighting positives with praise and encouragement, to help them monitor their progress as the lesson takes place. When the lesson finishes, give either a point or a half-point for each behaviour. This method can be combined with a home contact book so that rewards for good behaviour and encouragement can be reinforced by parents.

If the student has an allocated TA, ask this member of staff to write down three points at the start of the lesson, in order of priority, focused on tackling the subject of the lesson. This can help prevent procrastination and teach the student a coping strategy that they can take up independently in due course. For example, for comprehension, the three points might be: read, highlight key facts, and then answer questions.

Here are some other effective strategies you could try:

- Tackling constant fidgeting by giving the student some Blu Tack® or a small leather or foam ball.
- Sitting ADHD students next to a positive role model. The teacher can discreetly support the role model through the lesson.
- Helping ADHD students to dispel some of their negative reputation with peers by giving them small, responsible jobs to do. For example, ask the student to hand out or collect in worksheets.

Anger outbursts

Deal with anger outbursts in the classroom or the school corridor in a measured way. Anger outbursts are more common in secondary than primary schools. They can be a manifestation of an ADHD student's impulsivity (they don't think of, or they forget, the consequences) or sense of injustice (the feeling that it is always them singled out for misbehaviour), a form of attention-seeking, or even a deliberate attempt to be excluded from the lesson because other frustrations have built up and the student wants to get out.

Dealing with these outbursts as a teacher or TA is really challenging, but it is so important to bear in mind that your attitude affects the attitude of the student. Keep calm, don't shout and avoid going over old ground. Engage the student by coming to some sort of mutual agreement about current and future behaviour.

Sensory difficulties

Some ADHD students also experience sensory difficulties that can affect levels of hyperactivity. Health authorities have suggested a special cushion for the student, which helps their awareness of the chair and offers additional stimulation, addressing sensory issues that could be the cause of a student's desire to get up and walk around. But such cushions might attract too much attention, especially in secondary school. An alternative option is for the teacher to allow the student to get up every 25 to 30 minutes under the guise of doing a small job like handing out worksheets.

Each ADHD student has a personality they deserve the opportunity to develop. Understanding and responding to the condition and the context of the young person who has it (ADHD is often linked with challenging circumstances at home) will have a hugely beneficial effect on that person's current and future success.

Aspiration and self-esteem

All the students in your school who fall under the umbrella of inclusion will have two things in common:

1) They have specific needs. They might be looked after, newly arrived in the school or present any of a wide range of SEN. Some of these have already been discussed in this chapter.

2) As a result of these needs, whatever they are, they are likely to feel like outsiders: not 'normal' or like everyone else.

Consequently, despite the many wonderful programmes in place in our education system, there is an epidemic of what could be described as 'low self-esteem' that inhibits real attainment and progress. This 'outsider-ness' manifests in many ways throughout their educational life: too many children don't see SATs, GCSEs or A levels as applicable to them, let alone viewing university as within their grasp. They don't see that the 'system' is for them, and neither do their parents.

In some ways then, as we set about busying ourselves trying to narrow the elusive gap, the 'receiving end' may have absolutely no interest whatsoever. But this is fanned and given much oxygen – nearly always unknowingly – by everyone in a school.

Case study: Ava and Connor

Ava always presented as pleasant, smiling at her teachers, and drifting along two years behind the reading comprehension age of her peers. She was on the FSM register. None of her teachers gave thought to what aspiration meant for her. Her mum would come to all of the meetings and ask basically just one question: is she happy? This is what the TAs who worked with Ava also focused on. She developed two close friendships and her parents and the school were satisfied.

Connor's dad worked on a farm as a hand. So did his three uncles, just like his grandfather. His mum didn't work. He was not an FSM recipient, although he was arguably poorer than many of his peers whose parents didn't work. Connor assumed he would work on a farm. Connor's entire family assumed that he would work on a farm; in due course, so did his teachers. They saw school as a place for him to make and be with friends.

There are numerous factors that tie these cases together. A key issue for the purpose of this discussion is the belief of everyone around both Ava and Connor in the limitations of their life journey. The schools colluded with the parents' aspiration. The assumptions of adults surrounding these children were the key factors in the learning outcomes. It is by no means easy to tackle this. But our starting point has to be that it is possible and that it is worthy of a try. This idea translates off this page into an attitudinal shift that must be fostered by the leadership in schools.

Early on in my teaching career, I came across a student who came from a very poor background. I happened to have made a home visit at one point and it wasn't the lack of comforts that caused me to pause, but the deep sadness that polluted the home with the chronic depression of his only parent and his sibling who had schizophrenia and had attempted suicide numerous times. His were strong shoulders, and we have a label for that too – 'young carer'. He had thrown himself into his work as a distraction from the difficulties at home and had emerged with all As at GCSE. He said that he wanted to be an electrician. His teachers told me that he was headed for top marks at A level, that he could get into any university and he would be in with a good chance of getting into Oxbridge. I discussed these options with him but he said his mind was made up 'and anyway, I need to bring money into the home and do my bit'. I persuaded him to come with me to the University of Oxford for a visit and I set him up for a chat with one of the professors there who was very interested in him. The story ends in him being offered a place and him turning it down to become an electrician. I am happy for him to become whatever he wants but I realised then that he didn't perceive that he had options to choose from; life had chosen them for him. The failure here, my failure, is not catching this earlier. Not realising that options need to be promoted at the youngest of ages. Starting at age 17 is too late. How on earth can a student believe they can be more if we don't?

In general, our students are growing up in a society that is far more accepting. For example, it was commonplace 30 years ago for boys to make fun of their peers for their sexual orientation, and today students who self-identify as LGBTQ are very often accepted in England (plenty of challenges remain, of course, but the difference is stark). In nearly all cases, the school in which you work will be far more tolerant than the one you went to as a child. However, along with the growth of our understanding of SEN and sensitivity to a whole range of issues over the last 30 years, labels – and, with them, expectations of staff and the students themselves – impede aspiration. We have simultaneously become far more astute in recognising a broad gamut of needs and yet the sophistication of our collective aspiration for students with such 'labels' seems not to have grown. There are many books on this fundamental issue. Most people would think this a subset of the broader issue of 'aspiration'. I find the word 'aspiration' an easy catch-all that is simply unhelpful when it comes to practice. It is too broad and as a result dismissive of nuance – precisely that which we need to understand individual students and their own individual stories.

On a holiday in the US, and trying as hard as I could to get away from anything related to education, I took my own children to an aquarium. There I was impressed, bemused and provoked by something I saw: a group of about 20 children aged roughly 11 to 13 who must have been on a summer programme with leaders who seemed to be students doing a summer job. The children's bright yellow t-shirts were emblazoned with the phrase 'I promise to go to college' and the leaders' t-shirts said: 'I believe in you!' This was overtly tackling a problem – one that we experience the world over.

Before you, as I, guided by my British proclivities, was inclined to do, dismiss this out of hand, I'll pose a question: how many other really successful programmes do you know that build aspiration? How do you do it? What's the ingredient? Is it this American model example of overt indoctrination (why, you could write: 'I promise to get at least one PhD!')? Most schools opt for a trip to a museum or a play, as if cultural exposure would sort everything out. A whole-school, systemic approach to aspiration is rare to find.

After talking about this with one school, they decided that aspiration was so key it should emerge in every facet of the curriculum. For every new topic, they were going to invite in someone to speak about their job relating to it. When they started volcanoes, for example, they invited a geologist who showed them pictures of his field research. This approach recognises that the curriculum can be the launching pad to address aspirational horizons.

I think there are two foundational aspects of this broad term aspiration: the individual and the school. They cannot and should not be the same. School aspiration is what is written on the walls, said between points by teachers, an attitude seeping across the organisation, which evidently has a bigger mission for these children. The school approach needs to be persistent, overt, daily and manifest in as much of the school as possible. To make this slightly harder, every school should look and feel different in this regard, as it should reflect the personality of the school, the needs of the community and the shared language and beliefs of the staff. How do you know if it is successful? Because you ask this question as a team a lot and you tweak and add and evolve. A key factor has to be the changing hearts and minds of teachers and their aspirations for the children as seen in their lessons and language. Have you noticed any change in aspiration of the students or their parents?

Dean Ashton (CEO of Reach South Academy Trust) says to the school leaders of his academies, 'No child's aspiration should be limited by any adult's expectations.' He explains that the key to narrowing the gap in the schools that he has worked in has been to tackle both the aspiration of the staff for their pupils as well as building the self-confidence and skills of the students as critical learners. One headteacher he supported took over a very challenging failing school with a significant attainment gap. The outgoing head said to the new incumbent, 'These students simply cannot achieve any more; you can't expect anything more from them.' The new head inspired the staff with a different belief and culture. For example, every year he would insist, 'This new cohort is the highest attaining group of students that has ever started the school.' And lo and behold, like a religious prophecy that had been heralded by their shepherd leader, it would come true. Dean suggests that the very belief and aspiration of the headteacher can seep through every aspect of a school while recognising that this must be buttressed by a clear pedagogical strategy and by supporting staff in their development.

The other aspect of aspiration that I think of is very different. It is personal, private, almost a secret. The individual student has someone with whom to explore their own dreams and possibilities and, most importantly, the key factors inhibiting them as an individual. Start by asking, 'What are you passionate about?' and facilitate them to engage with this as a carrot for school engagement. This is commonly thought of as coaching, although I think there is a goal here that is about enabling the student to see beyond their limitations and is not something that can be done on a whole-class level. This 'nurturing' is more akin to a form of re-parenting, which evokes the notion of *in loco parentis* – which, here, is taken beyond its legal ramifications to be thought about as an approach to supporting children in emerging into a world with a sense of hope and personal belief.

The most obvious example of this is the *Billy Elliot* story, which shows the journey of a child to find his passion and use it to emerge from the limitations of his upbringing. The story misses the bigger point however: what about all of Billy's peers – what are they going to do? *Billy Elliot* is only a story because of the failing of most to find their unique path; if so many did find something that made them feel alive and impassioned then the story of Sir Thomas Allen would hardly have been worthy of dramatisation. Of course, the role of the dance teacher in the story is key; she is a model for coaching and belief in a child. I find the transformational experience of the teacher as profound as Billy's – and it is here that the two aspects I described above collide.

Conclusion

Each of the issues discussed in this chapter requires far more depth and nuance than I have given. Nonetheless, I hope I have made it clear that the best responses in all cases are, at a fundamental level, the same. They involve:

1. Getting behind the reasons for poor attainment and performance.
2. Dealing with causes rather than symptoms.
3. Focusing on overcoming barriers and exploring motivations.
4. Seeing students as individuals with unique sets of challenges and gifts.
5. Enabling teachers to understand and supporting them to grow in skill and aspiration.

The attainment gap has a diverse and challenging range of causes. Traditional, out-of-the-box responses fail to recognise this and are bound to fail, especially because core issues like self-esteem, attitude and aspiration are rooted in the home.

Schools need to expand the scope not just of their interventions, but also of their sense of the remit of their duty. Thankfully, there are few school leaders these days who still think that school is just where children go to learn. But schools need to invest much more creative energy in the ways they respond to what is undoubtedly among the most pernicious social issues of our age. The only solutions are bespoke.

3 Barriers to narrowing the gap

Having explored the factors that contribute significantly to creating the attainment gap in Chapter 2, in this chapter I look at the biggest barriers schools face when they try to narrow it. These are all systemic issues, from mismanagement of the SEN department to relationships with feeder schools and recruitment challenges in remote locations. Each has the potential to undermine a school's good intentions as far as the attainment gap is concerned, and more often than not the problems I observe in schools with which I work can be traced back to one or more of these problems.

Each of the barriers represents a really tough challenge. But a school's biggest problems are also, of course, its greatest opportunities. I have seen schools make fantastic improvements on their attainment gap by directing energy at one or two of these systemic issues.

However, while, more or less, schools have challenges in common, that does not mean that the same solutions work for all schools. I am sceptical of nationwide initiatives because they often disguise rather than illuminate the unique problems schools face. This should be borne in mind as a caveat for the chapter: the issues described are general mechanisms, the specifics of which will vary hugely from context to context.

Teaching assistants (TAs)

TAs have had a bad rap in the press recently. It's commonplace to hear senior leaders and policymakers questioning the value of them altogether. Figures such as '250,000 TAs at the cost of £4bn' distract from the simple fact that they are the lowest-paid people in the education system with a salary that is, on average, half that of a teacher (Stevens, 2013). But many teachers, students and parents would argue that TAs are one of the best things about our schools; with their individualised support, thousands of our children flourish.

I have worked with dozens of schools across the UK where TAs are barely utilised and given minimal guidance, support or training to be able to effectively engage with our most vulnerable children. I know of too many schools where the skills and confidence of their TAs remain untapped. As a result, TAs aren't able to build key relationships with parents and outside agencies, and they are rarely asked about the very students they know best. In other words, schools often simply don't know how to support and manage their TAs to allow them to contribute substantively.

One important element here is the SENCO: good SENCOs can offer critical expertise and support to TAs on a case-by-case basis. But the huge challenge of finding a good SENCO (see page 53) means that this key role is often held by someone without appropriate leadership skills, or is left unfilled altogether.

As a result of insufficient management and training, the TA-funding downward spiral begins (see Figure 3.1).

One school I visited had 35 TAs and I calculated within an hour that they only needed 15. The first thing the headteacher had told me was that the school was in massive debt – I think as a way of saying that he could barely afford this visit. We totted up the savings and it came to about £400K. I sometimes joke with my team and tell them they will gain a commission for every £100K they save a school. This is a frighteningly common occurrence.

Perhaps an obvious question that you could direct at a headteacher would be: why wouldn't you invest in all of your staff, particularly your TAs? While some heads might attribute limited TA support and training to a lack of time and funds, I'd add in lack of

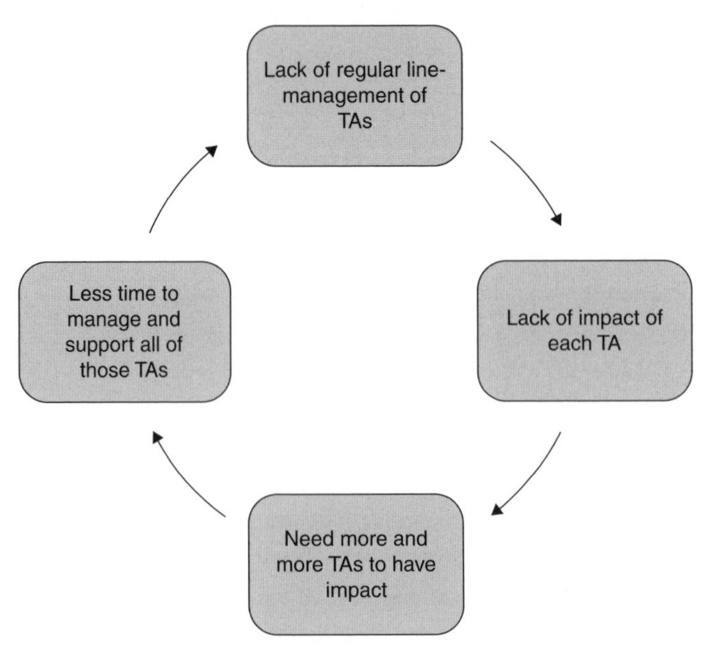

Figure 3.1: The TA-funding downward spiral

accurate prioritisation. There exists a commonly held notion that unqualified and untrained staff are of minimal worth; money spent on their development would be extravagant and an inefficient use of limited resources. In the triage of urgent issues needing to be addressed by headteachers, this one hardly figures. But TAs can actually have the greatest impact in solving schools' most time-consuming and money-haemorrhaging issues.

I've worked with schools and their TAs to establish systems that have massively impacted on attendance among the most vulnerable, improved the attainment of all inclusion groups and significantly reduced fixed-term exclusions. I have seen TAs solve a school's 'aggressive parent problem' precisely because they are perceived as unthreatening, are able to reassure parents and can create a special connection with their children. I have witnessed just how well TAs can support teachers in understanding their students, save them invaluable time in creating differentiated materials and even deliver provisions and small-group work to foster real, high-impact learning.

Key takeaway

Often under-trained TAs are an untapped – and potentially brilliant – resource in schools.

Here are three examples of great TAs with whom I have worked, and who with just a bit of investment have since inspired similar developments in many other schools.

Case study: Gail, Denise and Alison

Gail: a focus on pastoral support for vulnerable students

Gail, a 48-year-old mother of two and previously the owner of a market stall, seemed to naturally gravitate to the naughty students – and the gravitation was mutual, particularly when the students clearly disliked all other staff. I made this natural affinity into a job, gave her a room where she could meet students, and a desk and phone for basic admin, such as calling parents. We met on a weekly basis to discuss her cases and, as I supported her and her confidence grew, she honed her skills and broadened her reach.

Soon, she began to liaise with external agencies and services on behalf of the school. Gail now organises, attends and briefs around all significant pastoral meetings. She notices and actions hidden child protection issues, supports vulnerable students to succeed and attain good results, quickly addresses cases of bullying and saves the senior leadership team an immeasurable amount of time and energy each week.

Denise: supporting year 7 teachers and parents with transition into secondary

Denise, 38 and mother of two, suggested that the toughest problems were to be found in year 7; she rightly pointed out that the school didn't know its newest students well enough and that staff should work more closely with feeder primary schools. After asking her to suggest an action plan, she designed a schedule for meeting year 5 parents, and developed a transition programme and team that she trains and manages. She knows every year 7 student that has any form of need, as well as their parents, she liaises with all their agency support teams and she briefs all teachers at the start of the year.

This generates the best possible bespoke pastoral and learning support. Aside from creating an environment where new students can hit the ground running, she helps parents through the arduous process of getting much-needed statements and financial support in advance of coming to the school, and pre-empts a host of issues that would otherwise drain resources.

Alison: in-depth knowledge of students' learning profiles

Alison, 47 and also a mother of two, told me that we needed to know the students' learning profiles better; I asked her to help me to set something up. Before I knew it, she had come up with a way of running a whole-school assessment procedure. It didn't end there. She decided to tackle the cumbersome and financially draining examination access procedures. She asked to go on a short course so that she could personally conduct the assessments and run the system in its entirety. Try asking her, off the top of her head, to tell you about any sixth form student and the history of their learning profile. She'll rattle off an answer that is detailed, emotionally intelligent and sensitive to the broader background. It's hard to quantify the worth to a school of staff with this level of knowledge, but it can save its SEN department thousands of pounds and numerous headaches.

These real-life case studies exist through a belief in the worth and potential impact of TAs. Sadly stories like these are all too few. It's my strongly held belief that TAs should be valued – so they are made to feel important and that their voice counts. TAs should be trained – so they can realise their potential and give their maximum to the school. TAs should be supported with the right framework and management system so they can learn, develop and make a difference, just like their students.

Special educational needs (SEN)

It is notoriously difficult to hire good SENCOs – so difficult, in fact, that even some vulnerable schools choose to go without them for extended periods – and as a result there's a knowledge deficit about SEN that contributes to the issues described in the previous chapter. This can have a multitude of negative effects.

There is a great deal of confusion surrounding the role of SENCOs. I believe that this role should encompass leadership on narrowing the gap, and in schools where these two areas are partitioned between different staff, there is confusion, overlap and a lack of coordinated thinking. In so many of the schools I've visited, teachers have assumed that SENCOs deal exclusively with SEN students, and SENCOs are often treated as remedial teachers. I often encounter SENCOs in vulnerable schools still teaching in the 'old style', hiding in their office rather than working on the front line supporting their teaching colleagues.

This can lead to the following negative spiral of exclusion (in the name of inclusion!), which is also illustrated in Figure 3.2:

1. SENCOs are alienated from other teaching staff and focus on deploying interventions.
2. As a result of this lack of support, differentiation and personalised learning in classes are lacking.

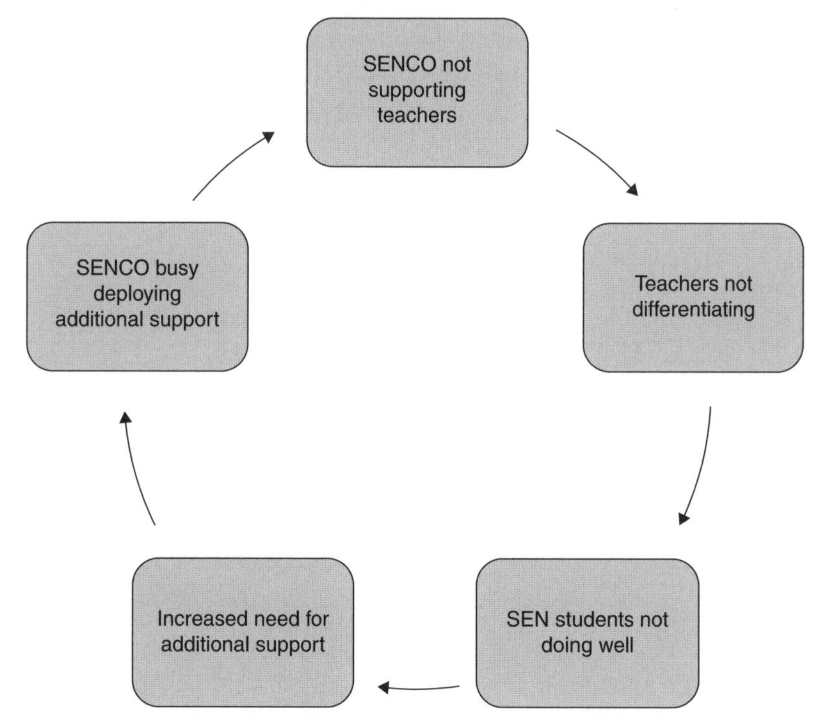

Figure 3.2: The negative spiral of exclusion

3. This lack of class-based work leads to SEN students doing less well than they could, which means they are perceived to need even more remedial support.
4. SENCOs have even more additional support to deploy and even less time to assist and train their colleagues.

In their 2016 survey, the National Association of Head Teachers (NAHT) found that only 17 per cent of SENCOs (and teaching roles with a teaching and learning responsibility) were recruited 'with ease', while 60 per cent were recruited 'with difficulty' and, in a depressing 23 per cent of cases, schools failed to recruit at all (NAHT, 2016).

We have waltzed into a national crisis and no one seems to have woken up to the problem, let alone be doing anything about it.

Since the SENCO role is so broad, what sort of person should schools be looking for, what do they need to prioritise, and what responsibilities can be delegated to avoid the negative spiral of exclusion detailed above?

The traditional SENCO

In the past, the SENCO was a sensitive, perhaps slightly eccentric (yours truly) soul, happy to be based in that room under the stairs or down the quiet corridor away from the bustle of normal school happenings.

Students needing extra attention were removed to this special room. The role required patience to work with socially awkward and frustrating students (and their parents), the ability to adapt resources for a broad spectrum of needs and healthy bouts of resignation to the lengthy paperwork, the outside agencies that were forever lacking and unavailable and, of course, the teachers who would expect SENCOs to take all the responsibility for any student with an SEN label.

You could hire that SENCO: it was clear what you needed and there were plenty out there.

The new SENCO

Thanks to Ofsted, the **SEND Code of Practice** and the **Teachers' Standards**, we have seen a significant attitude shift from keeping those SEN students in that back room to making them a central feature of a successful lesson. 'Substantial and sustained progress' of all groups, as Ofsted put it (Ofsted, 2016), is interpreted to mean that the students beyond the edges of the average need to be making significant progress in a teacher's class for it to be considered any good. When SEN students do not make adequate progress then it can call into question the ability of that teacher, but also the broader school system and its capacity to accurately identify needs.

SEN is no longer something that happens in the room down that quiet corridor; rather it is taking centre stage as a top Ofsted priority. Our SENCO needs to get this to happen – but not from the quiet of their office where they are busy slaving over yet more local authority paperwork and babysitting those same students who have been excluded from class again.

That sensitivity, which was the hallmark of the SENCO, is no longer a top priority. The new SENCO is someone who can think in whole-school leadership terms, has great communication skills with staff and has a deft ability to get your school into gear for the Ofsted challenge. That's a different SENCO altogether – a different job description requiring a different type of person.

What you need from your SENCO

The modern SENCO needs to be outstanding at the following aspects—and not just doing them, but doing them simultaneously:

1. Can not only get all the ridiculous paperwork done quickly but can actually manipulate the system to get what both the school and student need with tenacity, calm and a willingness to go the extra mile at every junction.
2. Can handle challenging parents, usefully share the burden, and support the senior leaders. They spend 90 per cent of their time managing the top ten per cent of students and know how to stop a bad situation spiralling out of control.
3. Can provide bite-sized information to teachers about their students on a regular basis, are available as a go-to person for continuous teacher support, and can even help nurture the relationship between TAs and teachers.
4. Can read, use and feel at home with whole-school data such as the Analyse School Performance service (previously RAISEonline).
5. Can support whole-school planning in senior leadership meetings and contribute to both pastoral and curriculum development.
6. Can be someone you can rely on to ensure you are compliant with the SEND Code of Practice, Ofsted and the latest policies.
7. Can deploy resources intelligently and can accurately and dynamically meet needs with high-impact and easily measurable provision.
8. Can lead on related issues such as looked after children, narrowing the attainment gap, EAL and so on.
9. Can deliver on being in and out of classrooms supporting teachers with their differentiation and personalised learning on a daily basis.

So, can you imagine advertising for such a candidate and managing to invite eight applicants to an interview day – all of whom could potentially do this job for you? I hear you laughing from here. Is it possible that if they are actually good enough to be taking on the duties described in the above list then they may as well be going for a headship? So what can we do?

Recruiting the right SENCO

Here are some tips to help senior school leaders recruit the right SENCO:

- It is a competitive market out there and your first gambit is simply to up the salary. Why should this job be isolated from normal market forces? Other schools will be doing it even if you don't, making recruitment all the more difficult.
- Think more in terms of a senior leader, possibly at the deputy head level. One headteacher told me they had advertised three times for an assistant head SENCO role with no success. I got her to reinvent the position at deputy head level and it was filled quickly. This does have implications for getting governors on board, and for budget, but needs must.
- In line with the previous point, think more about someone for their generic leadership skills, their proven capacity to coach teachers in teaching and learning, and whether they can demonstrate any prior sensitivity to SEN or vulnerable students. This takes us off piste from the usual SENCO to someone who is more of a generic whole-school leader. I think SEN specifics can be learnt in the role, whereas it is much harder for someone with a master's degree in SEN to learn the requisite leadership skills.
- The point above will make more sense if you expand the role to more of an INCO (inclusion coordinator) with responsibility for all areas of inclusion without forgetting the stretch and challenge end as well. Lay out your expectations that this role will involve getting all staff up to scratch with SEN.

Expertise versus leadership

The above steps challenge the common misconception that you need to hire someone who knows the most about, for example, dyslexia. Let me compound that problem even further by saying that the SENCO training course is worse than useless for getting your SENCO up to scratch.

They can read a book about dyslexia and after six months of dealing with a range of needs and reading the specialist advice and educational psychologist reports, they will know enough. The hardest thing about being a SENCO is managing it all: the paperwork, the meetings, the staff development. It is precisely these things that are not SEN-based per se and cannot be read in a book. They fall under leadership.

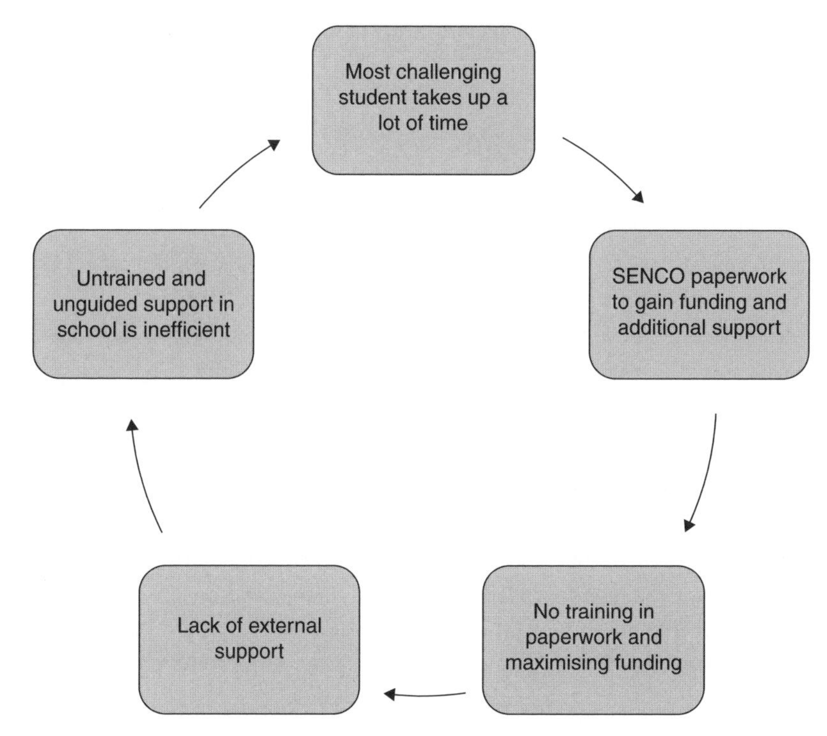

Figure 3.3: The negative cycle that can occur without the right SENCO

I am suggesting that you could invest in a good leader who has a broad responsibility for inclusion with a strong focus on staff development. Failing to do so can result in the negative cycle shown in Figure 3.3.

Many of the most challenging cases – which we know end up as NEET, and perhaps worse down the line – can be dealt with by hiring the right individuals who can avoid this negative cycle.

The annual reviews

I have written and argued vociferously time and again that many of the traditional SENCO functions can be carried out by **higher level teaching assistants (HLTAs)** under the guidance of the SENCO.

When I was a SENCO, for example, one of my HLTAs prepared all of the annual review paperwork both pre- and post-review, and my role was merely to check it and sign it off. We had a paperwork meeting once a week for two hours.

It is a waste of time for your SENCO to spend time on the phone trying to get through to the **Child and Adolescent Mental Health Service (CAMHS)** when one of the TAs can do that. Timetabling of TAs is another thing that the traditional SENCO did but which is better taken on by an HLTA. The traditional SENCO tasks have changed and many of these can be given to HLTAs.

Concluding thoughts

I hope this gives you some pause for thought about this role. The relevance of this new type of deputy-head-whole-school-leader SENCO that I describe will vary from setting to setting. There can't be a one-size-fits-all shape. Your SENCO should be someone who is able to facilitate and promote everyone else delivering SEN support, rather than shouldering it all themselves – as well as bringing all their knowledge and experience to narrowing the gap.

Early years foundation stage

A number of schools have a hidden hornets' nest of a problem at **early years foundation stage (EYFS)**, either in a feeder nursery or internally. One commonality that my team and I have identified is that the individual needs of students are often not picked up on early enough. In addition, there is a general misapplication of the EYFS framework. Primary school headteachers mostly do not have an EYFS background and, as such, may miss the issue. It festers, and costs a great deal of time, effort and expense later on.

It is well established that the attainment gap begins to open long before children arrive at school. Some of the evidence was explored in the previous chapter; in addition it is worth mentioning the Bercow Report (2008), which says that a large proportion of children start school with worryingly limited basic communication skills that are vital for effective schooling. Bercow highlights the direct link between young children's language and communication skills and their academic achievements down the line. Similarly, the Rose Review (2006) highlights the importance of developing children's speaking and listening skills, essential for the acquisition of literacy.

The findings of these studies haven't yet translated into a narrowing of the attainment gap. But I believe that two of the biggest barriers schools face in their work on the issue are linked to EYFS. They are:

1. Primary and secondary school leaders, trying to narrow the gap in their own settings, fail to communicate with or offer any support to feeder EYFS settings. If you are a primary head and the attainment gap is already there when your pupils are at the EYFS feeder down the road, there's both a practical and an economic argument to get on the phone to them and work out how you can offer support. This doesn't happen nearly half as much as it should.
2. More fundamentally, most leaders of multi-academy trusts, secondary schools and even some primary schools do not have a sufficiently sophisticated grasp of what help is necessary in the EYFS.

As a result of these two easily redressable flaws, the EYFS is left to face our country's most challenging problem without any significant support or investment from the broader educational fraternity. And the gap continues year-on-year without much of a glimmer of hope on the horizon.

I must confess that I fall foul of these problems myself. While I have experience and expertise within secondary and primary, my knowledge of EYFS only extends to what I have gleaned from my own children's early education. I have aimed to remedy this by speaking with two of my colleagues who run the EYFS division of my organisation, whose advice I will proceed to share. The aim isn't to offer an exhaustive compendium of all that is worth knowing about EYFS, but to provide a checklist of common mistakes that have the biggest impact on the attainment gap, in addition to suggestions of support that might usefully be offered to EYFS settings to help them narrow the gap.

My conversations were with Dr Sue Allingham and Hilary Solomon.

Sue's expertise and passion for teaching and learning in the early years started with her classroom experience and Senior Lead role as an Early Years Coordinator. As her career developed, she decided to research her subject, gaining an MA and then a doctorate in early years education from Sheffield University. She writes regularly and is Consultant Editor for *Early Years Educator* magazine, and has written a book, *Transitions in the Early Years*, which is now in its second edition.

Hilary has been working in special educational needs and disabilities for over 25 years. A qualified teacher and assistant head at Oakleigh School in Barnet, Hilary leads Barnet's Pre-school Inclusion Team alongside her work for Inclusion Expert.

The three of us came up with the following areas of focus:

1. importance of parental engagement and participation
2. importance of quality interactions
3. need for well-informed staff
4. need for a constructive environment to facilitate learning
5. outside environment versus the inside environment
6. need for simple planning based on learning not activities.

I will consider each of these areas in more detail below.

1. Parental engagement and participation

I assume this is an obvious point, although there are some nuances that we should focus on.

Home visits prior to the child starting their placement should be prioritised and can set a precedent for continuous positive and active communication. Parents should be encouraged to regularly come in to the school, via activities like coffee mornings (apparently cake works).

Most importantly, it is not just significantly increasing the engagement of hard-to-reach families that counts, but facilitating parents to understand and engage with their child's development and learning journey. Instead of just passively receiving reports, they should participate in the process.

A good learning journal should not just be full of photos, but should enable parents to understand the significant moments that inform their child's journey. This is the key: to recognise parents, and what goes on at home generally, as a critical element of the EYFS.

2. Importance of quality interactions

As Ofsted's 2015 report on narrowing the gap in the early years (Early Years Report 2015) says, teaching incorporates all of the ways in which adults help young children to learn. Effective EYFS leaders do not think of teaching and play as separate endeavours.

There are some mistakes that are seen on a regular basis. It is quite natural for adults to enable EYFS children to speak with simple, closed questions, and to fill the silences with their own speech. This closes down learning. A 'quality interaction' has many facets but, for the sake of this section, it means maximising (as opposed to actively minimising) the learning opportunity of every interaction.

Instead of asking, 'What does it do?' or 'What colour is this?', which can only lead to simple answers, ask open questions. Give time for children to respond rather than jumping in to fill silences. My team use the nine-second rule: allow children nine seconds to do anything before you jump in. Wait, listen and be patient.

Pepper the day with choices to promote thinking. We dominate children with the choices we make for them and this takes away thinking and articulating. Ask, 'What do you want to read?' rather than saying, 'Let's read this' and 'What do you want to wear?' rather than, 'Let's all dress up as pirates'. This is more of an attitude shift that facilitates TAs and teachers listening to children and promoting reflection.

Adapt to the moment rather than getting stuck with what you have prescribed. EYFS children are constantly bringing surprises into the setting about things they have discovered, want to know about or share.

One example of good practice I saw was an EYFS lead who, when a child came in with a patch on her eye to address the not-uncommon problem of lazy eye, adapted the lesson plan to make it pirate-themed.

The above pedagogical approaches are golden, impact-over-time things that cost no money. Interventions at the EYFS level look like this rather than 'a this or that type of group' that is the hallmark of boosting learning throughout the key stages.

3. Well-informed staff (especially the SENCO)

Cf. the previous section of this chapter! Many SENCOs haven't got a clue about EYFS and they just don't know where to start. It is a different way of understanding the relationship between curriculum and learning. The Statutory Framework for the Early Years Foundation Stage (Department for Education, 2017b) states exactly how teaching and learning must be approached, through the 'characteristics of effective teaching and learning'. Ofsted also expect to see this. Heads and SENCOs must be aware of this.

The pedagogical approach is that children should learn through experiences. Children need to develop aural skills before literacy; the Rose Review (2006) draws a direct link between language development and dyslexia.

Consequently, the SENCO needs to develop an understanding of EYFS development, in particular the difference between SEN and development. They should understand how the pedagogical approach necessitates an entirely different attitude and strategy for addressing needs, and how getting it right in the EYFS is going to have a massive impact on SEN throughout the rest of the primary school.

EYFS relies on a high ratio of TAs, whose role is very important. However, like in all key stages, TA deployment is only as good as their management. Helping them understand the cognitive, neurological and physical development of young children is foundational in ensuring that their hard work with their wards is meaningful and accurate.

When you walk into an EYFS room, TAs and teachers should be indistinguishable in their action. Their differences should be seen not in who is washing up the paint pots but in who is leading planning.

Assessing children's starting points should be based on constant reflection about what is deemed typical for each child given their chronological age in months, rather than years. Staff should frequently check and agree their judgements with one another and with other stakeholders. This should include the frequent sharing of information with and between parents and health visitors.

4. Constructive environment to facilitate learning

For those of us who are not trained in the art of EYFS pedagogy, this is one of the most different aspects of educational management. Environmental set-up is absolutely key to learning: who would have thought that where you put the chairs and tables could have such an impact on the attainment gap?

The aim is to set up areas of continuous provision such as a water area, sand area, discovery area (with opportunities for children to mix things), creative area, writing and mark-making area using lots of different types of implements, stage area with puppets, etc. None of this costs a lot of money.

These areas facilitate learning through play and activity. Each area should come with lots of suggestions for staff to facilitate key questions and vocabulary. More importantly, ask the children to feed back and evaluate. The entire EYFS space is a learning opportunity and so this needs to be carefully strategised, evaluated and managed.

An important and common example of the impact of not maximising the environment can be seen at Key Stage 2 in boys' writing. We know that boys are generally slower in their development than girls, but the EYFS environmental set-up can go against them. Most activities often tend to be on tables. However, in order to write you need core strength and shoulder stability. When boys sit on the floor, they use their arms and legs. Reception and nursery require sitting, but developmentally boys just don't have it. Therefore, they need floor-based activities that involve kneeling, leaning on arms, stretching up and so on to develop this key core and shoulder stability.

5. The outside environment is completely different

Both EYFS experts emphasise this point most emphatically as being a classic, common mistake. The mistake? To think of the outside environment just like the inside and adopt the same pedagogical approaches and use the same items from the inside. It is common for staff to bring out the play materials from indoors and conduct the same type of learning. Actually, the outside environment is rich with opportunities for different language acquisition and use as well as different types of thinking. Simple questions such as 'Where are those clouds going?' open up such rabbit holes.

6. Simple planning based on learning not activities

Teachers tend to look at the EYFS curriculum and plan accordingly. This certainly makes sense from a primary and secondary perspective. However, this is a significant error in EYFS delivery. Instead, staff should be looking at the children and then referring to the EYFS strategies to support their learning.

This upside-down way of thinking about planning is one of the harder aspects for the primary visitors to get their head around. However, without this child-led approach, the EYFS setting will not directly provide for the child's needs. This is the heart of the attainment gap in development.

Interventions

The process of schools trying to fit the round peg of a 'universal solution' into the square hole of their unique problems is one I see frequently. The schools I have worked with often do not know whether or not they are making progress with the attainment gap because they have no means of properly measuring or monitoring their interventions. Furthermore, lack of more imaginative or strategic interventions leads to a waste of resources and the excessive use of staff.

'Off-the-shelf' solutions are inviting because they appear a safe and inexpensive choice, but they constitute a false economy. Any savings in time or money that are made initially are almost inevitably lost. Such solutions rarely solve the attainment issues because they do not seek to address their underlying causes. The 'buying of a solution' is just an echo of the material, consumer-led-society approach we take with most other things in our lives. Surely, we can buy our way out of the attainment gap? In fact, most governments around the world throw money at this problem but in no way does the quantity of spending really impact the quality of the outcome. The process of narrowing the attainment gap must start with an understanding of the problems of the individuals in question and then, based on this, bespoke plans must be devised.

Far too many interventions end up having a long-term negative, rather than the intended positive, impact on students because they are based on exclusionary practice, which is not reflective of the main class learning environment. With this style of intervention, it becomes impossible to reintegrate the child into the main class because they develop a reliance on being withdrawn from their cohort.

If this style of intervention is allowed to dominate, a vicious cycle can develop as follows (this is also depicted in Figure 3.4):

1. The student is removed for extra support and taught in a separate room; crucially the intervention is often (due to lack of SENCO integration) based around non-curriculum activities.

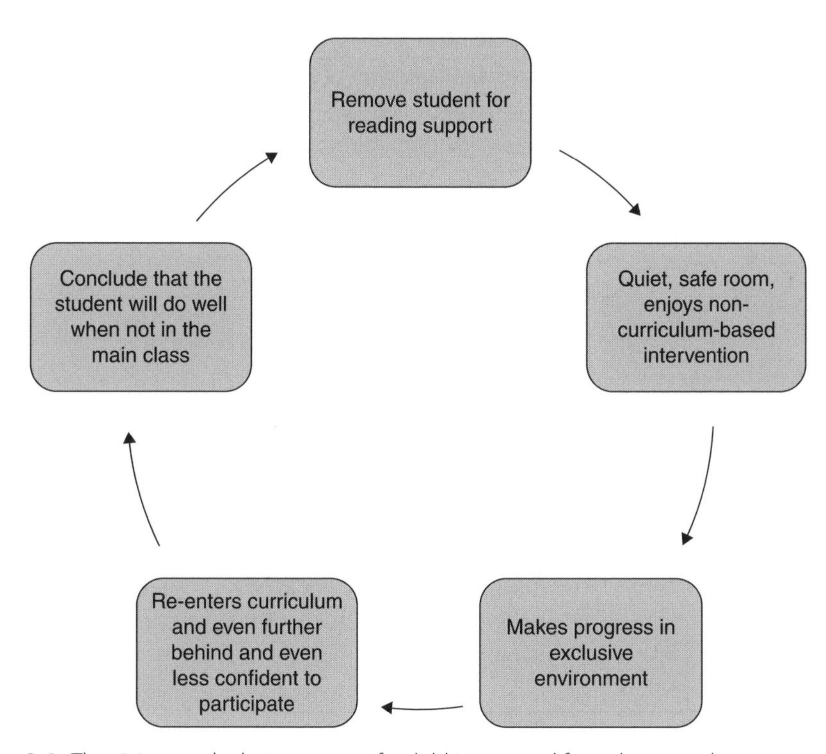

Figure 3.4: The vicious cycle that can occur if a child is removed from the main class

2. The child may then make progress in this exclusive environment but when they return to the main class they find that they lack the confidence to participate due to the fact that they are behind on the curriculum and not accustomed to learning in the main class environment.
3. It is then decided that the child cannot thrive in the main class and so they are removed again. The cycle continues.

What makes this situation worse is that SENCOs are often unable to navigate the challenging procedures that need to be followed to access external support; as such, applications for support from vulnerable schools are frequently refused and headteachers often believe that external help is simply impossible to access. This scenario often leads to the last-gasp measure of hiring yet more TAs to try to combat the problem – exacerbating the issues outlined in the section on TAs earlier in this chapter.

Key takeaway

One-size-fits-all interventions, and interventions that take the child out of the classroom for extended periods of time, can end up doing more harm than good. In the long run, the most cost-effective interventions are those that are highly bespoke, carefully monitored and regularly tweaked.

Schools seeking to narrow the attainment gap should be guided in their choice of interventions by the following principles:

- **Early and longitudinal intervention**
  What is necessary is an understanding of the student and longitudinal intervention – preferably starting with nursery school.

- **Understanding the issue not the symptoms**
  Staff must be trained to identify the reasons behind problems, not just the problems themselves.

- **Flexibility for schools to develop individual approaches**
  Each school should have the freedom to develop its own solutions within the framework suggested.

I will look at each of these in more detail below.

Early and longitudinal intervention

An obvious and powerful strategy is longitudinal collaboration across key stages: I would like to see nurseries, where the attainment gap first emerges, linked through primary schools all the way up to the end of statutory education, with cooperation and strategic thinking happening between stakeholders at every stage. It isn't unusual to find secondary schools working with their feeder primaries in specific ways: around transition, say, or sharing facilities. Another increasingly common collaboration is between staff of different schools working at the same key stage: sharing CPD and moderation, for example. As schools become increasingly federated, there is more space for communication and collaboration. But for the time being this remains uncertain territory and collective strategies are patchy, primarily focused on procurement. While there's some sense that collaboration should naturally carry through to inclusion issues, in my work with schools across the country I have seen very little evidence of this happening in a coherent and sophisticated way.

Understanding the issue not the symptoms

Staff must be trained to identify the reasons behind problems, not just the problems themselves. We must develop a policy of deriving interventions based on communication with the individual students. For example, a solution that worked well for a particular set of year 9 boys who were struggling with achievement was the employment of a gold-toothed, heavily tattooed, 'hard-man' boxing coach. The school had realised that none of the boys in question had a father and this man provided a male role model. Sanctions he introduced, such as refusing them entry to the gym if they got a detention, improved their effort during the school day. These boys all started out with low aspirations, which could, in part, be traced back to the lack of encouragement or expectation to achieve at home; however, the boxing coach told them that they could be great and, moreover, he expected it of them. He emphasised to them that school was their ticket to a better life and, as such, their level of achievement in school rose significantly.

Flexibility for schools to develop individual approaches

Notwithstanding the proceeding notion of a body of researched problems and approaches, each school should have the freedom to develop its own solutions within the framework suggested. The entire approach is personal, bespoke and depends on a deeper, more sensitive approach by the school. There is no reason that a strategy that works in one case or in one school would necessarily work in another.

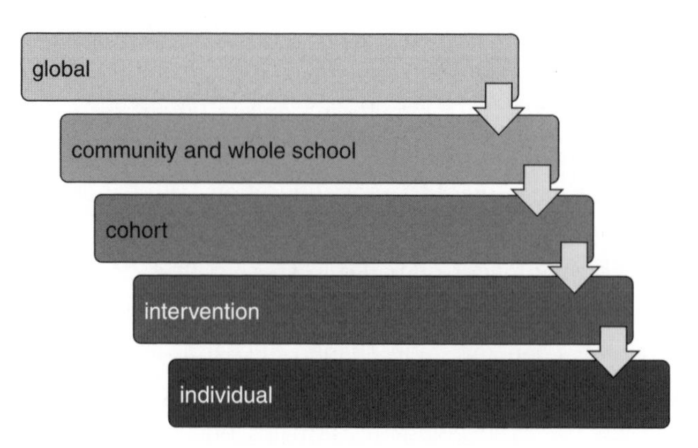

Figure 3.5: The usual approach to tackling whole-school issues

Looking at things the wrong way

I think the issue of schools feeling inhibited in devising innovative decisions is illustrated well by the following example. I recently visited a school in special measures, where I was asked what the best solution was to narrowing attainment gaps in other schools. I suggested that rather than trying to find a solution that had worked in other schools, they focus on identifying the underlying causes of their own attainment gap and address those instead. After much discussion and the creation of a tailored plan of action, staff asked, 'Are you sure we are allowed to do this?' In asking that question, they summarised the feeling of strong inhibition and timidity felt by many vulnerable schools.

Figure 3.5 depicts the usual process of thinking about how to tackle whole-school issues. It starts with outside influences such as Ofsted ('Global'), then what the school needs to do to meet the issue and then how that requirement applies to cohorts. At this point, schools will buy or devise an intervention and only then decide which students they can use it for.

Think about how this process prioritises the school's issue rather than what causes the issues. This is a major flaw in the thinking of schools in addressing the gap. Really, it doesn't so much matter what outside factors, pieces of research or letters from the Department for Education to the school demanding action say when they cause generic responses to issues that are actually a conglomeration of lots of specific issues. What I am saying may make sense on this page but in the real-life context of a school it feels normal to do it the 'wrong way' and counter-intuitive to rethink a problem in the way I am about to describe.

Figure 3.6 shows an alternative road into whole-school issues such as narrowing the gap. We are not creating systems to fit individuals into, but making them our starting point and our reference point for further review. You could call this a 'soft-data approach' since it is predicated on reasons, barriers and motivators. Start with individual students, build up to cohorts and work out how you can address individual needs on a larger group level. Eventually, build systems around your organic practice.

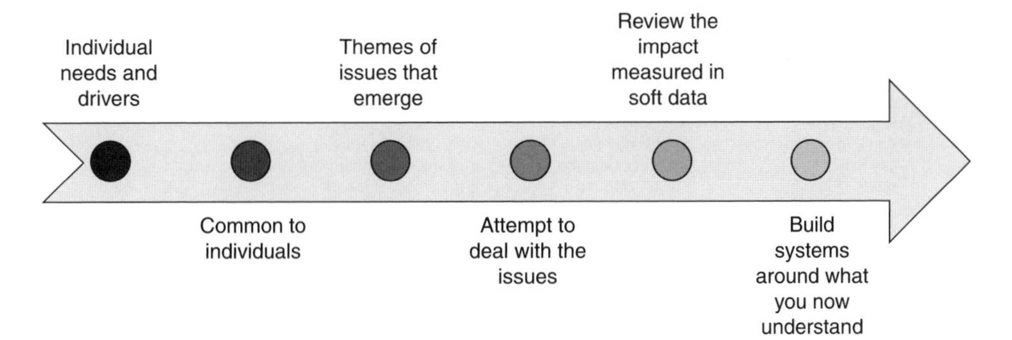

Figure 3.6: An alternative approach to tackling whole-school issues that begins with the needs of individual students

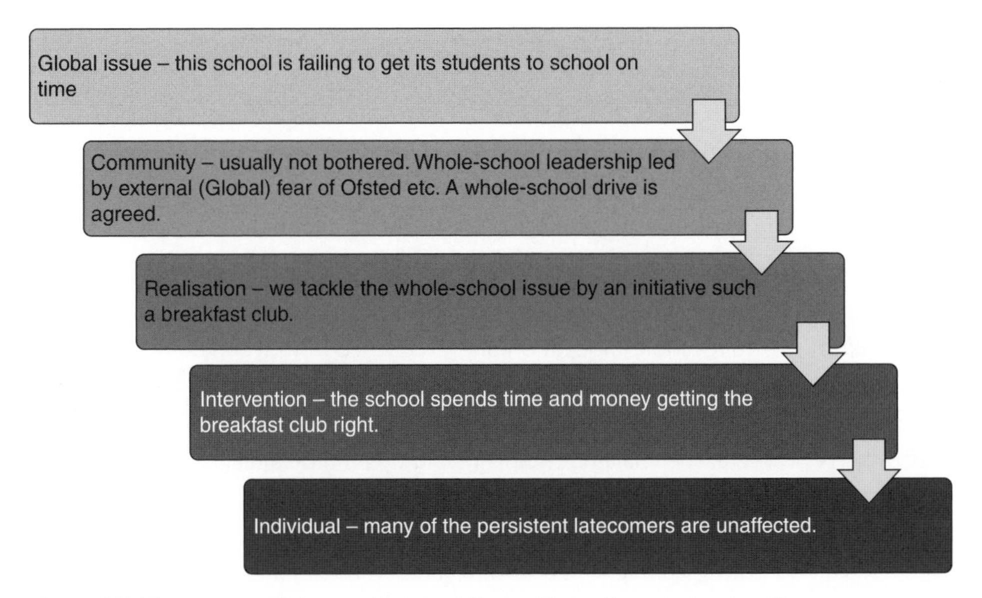

Figure 3.7: The outcome if 'the usual approach' is used to tackle a whole-school issue

Take the same problem as processed through each view. The outcomes are very different, as can be seen in Figures 3.7 and 3.8.

If it were up to me, when heads take on their first school they would be made aware of these common patterns and be told to look out for them in their schools. The real problem is being isolated, unaware and unsure of where to look. Every company is trying to sell them a quick-fix solution and somehow, their nearest outstanding school simply doesn't understand the quagmire because they were never in it themselves. All of these problems must be dealt with from the unique vantage point of the school; moreover, from the vantage point of the individual child.

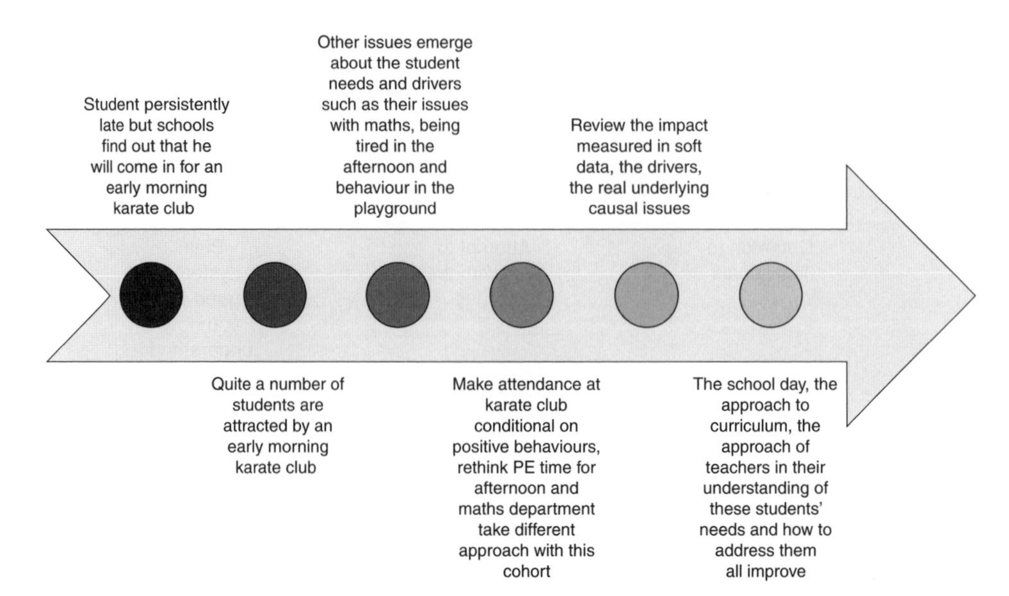

Figure 3.8: The outcome if 'the alternative approach' is used to tackle a whole-school issue

Maths

It took me three attempts to pass maths GCSE. The subject is challenging in a multitude of ways: it's conceptually difficult and potentially dry; it has traditionally been thought of as 'boring'; it requires more innovation and excellence from teachers than perhaps any other subject, and yet struggles perhaps more than any other to attract willing recruits. Unsurprisingly, the attainment gap in terms of pure grades is often bigger in maths than elsewhere. The challenges of resolving this can be a real barrier to broader progress.

The notion that the answer lies in intervention through remedial lessons in students' free time is like giving extra salad to children who won't eat their vegetables: seemingly logical and actually pointless. Such a response is usually based upon three tacit assumptions. Firstly, that the socio-economic circumstances of students are external variables; they cannot be changed. Secondly, that a school's role is to teach, so intervention must be led by the curriculum. Thirdly, the intervention must be based on a generally applicable rubric, so that consistency can be guaranteed. Each of these assumptions is in part, or in whole, mistaken.

Schools cannot expect to change the socio-economic background of children, but they can work to address the specific effects that arise as a result of children's backgrounds. The effects of a child's socio-economic background come in many shades and can be as diverse as: low self-esteem and aspiration, poor language comprehension or practical problems with access to regular meals and reliable transport to school. To illustrate this diversity, I would point to the following case study.

Case study: year 9 boys in Norwich

I was impressed recently by the investigative efforts of a school in Norwich, where a group of year 9 boys had been struggling with maths for quite a while and was falling further and further behind. The school found that common to 17 out of the 20 lowest achieving boys was some sort of speech and language difficulty. They decided to buy in SALT (speech and language therapy) support for their maths teachers, who learned just how difficult the boys found the ***language*** of maths – rather than the concepts, at which the majority were surprisingly good.

Differentiation and personalised learning

It can be tough to teach whole classes of impoverished children, or any children with challenges, and there is a correlation between the extent of the attainment gap and quality of teaching. But how can school leaders tackle this effectively? Many schools have ongoing support and training in-house or more recently from a **teaching school alliance**. But does this really work?

Differentiation is accepted as part of teaching, but too often we don't offer true differentiation to all students, especially those with SEN. This section sets out a more nuanced and investigative approach to differentiation.

Challenging classroom behaviours usually come down to two factors: the attitude of the teacher and the degree to which instruction is tailored to the individual – we of course call this differentiation.

It is my strongly held belief that if the teacher comes to class with a positive mindset, effective differentiation takes care of the rest. Look through any classroom window: the disengaged learner is easy to spot. He or she has their back to the teacher, trying to distract their classmates or they are doing their very best to go unnoticed, making movements that look like writing or pretending to read.

There is always a subtext to this story. These students may simply not be getting learning that works with their natural disposition. They are simply not able to absorb that which doesn't play to their strengths.

What does effective differentiation look like?

Throughout my career, I have observed that the vast majority of teachers have a strong and sincere desire to differentiate, yet too often they rely on a flimsy understanding of the underlying principles. They may have gleaned ideas from the Internet, or attended CPD or twilight sessions that reference the topic in vague terms, but they lack the tools to implement a nuanced articulation of individualised learning.

I have seen so many sincere attempts at differentiation that I believe amount to no more than window dressing: an example I keep running into is the addition of explanatory visuals to complex task instructions, in the hope that this will penetrate language processing difficulties.

Other common examples of well-intentioned but ineffective attempts at differentiation include:

- Increasing the size of a font, or of a worksheet itself, in the hope that the student will suddenly 'get it' because it's larger.
- Double-spacing text, again without altering vocabulary, only to find that the student with general learning difficulties is still unable to complete the work without support.
- Using TAs to explain text, without thinking about how work could be pitched so that pupils use more independent thinking.
- Expecting students with language processing difficulties to successfully interpret poetry because the teacher has given the student a choice of descriptive words – of equal inferential complexity – that could fit into a sentence gap.

Real differentiation is about devising and implementing strategies that scaffold the kind of nuanced support that is expected in the modern classroom. Examples of effective differentiation might include: timed learning targets; writing patterns of behaviour into support – as opposed to simply trying to quash challenging behaviours with carrot or stick; giving autism spectrum disorder or ADHD students 'fiddle time' between tasks; allowing time out from learning when needed; or qualifying subject-specific vocabulary for students with short-term or working memory difficulties.

Key barriers to quality differentiation

Again from my experience, the key barriers to effective differentiation are:

- The teacher doesn't have enough time to make elaborate resources.
- The teacher doesn't know their students well enough.
- The teacher takes the easy road in using generic 'differentiated' materials, which do not meet the needs of individual students.

The biggest factor in my experience is so often that bugbear of educators everywhere: teachers are overstretched as it is, and simply don't have the time or energy to prepare effective materials or to devote to one or two students that need help.

An example: a young teacher at an inner London school I worked with couldn't explain why two of his students were having difficulties, and he didn't know how to go about accessing the information that could help him. He also understood that even if he were able to access relevant files or documents, he was ill-prepared to address the issues. He was frustrated that although he was trying hard to support the students by downloading resources from the Internet, the challenged students were still unable to participate in his lessons and he could not afford the time to produce resources to help them.

Why most differentiation training doesn't stick

I believe that most differentiation training is too generic and is delivered in lecture format or in abstract fashion, where the only resource is a book, which doesn't address key barriers faced by individual students.

In-school CPD training is nearly always delivered to cohorts of teachers within subject groups – or even generally delivered. Usually an 'in-the-know' lecturer will stand in front of the group, brandishing a clicker, and will flick through a sophisticated PowerPoint presentation. Occasionally the delivery of information will be more dynamic, with the lecturer facilitating interaction and discussion, which will of course excite and empower teachers to incorporate new ideas.

However, these ideas and methods, sometimes brilliant for whole-class advancement, are rarely pitched towards those one or two students with specific needs.

An investigative approach

So how about a more investigative approach? Why 'investigative'? Well, it is about talking to teachers to identify their needs. We should encourage teachers to seek more feedback from their students in order to broaden their understanding of the difficulties they face.

How might you deliver this? After an initial 'back-of-class' lesson observation, a discussion with the teacher on what has been observed can take place to delve deeper into perceived successes and difficulties that the teacher identifies. This dialogue should centre around the ways in which a teacher's current provision meets the needs of students experiencing difficulties, what changes can be adopted to increase both student access to the curriculum and the working knowledge a teacher could benefit from. It is only after this meeting that a nuanced and personalised differentiation can be planned according to the needs of the SEN individuals in each class.

Going back to the example of the London teacher: during a classroom observation, it was noted that a student with autism sat with her fingers in her ears and her eyes closed during the viewing of a loud and frenetic video. When this observation was fed back to the teacher, he responded, 'Oh yes, she often does that to get out of doing the work.'

It was obvious to us that the teacher had scant understanding of the traits and common behaviours associated with the autistic spectrum, and of how students with autism can often respond to sensory overload. The teacher had misinterpreted the student's response as bad behaviour. As a result, time was spent with the teacher addressing this and then planning ways in which their new knowledge could be put into practice to get more positive outcomes.

So what are the key tenets of an investigative approach?

Nuanced understanding

The teacher should seek a deeper, more nuanced understanding of their students as a foundational step. Usually a teacher is easily able to identify students in their class who obviously present with either challenging behaviour or lack of engagement. In many instances, a teacher will point out a student with more specific needs such as Asperger's or dyslexia, but yet are seen to be providing them with the same resources as their peers. The process should work collaboratively with the teacher, by establishing what knowledge they do have, then supporting them with additional information. The teacher is then supported to model resources, which are often immediately effective.

Applied to all lessons

Any time spent planning for specific students is valuable and scarce, so inherent to success is that all knowledge imparted and resources planned are useful not just for the SEN or gifted and talented students, but are the foundation of good practice within the general classroom setting too. Instead of coming up with new materials, teachers should be able to adapt the resources they already use.

Small groups

Rather than deliver generic advice to large groups of teachers, try working with smaller groups of identified staff who are in a great position to cascade ideas to their colleagues. By working in this way the facilitator can address case studies brought to the meeting, understand the learning that has been provided thus far, and acknowledge successes and good practice while helping to develop new methodologies with which a teacher can progress effective bespoke differentiation.

Teaching assistants (TAs)

The SEND Code of Practice encourages both TAs and teachers to work collaboratively in meeting the needs of their students. No longer should a TA be used to 'babysit' a student, to sit with them in a 'velcroed' manner, or to give relief to the teacher by removing disruptive students from the classroom.

Instead, lessons should be planned in such a way that the TA is aware of what is being taught and is proactive in the delivery of materials. By giving the TA an integral role as the lesson is planned, they become an inherent part of the teaching team, imparting their knowledge of the students as part of the discussion.

Conclusion

By way of conclusion, I want to offer four approaches to the challenges explored in this chapter. I don't see one solution per problem; rather, I think that a few broad-stroke approaches can bring the very different issues together into a virtuous cycle of improvement.

Approach 1: celebrate

One thing these difficult issues have in common is that they are all topics mired knee-deep in disparagement, negativity and a general lack of hope. One example is the mental health of children (and indeed staff and the community): most heads could wax lyrical about the sheer lack of support, resources and the bleak state of the broken system. While it won't solve the problems, heavy doses of belief and optimism do go a long way.

I tried an experiment in one school where the lack of differentiation and personalised learning was very much at the heart of the 'requires improvement' Ofsted grade. The headteacher started sending an email out to all staff praising one or two teachers who had done a fantastic piece of differentiation, and sent them individual 'fantastic work' thank you cards. After a few weeks, the message was planted among the staff that recognition and reward were available. This obviously has to be coupled with some training and support.

This is the other side of the coin that says 'my way or the highway', which I have sometimes heard heads espouse proudly, as if an iron fist is the only hallmark of robust leadership. The problem with such an approach is that it fosters little goodwill, creativity or imagination and staff turnover tends to be high.

My contention is that you get out of your staff whatever you put into them, and if you are full of praise and encouragement you are usually rewarded in kind. The experiment we tried continues to this day and there is an atmosphere in the school that good teaching is warmly celebrated.

Similarly, celebrating your achievements loudly could be more than just a nice thing to do; it could be a priority. One school called me because they were expecting Ofsted. There wasn't much time to address the problematic blue items on RAISEonline, so I asked them instead to take me to the room where the inspectors would be based. It was a meeting room with bare walls.

By the end of the day, it was covered floor to ceiling with every possible positive thing the school could say, from a quote by a student about how great the breakfast club was to how much another student had enjoyed reading a book for the first time, to a newspaper clipping about a competition some students had won. The room shouted: 'we love our school'. We then replicated this in the entrance hall.

Something I have learned by visiting schools is that the attitude of the whole school is written on the walls of the entrance area. You can tell an outstanding school because they are so proud and shout about it from the moment you walk through the door. You can replicate this trick regardless of your Ofsted rating. Be outward-facing to the press and celebrate everything very publicly. Why? Because every function of the school requires a belief that you can do it, from leadership in curriculum to engagement of families. If you want parents to engage more, then make them proud of your amazing institution by declaring it in multi-colour on a regular basis.

Remember, your staff and all of your stakeholders walk through that entrance too. Celebrate them and they will show you goodwill in turn. The naysayers will claim that this has nothing to do with pedagogy and is just a marketing trick. That would be true if it were done in isolation, but if you are in the process of change, it will ultimately become much more than varnish atop a festering mess; and it can make the difference between Ofsted grades.

Approach 2: think of SEN anew

The kind of reinvention SEN needs in order to meet the SEND Code of Practice is not cosmetic. However, it is possible to meet the Code of Practice's requirements and still miss the point. The point? Make SEN a whole-school venture, not the sole domain of the appointed SENCO.

The old SENCO role died a few years ago and yet in most schools I visit, it persists like a ghost. The reason for this, the real issue we have to deal with, is teachers' perception of their role around SEN. A strategic starting point for your leadership team might be for you to imagine that you do not have a SENCO, interventions or even TAs and that all SEN is to be dealt with by the teachers only (okay, assume just for the exercise that you have a visiting SENCO to take care of the SEN panel paperwork!).

In this scenario, what would your teachers need in terms of training and planning to rise to this challenge? When you can answer that question and work out how you can implement it, then you are on track to what 'think of SEN anew' actually means in reality.

It could be that you would want to dedicate one member of staff to help the teachers get their differentiation just right – and that would be the new SENCO role. It could be that TAs would be deployed more infrequently and be used only when they have had solid training and regular line management to ensure they are not simply unburdening the teacher.

I appreciate that this is a larger topic than just this one exercise – but the key point is the need for reinvention and what that actually means in reality for your school.

Approach 3: EYFS expertise

Quickly admit what you don't know. If you are not EYFS-trained then you don't know EYFS well enough to recognise problems. Two common problems are that primary heads often have to be persuaded that their EYFS staff don't have sufficient training, and that EYFS leads in schools are sometimes not great managers: so whereas they themselves may be knowledgeable, their staff might not be. This leaves primary headteachers vulnerable to misinformation or even unaware of the lack of information (they don't know what they don't know). I don't know a magic trick to get out of this conundrum but I think it may start with being honest.

For any school that has struggled to make progress from their current Ofsted category to the next, I strongly recommend that they consider an independent, warts-and-all EYFS review with a strategic implementation plan specifically written for the headteacher to use for line management.

Approach 4: be sceptical and creative

It is a hallmark of low-Ofsted-grade schools that they perpetuate interventions that are not regularly managed or critically evaluated. Ask your SENCO, teacher and TA to come up with an intervention that meets the needs of the students of that particular class, track it every week, review it every six weeks and assume it should not last longer than two terms. This easy formula has produced some fantastic results. Remember the key here: interventions have to be line managed and held to account very carefully.

Ultimately, my advice to schools for breaking down the barriers to inclusion outlined in this chapter is this – ask 'What do our students actually need?' and work from there.

What works for your unique setting has to be bespoke. The capacity of the staff to deliver and how often and how well they are line managed are as much factors as the intervention itself.

PART 2

Actions

4 Getting everyone on board

Having set out the context and causes of the attainment gap issue in Chapters 1 to 3, this chapter and the following chapters are structured slightly differently: they outline practical steps that you can take in your setting and conclude with a list of action points. This chapter reflects on the people you can involve in your strategies to narrow the attainment gap and the best ways to approach and communicate with them.

Promoting social migration at the stage in life at which it is most achievable requires understanding and cooperation across each aspect of a disadvantaged pupil's background: their life in school, at home and in their local area. Allocating resources for disadvantaged students is, in this sense, a community-wide project.

Your disadvantaged students are influenced by their interaction with a wide range of people, both in the school and in the community. This means that it is highly beneficial to involve as many people as possible – not only from within the school, but also parents and other members of the wider community. These people are your stakeholders. An effective spending strategy must reflect and utilise this web of relationships.

Gathering stakeholders will help you build a picture of the context of your school, particularly of the challenges of and interplay between different groups in your area. Every school is different, even in terms of how a shared issue might present itself: impoverishment in an inner-city school in London doesn't function in the same way as impoverishment in a small coastal town. The goal of gathering stakeholders is to really get to grips with these quirks and nuances. This needn't be a drawn-out process of consultation; the idea is simply to have conversations. Get in touch with a wide range of people, tell them about your aims to narrow the gap, and get feedback from them on key local issues. The more perspectives you can bring on board, the fuller your picture will be.

Identifying and gathering stakeholders

Within the school itself, try to involve a range of people who know the students in different settings in your strategies to reduce the attainment gap.

There is no need to collate this information in any particular way, although it is definitely worth making notes of your conversations, and it could well be useful to write them up afterwards. The focus, instead, should be on speaking to as many people and gaining as much perspective as possible.

All of the following people will have differing and useful perspectives to offer:

- senior management
- heads of year
- heads of department
- class teachers
- form teachers
- TAs
- SENCOs
- extra-curricular staff (e.g. musical instrument teachers)
- staff involved with school data and paperwork
- accountant/bursar.

Governors

Governors could well be included in the list above, but it is important to focus on them in a slightly different way. In England, Ofsted have increasingly been grilling governors on the issues relating to the pupil premium. As such, it's important that governors are kept in the loop.

Keep them updated with your findings at each stage; they are *obliged* to know about core data details of money, provision, attainment and progress.

Governors' report

It is good practice to produce a report on the issue of the attainment gap for submission to your governors. This further ensures that the issue is being talked about at every level, and creates a paper trail to prove it. Governor enthusiasm and involvement are obviously beneficial, and can go a long way towards putting structures in place to help disadvantaged students.

How you create the report is up to you, but it should contain:

- basic data (student numbers and other hard data)
- a summary of the key concerns and successes from the beginning of the year
- financial details

- how the money was spent
- the results.

This report, with the minutes of the meeting at which it was discussed if available, would be a valuable addition to the Ofsted or equivalent folder.

Governors are interested in overall policy and direction, rather than the nitty gritty of a school's work on the attainment gap. As community representatives, they should be especially active in helping the school understand its community and ensuring that the school is responding to community issues.

Students

Even the peers of disadvantaged students can be effective stakeholders. For example, peer-to-peer coaching is often, surprisingly, more successful than the use of highly trained educational psychologists, especially in areas of social ability and self-esteem. A sixth former from the same area and background as a younger student – perhaps even one who knows them – can often get through to that student, or act as a role model for them, in a way that a paid staff member could not. As well as being effective, such coaching is also completely free (although it may be that the sixth former requires some level of support from staff).

I've seen this in play in a number of schools, and what's particularly remarkable is the impact that a well-managed peer-to-peer programme can have on the older student, as well as the student being mentored. The older student is given responsibility and a sense that they have a role to play and are being trusted and respected by teachers, all of which can have a huge impact on their motivation to work hard and engage in learning.

Parents

Parents of disadvantaged children are frequently let down by the education system. They can feel intimidated in school meetings and generally distrustful of an education system that may have let them down during their own childhood. Challenging meetings, for example, where a parent gets worked up and aggressive, might be understood as playing-out a time in that parent's own experience of education when he or she wasn't able to stand up to a teacher he or she disliked. Likewise, parents who refuse to engage might still be fighting a deeply embedded aversion to school.

At the same time, most parents are full of anxieties around their child's future, and many feel powerless and overwhelmed. They might experience frustration at their inability to get hold of anyone at the school who can really help, answer their questions or reassure them. As a result, these parents often disengage with the school – unlike parents of better-off children, who might be more able to 'battle the system' and get what they want for their child.

All in all, it's not just a matter of setting up opportunities for engagement and seeing to the parents who turn up. Schools need to reach out and actively win parents' trust.

Anyone who has worked in a school knows that the more that homes are involved, the better students perform. This was confirmed in the Lamb Inquiry of 2009. Engaging hard-to-reach families (families that keep their distance or deliberately avoid engaging with the school) is especially important, because there's a slight correlation between these families and students with lower attainment. But doing so requires quite a lot of skill and needs to be bespoke to each community.

A few years ago I worked with a school in Staines, West London that reached out to parents who never came into the school by setting up a table in its local supermarket. The table was manned by TAs from the community who spoke the relevant languages, and offered free hot drinks and biscuits to parents who paused to chat about the school. (Staffing drop-off and pickup time is another good way of getting hold of parents who don't normally engage.) There are many examples, more fully explored in Chapter 5, of schools making positive progress through an effort to involve parents and make them feel central to their children's success.

The starting point must be the assumption that parents care more about their child's progress than indulging their own emotions and needs – even though this might not always appear to be the case from the school's perspective.

We need to encourage teachers to engage with parents empathetically. We are not asking staff to become counsellors or shoulders to cry on; however, staff should be trained to be more aware of parents' feelings, and learn how and why these feelings can prevent the parent from being reasonable or cooperative even if this is to the detriment of the child. Teachers can then be given strategies and resources on how to support a parent. I have seen many cases of staff who, after receiving training in parent relationships, note positive impacts on the student both emotionally and academically.

Ask parents about their own children and about their impressions of the school and wider community. There's no need to focus specifically on the attainment gap. The aim is to develop an understanding of the broader issue of disadvantage and social mobility in the area. But at the same time, parents of course have a unique knowledge and understanding of the issues affecting their child, so it's important that they are brought on board and kept engaged.

Key takeaway

Parents have invaluable insights to offer, about both their child and the attainment gap issue as a whole in the local area. But many parents are distrustful of the education system, as a result of concerns about their child or bad experiences during their own schooling. Schools should engage with parents in an active and empathetic way.

Services

Social workers and educational welfare officers will have invaluable insight into individual pupils and the wider context of the school. They don't need to be invited – they come to the school anyway – but the goal is to get their views on community-wide issues and dynamics, rather than the specific individual cases they might be working on. If they can be encouraged to step back and take a view, they are likely to have fantastic insight to offer.

Two other really valuable service providers, who know a great deal about their communities, are GPs and local government officials (including MPs). Invite them in for a meeting: they will have a behind-the-scenes perspective on things the school might otherwise never see. They are of course extremely busy people, but in my experience GPs in particular are surprisingly willing to help out local schools, as a way of supporting the local community as a whole.

As ever, record minutes of stakeholder meetings and publicise them on the school website if possible.

Wider community

Consider speaking to youth workers, local religious leaders, people involved with out-of-school sports clubs, and so on, who have contact with significant groups of your students.

Let people know that you are spearheading an important process within the school and ask if they can be supportive. Bringing a wide range of people on board will help concrete an understanding of the school's position at the centre of the local community. It will also establish a network of people to advise and support you and the school with the attainment gap both now and in future.

Two brilliant examples here are, first, a Church of England school with a significant number of Muslim pupils, which invited the local Imam to work with governors and senior leadership on better understanding the dynamics of its students.

Similarly, I worked with a primary school in Wolverhampton a couple of years ago that had a large number of Sikh students. They were struggling with their attainment gap and, as part of their strategy for improvement, reached out to a Gurdwara in the area to build ties with parents and the community as a whole.

SENCOs

I haven't encountered any school that has been successful in narrowing the gap in which attainment and SEN are managed separately. Lack of coordination leads to duplication of both staff time and resources. In one extreme example, I conducted an attainment review for a school and as part of the process helped them build a provision map that allocated resources to all their disadvantaged students. I returned a few months later to run an SEN review. It quickly transpired that the SEN team hadn't even been told about the provision map, even though nearly all their SEN students featured in it. If SENCOs aren't involved early on in your work on narrowing the gap, you will end up wasting time and money and are much less likely to be successful.

In all honesty, I wouldn't recommend anyone to become a SENCO. It's not a job for someone who values their work–life balance. I fell into the role many years ago rather unknowingly, and when I first started I decided to visit a couple of schools to chat with peers who had been in the role for more than ten years. I still remember what Mike (who recently took early retirement) told me in his strong Northern Irish accent: 'The thing is, Daniel, to be a good SENCO, you have to always prioritise your mental health.' I recall thinking at the time that this must be rather unique advice to receive in one's first week in the job. But since then I have worked with hundreds of SENCOs across the UK and, I have to say, I think he was right.

SENCOs are often frustrated in their dealings with both school and parents. Few headteachers reached the top through the SENCO route, and they often lack an understanding of the challenges the SENCO faces. They may struggle to handle parents who phone too much and appear overly demanding. The SENCO might resent the parents' apparent anger and search for someone to blame over the school's failure to meet their child's needs. At times, the SENCO may become scared or upset with angry parents and will understandably avoid talking with them, yet this avoidance only makes the situation worse for all involved, especially the child in question. Though a difficult situation may soon be escalated to the headteacher, their authority may not be enough to overcome their lack of real knowledge about the student, and the head all too often ends up dealing with the frustration rather than the cause of the frustration and potential solutions.

The role of the SENCO spans both the micro and the macro; covering people, provisions and budgets, SENCOs have the fullest involvement with individual students, run the largest department, and take responsibility for whole-school leadership issues such as lesson design by teachers. Every SENCO will lack skills or training in at least one of these complex areas of management; even a management trainee at a leading company would be overwhelmed. As a result, something gets dropped, whether successfully influencing the headteacher or continuing to support vulnerable students.

To solve this, schools need to train and support SENCOs to lead on whole-school issues in the same way as other senior staff.

Key takeaway

SENCOs have a critical role to play in narrowing the gap, but to perform it they need effective management and plenty of support.

Teaching assistants (TAs)

When it comes to the really challenging cases – those involving the most disadvantaged students – TAs are the front line. That makes them a goldmine of soft data. I wrote in the previous chapter about the importance of ensuring that TAs are properly trained and supported. It is equally important to include them in any big vision for narrowing a school's attainment gap. TAs can often feel disregarded, at the bottom rung of a large and siloed school hierarchy. Schools should make an effort to include them – to ensure that they understand the project and feel valued for the critical role they play in it. I find that the best way to facilitate this is sharing information about students and families at regular facilitated TA group meetings.

TAs are also often better informed about the local community than teachers because, generally, they come from it. This is why I advocate that TAs call home regularly with positive news about student performance. Most schools contact home when there's a problem; contacting with good news ensures that when there is a problem, the pathway of communication is already there. This is best done by TAs because they speak the same language – often literally, and in terms of a shared background, class and community that helps them get parents on side.

Home visits

I encourage all school leaders, both senior and middle, to do occasional home visits, so that they encounter parents of the community they serve in their real settings. In these visits they will see real people and real poverty, and understand the needs of vulnerable students first-hand. Generally home visits are met with scepticism by parents or carers the first couple of times, but I find more often than not they're welcomed from the third visit onwards.

Obviously home visits should never be done alone, and should be run in line with proper protocols and safeguards. Sometimes home visits can be traumatic – I've known quite hardened senior leaders to come back tearful. As such, if appropriate, proper support should be made available for staff.

Communicating your goals and progress

A key step in getting everyone on board is communicating clearly and effectively with all the stakeholders in your school community. Below are some thoughts on keeping track of what you know, and telling the right people about it.

Consolidating and sharing your information

As previously mentioned, it may be difficult to properly consolidate and structure the various strands of information that you gather from your conversations with stakeholders.

Nor is there any particular call to do so in a formal way. Of course, having notes to which you can refer back will likely become useful, and it may also be valuable to write up one or two paragraphs summarising your findings. Distilling your research in this way is an apt conclusion to the process, and could help to crystallise your sense of which are the most significant of your findings.

You might email these paragraphs to everyone with whom you have spoken; this keeps them engaged and makes them feel part of a significant and ongoing process. For stakeholders outside of the school, it will probably also be helpful to include information that you take for granted.

Since there's a statute in England that information about a school's use of the pupil premium grant must be publicised on its website, anyone coming in to inspect a school will read it. Probably no one else will – parents generally don't. But it's a backdoor to the hearts and minds of inspectors. Write as much as you want, and make it fantastic; it's pretty much a unique opportunity to demonstrate that you've really worked to engage stakeholders, to understand how your school is unique, and to respond accordingly. This is non-challengeable, because the inspectors coming into your school aren't going to claim they know your community better than you do. They just want evidence that *you* know your community. Don't be afraid of writing at length and including minutes of stakeholder meetings, records of home visits and so on.

Exemplary data

Along with the broader data, include a number of exemplar documents that give a much more precise level of detail. These provide not only a more specific but often a more accessible insight into one or two of the interventions that the school is using. It allows readers to engage with specific programmes and targets, and to see the students that these are benefiting (or, equally importantly, not benefiting). Such documents also demonstrate the level of care in the micromanagement of the whole project. They can be given to your team, to senior management, to governors, and even posted on the school website, providing individual names are removed.

Beyond statutory requirements

Encourage your school to celebrate the progress it makes in narrowing the gap. After all, the results you achieve don't only represent money well spent, but also effective work on the national issue of social migration.

Keep parents and other external stakeholders in the loop: mention the issue in newsletters and emails, and perhaps even link to the relevant section of the school website in your email signature. Post information and positive results on boards in the school. Preface the information on your website by saying that the issue is a high priority for the school. Beyond the information necessary to fulfil statutory requirements, consider including:

- a list of your interventions, mentioning that these are in regular review
- the specific documents discussed above (edited to be in accordance with data protection regulations)
- some success stories.

School Improvement Plan

The attainment gap is not a separate topic from the major pillars of running a school: curriculum, teaching and learning, and pastoral care. It's influenced by and influences what's going on in every single classroom at a particular point in the day. Everything, save perhaps budgeting for roof repairs, is an attainment gap issue.

Push for attainment gap issues to be included in your School Improvement Plan. This helps to ensure that they will continue to be prioritised in future years, and demonstrates to any inspectoral eyes that the gap is high on the school's agenda. But ideally go further and root the entire Plan in the perspective of narrowing the gap.

This could be done by drawing out a key theme – one school we worked with focused their whole Plan around the issue of language acquisition, because it was common to nearly all attainment gap students and those students were a majority of the school. They decided to run a theme of a 'language-rich' school: they taught new words every day and students were encouraged to find new words of their own accord and to be excited by them, to make personal dictionaries, and so on. Students with pastoral support needs were encouraged to learn new words for expressing themselves. This is a fantastic example of a multi-track, intersectional vision, and the results were fantastic.

An example school

The Fort Royal Special School is in Worcester and is led by Ed Francis. Ed and I worked on the school's attainment gap, with a focus on engaging stakeholders. His leadership team wrote the following report about the school for its website, to be shared with stakeholders.

The Nature of Disadvantage and Vulnerability at Fort Royal School and a Rationale for the Deployment of the Pupil Premium Grant

(Reproduced with the generous permission of Fort Royal School)

'The sheer quantity and high-quality provisions at Fort Royal School is unusual and outstanding'

D. Sobel – independent advisor who led our School Pupil Premium Review in January and February 2016

As can be seen from the government advice (below) it is imperative that the Pupil Premium Grant (PPG) is focused to support the learning of the most disadvantaged and vulnerable in school.

> *'The pupil premium is additional funding given to publicly funded schools in England to raise the attainment of disadvantaged pupils and close the gap between them and their peers [...] The pupil premium is paid to schools as they are best placed to access what additional provision their pupils need.' Department for Education, March 2014*

The nature of disadvantage and vulnerability at Fort Royal School (FRS) is, however, an extremely complex picture. Pupils who receive the PPG make up just over 43 per cent of the whole school population. This compares to only 28 per cent nationally and puts us in the upper percentile. Our school deprivation indicator, however, is only 0.22, which is exactly on par with the national average and so sits squarely at the mid percentile.

Our school catchment area covers a large part of the south of the county and includes rural, urban and semi-urban areas and no one socio-economic background is more prevalent than any other (as our deprivation indicator suggests).

These statistics inevitably raise the following questions:

- Why do we have such a high proportion of pupils who receive the PPG and
- What is the nature of their disadvantage if it is not necessarily social deprivation?

We need to be able to answer these questions in order to accurately focus our PPG and adequately support our disadvantaged and vulnerable learners.

To help us answer these questions we began by sending out a survey to other agencies (health, social services and education) who work with our pupils and families to glean information from their data, knowledge and expertise.

From this exercise we have been able to identify the following four factors which we feel explain our increased prevalence of pupils eligible for the PPG above that which would be expected from our mid percentile deprivation score.

1. The additional pressures and challenges of having a disabled child in the family sometimes lead to parents deciding not to work or work only part time in order to

support their child. This may lead to reliance on disability benefits and grants provided by the government, which include factors which would qualify their children for the PPG.

2. This issue is even more prevalent if the child also has complex health needs and requires 24-hour care and frequent appointments with medical professionals.
3. Although we are not able to collect specific data on this issue, it is clear that some (and above average expectations) of our pupils' parents also have a disability or learning difficulty. Employment prospects are not good for those with learning difficulties.
4. Within the general population a higher proportion of pupils who have a learning disability are cared for within the looked after system.

These factors all contribute to a very complex and intertwined picture of disadvantage and vulnerability of FRS which the school must address. Viewing the issue as purely a PPG issue is clearly too simplistic. The vulnerability of many of our learners is prevalent within the PPG population and the nature of the factors which enables many of our learners to qualify for the PPG also makes them very vulnerable but it is also clear that this vulnerability also goes much further into the wider school population.

An analysis of the various significant factors which may have an impact on vulnerability of pupils at FRS or on which vulnerability can impact such as:

- attendance
- ethnic background (EDL)
- progress and attainment
- safeguarding concerns
- emotional health and wellbeing
- health needs
- nature and severity of individual disability

all indicate that there is no one particular common need of the cohort of pupils who receive the PPG that separates or distinguishes them from their peers which would indicate a specific route to targeting our PPG. Our pupils who receive the PPG are on a par with their peers; there is no discernable difference between the cohorts in terms of attainment or any of the factors listed above. The issues that are pertinent to vulnerable learners within the school are also pertinent to the PPG group. The pupils who receive the PPG in fact form a subsection of this wider vulnerable group with similar and overlapping needs.

Therefore we can be confident that the intervention and provision we plan for our general population of vulnerable learners will also have a significant impact on the PPG group.

So although we do target PPG funds for specific resources and activities for individual pupils who qualify if deemed appropriate, we also use the funds to expand the whole-school provision and interventions we plan for all our vulnerable learners in the sure and certain knowledge that pupils in receipt of the PPG will benefit.

Parent support and engagement

The four factors which we feel explain our increased prevalence of pupils eligible for the PPG (see above) all indicate that we need to invest much time and effort to support parents with their extremely difficult role of bringing up a child with a disability or learning difficulty, especially if they have their own difficulties. Much of this work comes in the form of time supporting parents and is not necessarily planned, costed or evaluated and derives from the general school provision and is integral to our ethos and to the way we function. It includes, among many others, the following:

- A general collaborative and team approach to working with families.
- Parent support groups and family clubs.
- A school-based family support worker, who supports parents with care routines and behaviour strategies in the home; this work can be referred by the school or by the parents themselves.
- Regular parent training sessions such as Triple P – Stepping Stones (a specialist behaviour programme for parents of a child with a disability).
- Sign-along training to provide parents with a means of enhancing their communication with their child.
- Close liaison with a range of professionals who are all provided with work bases in school and can support parents in the home, such as speech and language therapists, occupational therapists, wheelchair technicians, physiotherapists, the school nurse and various other medical professionals who visit the school, a specialist social worker team (who have a pod on site) and also the CAMHS team.
- Additional time for parents at family conversations, EHCP or statement reviews, parents evenings or through numerous other meetings we arrange in school to support parents such as for behaviour support.
- Regular telephone contact (two way) encouraged.
- Regular invites into school to celebrate their child's work and also to provide opportunities for parents to meet staff to express concerns or ask for help.
- Help with completing official forms such as disability living allowance or DVLA car allowance form.
- Supportive attendance at Child in Need meetings and other meetings arranged by social services.
- Support for parents so they are more able to support and extend their child's learning at home.
- Personalised resources to support communication and behaviour at home.

Key priorities of our vulnerable learner group which should be addressed in the targeted interventions we plan

Beyond supporting parents, most of our targeted and costed energies designed to support our vulnerable learners and PPG pupils take the form of specifically targeted interventions, which are designed to address the key issues presented by the pupil's vulnerability which act (or may act) as a barrier to learning. These key issues become our core priorities for supporting vulnerable pupils and those who receive the PPG.

The five key priorities we address with our intervention work are:

1. To support **parents** in order to support their child's learning and development.
2. To support the **health needs** of pupils so they are ready to learn.
3. To support the **physical needs** of pupils so they are ready to learn.
4. To support the **social/emotional needs** and self-regulation needs of pupils so they are ready to learn.
5. To support the **communication needs** of pupils so they are ready to learn.

How we identify our most vulnerable pupils to prioritise for interventions

We run a spreadsheet that contains details for each pupil in school. Each can be cross referenced against the various factors we see as indications of vulnerability (see above) such as being in receipt of the PPG but also other factors such as complex health needs, emotional needs, lack of expected progress and safeguarding concerns. Key staff RAG (red, amber, green) rate each pupil against each factor and from this, a view of overall vulnerability across several factors emerges, which is then used to highlight the most vulnerable who are given priority access to the menu of interventions available.

Interventions menu

Taking account of these key priorities, we have created a range of sharply focused interventions which go beyond our general class-based provision and are designed to help pupils with these particular needs more easily access learning. The balance, style and number of these interventions change over time to keep pace with: new innovations and ideas, feedback from providers and the pupils, the quality of outcomes and the changing nature of the cohort of pupils. A professional independent audit of this provision has noted its high quality (see quote at top of this document).

How identified pupils are signposted to an intervention

A combination of teacher referrals and SLT (senior leadership team) referrals after scrutiny against the vulnerability spreadsheet is used to identify candidates for intervention. Priority is always given to those pupils deemed to be most at need after the RAG rating process. Referrals are made on the basis that any particular vulnerability or collection of different vulnerability factors presents a barrier for learning and a referral is selected from the intervention menu which is likely to best address that issue and help that pupil be more ready for learning.

How these interventions work

Most of these interventions take the form of small groups run by a TA (sometimes a specialist or specifically trained TA). They run for between ten and 30 minutes per session. Most take place either at the very start of the school day, at lunchtime or at the beginning of the afternoon in order to prepare the pupils for the session ahead and so that they arrive more focused and ready to learn.

Most interventions run for half a term and then are evaluated for impact. An intervention planning and review form is used to identify the entry and exit criteria for each participant (what the intervention is trying to achieve and the impact on learning that will be expected back in class). This is done by the intervention lead in conjunction with the pupil's class teacher. They will also agree how success and impact will be measured. A separate intervention tracking form is used after each session to identify 'what went well' and also an 'even better if'.

Specialist-run interventions

Some of the specific interventions run by our specialist TAs or professionals can run at any time of the school day and work on a withdrawal or in-class support basis for individuals and small groups. Examples of this work are shown in the following tables:

- Table 4.1: Specific interventions run by specialist providers (page 93)
- Table 4.2: Detailed list of interventions addressing key priority areas (page 94)
- Table 4.3: Intervention planning and review form (page 100)
- Table 4.4: Weekly impact of intervention tracker (page 100)

Table 4.1: Specific interventions run by specialist providers

Specialist provider	Interventions offered	Target group	Expected impact
Specialist TA for communication	Language groups Communication work in conjunction with SALT	Pupils identified by SALTs	On target (UQ) development in communication skills as measured by FRS assessment framework
Specialist TA for language and communication resources	Creation of individualised resources to support communication for home and school Eye gaze AAC	Pupils identified by SALT after discussion with parents e.g. at EHCP meetings	On target (UQ) development in communication skills as measured by FRS assessment framework
Specialist TA to support sensory learning	High-quality and focused access to the school specialist sensory resources for pupils with complex needs and very early developmental skills	Pupils working at the earliest developmental levels	On target (UQ) development in early developmental skills as measured by FRS assessment framework
Two specialist TAs for development of physical skills (these staff are also trained in all the various medical competencies to support class staff)	Physical programmes as designed by the physiotherapists Support individual pupils using specialist equipment Run specialist physical intervention groups Manage morning intervention and sensory swim clubs	Pupils identified by physiotherapists Pupils who are provided with specialist equipment Vulnerable pupils identified in need of intervention groups	Improved physical skills and strength Maintenance of physical skills and prevention of more rapid deterioration
A specialist outdoor learning TA	Outdoor learning sessions for the whole school Also intervention work for individual pupils and small groups to help with emotional regulation difficulties Forest skills extension work for more able pupils	Vulnerable pupils identified in need of intervention groups	Improved self-regulation and an increase in self-esteem and self-confidence Pupils ready for learning on return to class
Qualified OT who specialises in sensory integration and regulation	Sensory regulation assessment Development of sensory passport Support for class staff and parents to implement sensory programme Suggest equipment purchases	Vulnerable pupils identified in need of intervention groups	Improved self-regulation Pupils ready for learning Improved transitions Improved wellbeing and independence

Abbreviations: AAC: alternative and augmentative communication; EHCP: Education, Health and Care Plan; OT: occupational therapist; SALT: speech and language therapy; UQ: upper quartile

Table 4.2: Detailed list of interventions addressing key priority areas

Key priority area addressed	Intervention title	Who is it for	Details	What success will look like/ expected impact
1,3&4	Individual small group **sensory food sessions;** sensory tastes, extra snacks	Pupils identified by SALT Pupils who are vulnerable because of poor eating habits and selective diet	Run as a lunchtime club and also in distinct class sessions, especially at snack time and during messy play sessions	Improved access and tolerance to an increasing range of healthy foods
1&2	Focused and targeted individual sessions with **specialist physical TA**	Pupils identified by physiotherapists Pupils who are provided with specialist equipment Vulnerable pupils identified in need of intervention groups	Physical programmes as designed by the physiotherapists Support individual pupils using specialist equipment Run specialist physical intervention groups Manage morning intervention and sensory swim clubs	Improved physical skills and strength Maintenance of physical skills and prevention of more rapid deterioration
2	**Specialist equipment** (trikes, cutlery, class chairs, mini tablets, trampettes, etc.)	Pupils identified by SALTs, physiotherapists and sensory and medical occupational therapists	Individual equipment purchased to support and enhance special programmes, increase independence and build core strength and coordination Also some equipment for improved access to communication and technology	Improved physical skills and strength Maintenance of physical skills and prevention of more rapid deterioration Ability to communicate pretences and feelings Improved confidence, self-esteem and access to learning
1,2,3&4	**Sensory trail sessions**	Vulnerable pupils identified in need of intervention groups – especially in regard to self-regulation	Early morning use of sensory trails within school grounds, to encourage pupils to become more aware of their environment	Improved self-regulation to be ready for learning on return to class
1,2,3&4	Additional **sensory swim sessions** in hydrotherapy	Vulnerable pupils identified in need of intervention groups – especially in regard to self-regulation	Early morning use of the hydrotherapy pool to enable pupils to self-regulate in an active environment	Improved self-regulation to be ready for learning on return to class

Key priority area addressed	Intervention title	Who is it for	Details	What success will look like/ expected impact
2&3	Early morning **playground group**	Vulnerable pupils identified in need of intervention groups	Early morning use of outdoor equipment such as bikes and swings within school grounds to enable pupils to self-regulate in an active environment	Improved self-regulation to be ready for learning on return to class
1,3&4	**Breakfast clubs**	Vulnerable pupils identified in need of intervention groups, especially those who have missed breakfast or were not ready to eat breakfast at home	Usually in individual classroom; healthy food options are offered such as cereal bars, fruit and milk	Improved concentration and readiness to learn
2&3	**Horse riding** sessions with the RDA	Vulnerable pupils identified in need of intervention groups, especially those identified by physiotherapists for physical needs or those who require further sensory integration exercise	At specialist RDA provider off campus supported by additional staffing; group is identified from vulnerable pupil list by priority needs and waiting list	Improved physical skills and core strength Maintenance of physical skills and prevention of more rapid deterioration Improved confidence, self-esteem and access to learning back in school Developing quality relationships and communication
2&3	Focused and targeted individual or small group multi-sensory room sessions with **specialist sensory TA** (or other)	Pupils working at the earliest developmental levels	High-quality and focused access to the school specialist sensory resources for pupils with complex needs and very early developmental skills	On target (UQ) development in early developmental skills as measured by FRS assessment framework
2&3	Focused and targeted individual or small group **active learning** sessions/club with specialist sensory TA (or other)	Vulnerable pupils identified in need of intervention groups especially in regard to sensory integration	Focused session in sensory gym, following progress agreed by OT	Improved self-regulation to be ready for learning on return to class Improved confidence, self-esteem and access to learning back in school

Key priority area addressed	Intervention title	Who is it for	Details	What success will look like/ expected impact
		Some identified by sensory OT	High-quality and focused access to the school specialist sensory resources for pupils with complex needs and very early developmental skills	Developing quality relationships and communication On target (UQ) development in early developmental skills as measured by FRS assessment framework
2&3	**Morning club in lower hall**	Vulnerable pupils identified in need of intervention groups especially in regard to sensory integration	Pupils follow a sensory curriculum in the lower hall – based on a sensory integration model	Improved self-regulation to be ready for learning on return to class Improved confidence, self-esteem and access to learning back in school Developing quality relationships and communication
2&3	**Active learning club**	Vulnerable pupils identified in need of intervention groups especially in regard to sensory integration	An early morning session to enable pupils to self-regulate in an active environment	Improved self-regulation to be ready for learning on return to class Improved confidence, self-esteem and access to learning back in school Developing quality relationships and communication
2&3	**Sensory integration assessment and diet** via specialist OT	Vulnerable pupils identified in need of intervention groups	Sensory regulation assessment Development of sensory passport Support for class staff and parents to implement sensory programme Suggest equipment purchases	Improved self-regulation Pupils ready for learning Improved transitions Improved wellbeing and independence

Key priority area addressed	Intervention title	Who is it for	Details	What success will look like/ expected impact
3	**One-to-one nurture time** to build relationships	Early developmentally functioning pupils who still need to develop intentional communication and awareness of others Higher functioning pupils who have difficulty forming relationships and need to develop self-confidence	Individual time with adult to develop targeted skills at an intensive level	Improved confidence, self-esteem and access to learning back in school Developing quality relationships and communication
3	Small group or individual outdoor learning session with **specialist forest school TA**	Vulnerable pupils identified in need of intervention groups	Outdoor learning sessions for the whole school Also intervention work for individual pupils and small groups to help with emotional regulation difficulties Forest skills extension work for more able pupils	Improved self-regulation and an increase in self-esteem and self-confidence Pupils ready for learning on return to class
3	Support for **out-of-school activities** (e.g. stage coach)	Individual identified pupils after discussion at EHCP or LAC meetings	As per agreement	Improved confidence, self-esteem and access to learning back in school Developing quality relationships and communication
N/A	**Outdoor learning mornings and Friday club**	Vulnerable pupils identified in need of intervention groups especially in regard to emotional regulation	An early morning session to enable pupils to self-regulate in an active environment and become aware of their environment	Improved confidence, self-esteem, self-regulation and access to learning back in school Developing quality relationships and communication
3	Support to attend **holiday clubs**	Vulnerable pupils identified in need of additional support	Clubs run in holiday to maintain skills, routines and relationships over the holiday period Maintain physical programmes	Improved confidence, self-esteem, self-regulation and access to learning back in school Improved transition back to school Maintenance of physical skills

Key priority area addressed	Intervention title	Who is it for	Details	What success will look like/ expected impact
N/A	Financial support for **school transport**	Individual identified pupils after discussion at EHCP or LAC meetings	Support with cost of transport to school for pupils whose parents do not qualify	Improved school attendance and punctuality – knock-on positive effects on behaviours and ability to learn
3	Financial support for **school uniform**	Individual identified pupils after discussion at EHCP or LAC meetings	Support with cost of uniform for pupils whose parents do not qualify	Improved confidence, self-esteem
3&4	**Pet therapy**	Vulnerable pupils identified in need of intervention	Care and nurture for school pets	Improved confidence, self-esteem Developing quality relationships and communication
4	Small group language and speech sessions with **specialist communication TA**	Pupils identified by SALTs	Language groups Communication work in conjunction with SALT	On target (UQ) development in communication skills as measured by FRS assessment framework
N/A	Parent sign along training	Individual identified parents of pupils after discussion at EHCP or LAC meetings	Ten-week structured course led by qualified sign along tutors	Improved communication and relationships at home Improved communication between home and school
N/A	**Specialist TA** to support class staff with the creation of individualised resources to **support communication needs** at home and school	Pupils identified by SALT after discussion with parents e.g. at EHCP meetings	Creation of individualised resources to support communication for home and school	On target (UQ) development in communication skills as measured by FRS assessment framework Improved communication and behaviours at home
3&4	**Intensive interaction sessions**	Pupils identified by SALT Pupils working at very early developmental levels	Individual or small groups session started by specialist communication TA usually with aim of upskilling class staff to take over	Developing quality relationships and communication

Key priority area addressed	Intervention title	Who is it for	Details	What success will look like/ expected impact
N/A	**Eye gaze sessions**	Pupils identified by SALT or teacher sensory impairments Pupils working at very early developmental levels	Individual session supported by specialist TA or class staff	Developing quality relationships and communication
N/A	**Additional communication and language (SALT) assessment,** modelling language session with staff and staff training	Pupils identified by SALT	Additional SALT provided by the school	On target (UQ) development in communication skills as measured by FRS assessment framework Developing quality relationships and communication
N/A	**Lunchtime clubs**	Accessible for all pupils but vulnerable and PPG pupils are prioritised	Clubs decided by school council representing pupil opinion; led by school staff	Improved confidence, self-esteem, self-regulation and access to learning back in school Improved transition back to school in the afternoon Maintenance of physical skills Improved access and tolerance to an increasing range of healthy foods

Abbreviations: EHCP: Education, Health and Care Plan; LAC: looked after children; OT: occupational therapist; RDA: Riding for the Disabled Association; SALT: speech and language therapy; UQ: upper quartile

Table 4.3: Intervention planning and review form

Intervention Planning and Review Form		**Intervention title**________		
Lead________ **Start date**________ **End date**________ **Details of intervention (please describe briefly in two or three sentences)**				**Key vulnerability priority this intervention will target**. 1. Heath needs. 2. Physical needs. 3. Social/ emotional needs. 4. Communication needs.
Pupil name	**Entry criteria:** What is this intervention trying to achieve for this pupil? Think especially in relation to learning back in class and discuss this with teacher.	**Exit criteria:** What will success look like? Think especially in terms of impact back in class.	**Evaluation and feedback (impact):** 1. What do you think? 2. What does the teacher think? 3. What does the pupil think? (if appropriate)	
How many pupils made progress? **How many graduated?**		**What went well?** **Even better if**		

Table 4.4: Weekly impact of intervention tracker

Weekly impact of intervention tracker *(use this form in conjunction with the intervention planning and review form)*

Intervention title:				**Exit criteria:**		
Start date:		**End date:**		**Staff:**		
Pupil						
Week 1	WWW EBI	WWW EBI	WWW EBI	WWW EBI	WWW EBI	WWW EBI
Week 2	WWW EBI	WWW EBI	WWW EBI	WWW EBI	WWW EBI	WWW EBI
Week 3	WWW EBI	WWW EBI	WWW EBI	WWW EBI	WWW EBI	WWW EBI
Week 4	WWW EBI	WWW EBI	WWW EBI	WWW EBI	WWW EBI	WWW EBI
Week 5	WWW EBI	WWW EBI	WWW EBI	WWW EBI	WWW EBI	WWW EBI
Week 6	WWW EBI	WWW EBI	WWW EBI	WWW EBI	WWW EBI	WWW EBI
Outcomes						
Evaluation						

Guidance notes for use of the intervention planning and review form and the weekly impact of intervention tracker

- The purpose of these two forms is to enable you to accurately and succinctly measure the impacts of the interventions you are responsible for.
- The purpose of these interventions is to address barriers for learning so that the pupils are more ready to learn in class and access and participate in the curriculum.

Entry and exit criteria: Please discuss these with the pupil's class teacher. Establishing entry and exit criteria brings meaning to why you have chosen this intervention for this pupil. It will enable you to keep focused on what the goal is. The entry and exit criteria should be the same, for example:

Entry criteria: For pupil to attend and contribute to class group activity for ten minutes.

Exit criteria: Pupil will attend class activity for ten minutes and will make a contribution when requested.

WWW and **EBI: W**hat **W**ent **W**ell and **E**ven **B**etter **I**f. These are common terms to refer to the progress that was made and how things could be better next time.

Reflections on the example school

Fort Royal in Worcester is not a school the vast majority of people will visit, and yet you get a sense that the attainment gap is something they take seriously and, most importantly, is a challenge to which they have crafted a bespoke response. You get the sense that they have prioritised how they communicate with stakeholders about this issue and that what they are writing is a result of a lot of thinking and careful planning. How they conceive of and track interventions is intelligently done with a clear, simple formula.

The example is purposefully a special school because I wanted to demonstrate that even schools with the most challenging of cohorts can also engage in this process. This entire chapter could be misconstrued to be the 'outward facing' chapter. Actually, I think of this as a process of discovery for your leaders to go through. Ed found his senior leadership team benefited from thinking this through and for those who are interested in management speak you could say that this is an example of where the 'process' is the solution rather than just the 'end product'.

Conclusion and actions

The action timetable on page 102 can be used as a model to delegate tasks and set deadlines for getting your system up and running.

Table 4.5: Action timetable

Task	Assigned to	Report to	Deadline
Identify key stakeholders.			
Research, write up and share information on your local community (demographics, trends, socio-economic factors, etc.).			
Speak to other schools about their understanding of the local community.			
Speak to staff and governors.			
Speak to specialist outreach workers, educational psychologists, social workers, educational officers and any other local service providers.			
Speak to youth workers, local religious leaders, or people involved with out-of-school sports clubs or the like, who have contact with a number of school pupils.			
Delineate between information about specific students and cohorts versus the general picture.			
Write up one or two paragraphs summarising your findings.			
Distribute your findings to your stakeholders and ask for any further comments.			
Make this available in your Ofsted file.			
If relevant and appropriate, publish this information on your website (ensuring that no individual is referenced).			

What you hear in the course of your conversations with stakeholders will be disparate. It won't always be useful. But ultimately what matters is encouraging the conversations in the first place. In my experience, schools that bring their staff and local communities with them in their work on the attainment gap are by far the most likely to be successful. The more people discussing the issue and sharing their thoughts, suggestions and expertise, the richer the pool of insight you have to draw on in your development of strategies and interventions.

5 Data

This chapter will look at data: how to capture it, communicate it, and use it to develop strategies for closing the attainment gap. Data collection is integral to helping disadvantaged students keep pace with their peers. Both concrete figures about academic progress and more general information about a student's school and home experience have their part to play.

The chapter opens by recapping a couple of concepts and looking at good data practice in general, then focuses in on specific techniques for collating and presenting data. Finally, it goes over ways you can analyse your data that further your goals as a school, and that help you to shape a whole-school, whole-community strategy for closing the attainment gap.

Hard and soft data

To reiterate what I set out in Chapter 1 (page 19), hard data is concrete figures about the situation or performance of pupils, classes, years and so on. Hard data is generally numerical (e.g. 'proportion of FSM students in year 10 History') or binary (answers to yes/no questions, e.g. 'does this student receive FSM?', 'did the student meet their target?'). These figures come from external and official in-school assessments and, in the UK, from RAISEonline or its replacement the Analyse School Performance service.

Your school will already have all of this data on record; the task is just to make sure it is collated and presented effectively and shared with stakeholders.

Soft data refers to the educational, social and personal information about a student beyond simple figures and test results. Soft data is less direct than hard data but in many ways more important, because it gives so much more insight into the needs of individuals. Collating and presenting it in such a way that it is clear and flexible, and bringing it to the attention of all relevant parties, is an essential part of developing effective strategies for closing the attainment gap in your school.

Most schools are getting better at managing their hard data, but even outstanding schools still struggle with their soft data – not least because there tends to be so much of it, it's mostly non-numerical, and the vast majority will be irrelevant to the making of any one given decision.

My approach to data is to guide schools in combining soft and hard data in order to understand the attainment gap in their setting and find the provisions that most effectively – and cost-effectively – help close it.

Key takeaway

'Hard data' refers to numerical performance figures; 'soft data' refers to all other relevant information. Both are useful for understanding the attainment gap.

The gap in your data – intersectionality

Students' needs may not only be educational. 'Intersectionality' is the concept that our lives are governed by the crossover of a wide range of economic, social, physical and psychological factors. A disadvantaged student struggling to meet educational goals is not only affected by poverty but also potentially by race, gender, sexual orientation, SEN and so on. In deciding how best to support that student, the school is implicitly involving itself with a wide range of other community, family and personal forces.

On top of this, as well as existing within communities, schools are communities in their own right. They often bring together groups and individuals who live very separate lives outside of the school gates. This could precipitate issues in itself: for example, students who, on some level, experience a clash of cultures or backgrounds when trying to interact; students who find it hard to learn in particular class environments; or at the most basic level, students who distract one another.

Table 5.1 can be used to map intersections for both individuals and cohorts. It's an interesting exercise and can be quite revealing in terms of highlighting groups within the cohort of attainment gap students that warrant further attention.

Table 5.1: 'Intersectionality' map

	SEN	EAL	Lateness	Absence	Child protection (CP)	Education maintenance allowance (EMA)	G&T	Refusing school	Mid-phase
SEN									
EAL									
Lateness									
Absence									
CP									
EMA									
G&T									
Refusing school									
Mid-phase									

Working with data – best practice

Hard data may be the best indicator that an attainment gap exists and the best tool for tracking whether it widens or narrows. Soft data is the place to look in order to understand why there's a gap in the first place and how you might be able to fix it. But soft data is much trickier to capture and communicate than hard data, depending as it does on unquantifiable information and subjective experience. The following section addresses general best practice when collecting data, and then focuses on ways to present and collate both hard and soft data that increase their utility for developing strategies in your school.

Dealing with data

The data that you collate in your school will be the bedrock of your work on closing the attainment gap. All of your spending strategies and many of your approaches regarding individual students will be based on it. It will tell you about trends in disadvantaged student performance and provide the benchmarks against which changes can be measured. In England and Wales, and in various other jurisdictions, there is also a requirement to publish data on your school's website and share it with inspectors in order to meet accountability criteria.

It is therefore essential that all of your data is accurate, comprehensive, clearly presented and structured in a way that is useful. The three key words to remember when collating data are:

- accessibility
- presentation
- flexibility.

The importance of each of these words is explained in turn below.

Accessibility

There are two sides to making your data properly accessible:

1. Ensure that it is presented in a way that is clear and easy to understand. Anyone who opens your database or spreadsheets should be able to make sense of the information within. (See 'Presentation' opposite for more on this.)
2. Ensure that information is always accessible to those to whom it is relevant.

If a number of students are underperforming in English, it isn't enough for only their English teacher to know about it. Different types of support can be introduced by different people in the school, so the information should also be shared with the head of English, the students' head of year, potentially the SEN department or relevant TAs, and so on.

Each time you come across an important piece of student information, check that all relevant staff are aware of your findings. Aim to encourage an atmosphere in which any such information is shared not only with you, but also directly between different members of staff and departments. Creating a strong data network can hugely improve support for struggling pupils, and it requires no additional government funding whatsoever.

Presentation

It's really important that your findings are presented in a clear, usable way. A common theme of schools struggling with managing their gap is that senior leaders don't understand how to organise and share data. Data, however comprehensive and thoroughly researched, is basically useless if it isn't well presented – and equally useless if there's far too much of it.

Data has been presented well when:

- It is easy to understand.
- Everything is labelled so that it is clear what each item of data is or refers to.
- Trends and anomalies are easy to spot (making it simple to analyse).
- It can be referred back to quickly if you need to check your facts.

Guidance, tips and walked-through examples for presenting both hard and soft data can be found in the relevant sections in this chapter. However, there are some general points that it is worth considering at this stage:

- Label everything as you go along, so that it is clear what each item of data is and to what or whom it refers. Make sure that these labels are clear and stand out (e.g. increase the font size or colour-code them).
- Documents (particularly spreadsheets) that are bigger than a single A4 sheet tend to be overwhelming and difficult to process. Break them up using clear division lines, colours, fonts and so on.
- On spreadsheets, make sure that there aren't so many columns going across that the sheet can't be printed on A4.
- As far as possible, store your data in a single location.
- Set standard formats and stick to them rigorously. It can be easy to slip from storing pupils as 'Jones, Michael' to 'Michael Jones' without thinking about it, but this can really confuse the data when it needs to be sorted or searched.
- Back up your data.

Flexibility

Flexible data can be easily reorganised to support a variety of different points of focus: a single pupil, a single teacher, a year group, a department and so on.

Data that can be manipulated in this way is far more useful than the very same figures set out in a way that's rigidly focused on one metric.

With a flexible system, even straightforward hard data, such as Key Stage 2 results, could be the basis of a comparison of the success of disadvantaged students between form groups, then between departments, then between individual teachers.

Start with the end in mind: we're looking for *x*; therefore we need to collect data on *abc*.

Another question that sometimes comes up is how to tell if you have enough data. Realistically you probably already have too much (hard data at least); most schools do. It varies from setting to setting, of course, but if you are making use of your data and it gets you the information you need, you've got the right amount.

The most important practical step in making your data flexible is to categorise each pupil's record as thoroughly as possible. This makes it easily searchable and allows you to sort it into a wide range of different groups for analysis.

Before recording any new data or making changes to what you currently have on record, check again through the points above. Make sure you are happy with your system and that you trust it. Dredging data from a poorly designed system is nightmarish.

Key takeaway

How you store and present data will have a huge bearing on how useful it is. Data should be accessible, clearly presented and flexible.

In addition, meet with the person in charge of data in your school. Discuss what data is currently held and where and how it is available. Look together at the school's data handling systems: ensure that you can work them, and find out how the information they contain is usually presented (the school may have a standard format on which your work needs to be based). If possible, you should moderate data by comparing it across departments and with other schools in your area.

Finally, make sure that you are working in a way that is fully in line with data protection regulations. For information about UK regulations, visit www.gov.uk/data-protection.

Using hard data

This section works on the assumption that your school already has available all of the hard data that you will need including RAISEonline/Analyse School Performance (ASP) (or equivalent) and your school's internal data programme (SIMS or equivalent). It is nonetheless worth checking that the level of detail is sufficient. End-of-year or even end-of-term assessment grades are not necessarily very useful in trying to pick out points of change in a pupil's performance. Ideally, you should have some kind of performance record for the beginning and end of every half term.

Attainment and progress

It is important to draw a distinction at this point between 'attainment' and 'progress'. The examples below are taken from a secondary setting but the principles apply across the board.

- Attainment is the measure of academic achievement of a pupil: whether she gets an A* or a D in a GCSE exam, for example.
- Progress is the achievement of a pupil relative to the targets that have been set in light of his potential: if he has been deemed capable of a B, whether he gets an A (strong progress), B (progress as hoped) or C (poor progress).

Government discussions generally refer to an attainment gap between disadvantaged and other students. This is because they work on a collective scale: disadvantaged students as a group have no difference of baseline potential from other students, so it is correct to say that, overall, there is an issue of attainment. When talking about individuals, however, it is the progress figures that are important. There's no expectation that every pupil will get top grades. What matters is whether or not they are meeting their potential, and disadvantaged students are significantly less likely to do so than their more affluent peers.

Ultimately, on your school's website, you will need to publish a summary of how well your vulnerable students have done relative to the expectations set by RAISEonline/ASP or other sources.

Presenting hard data

Later in this chapter we will deal with how to analyse and use RAISEonline or equivalent data, but first, some recommendations for presenting it clearly. This might seem trivial, but how well-organised your data is – how quickly it can be understood and processed by stakeholders, including those who aren't confident working with spreadsheets – will make a big difference to your ability to bring people on board and keep them up to date with your work.

A useful tool for the purpose is colour-coding. Unfortunately, because this book is printed in black and white only, I have had to replace colours with shading in the examples on the following pages. It works okay but colours are definitely preferable.

In Example 1 (Table 5.2) the effects of a basic shading- (or ideally, colour-) coding system are demonstrated. The eye is immediately drawn to certain areas of interest:

- Maths and art, where the lack of shading denotes that progress is good, with 85 per cent and 91 per cent of students respectively meeting or exceeding targets.
- Mandarin, where dark shading highlights poor performance: less than a quarter of students are meeting targets.

Table 5.2: Example 1 – drawing attention to outliers

Year 10 – SUMMARY OF ATTAINMENT / PROGRESS – Met or exceeded target grade									
INCLUSION GROUP	**CORE**		**HUMANITIES**		**MFL**		**BICT**		**ART**
	English	**Maths**	**Geography**	**History**	**Mandarin**	**Spanish**	**ICT**	**Business**	**Art**
Free school meals	23/34 67.6%	29/34 85.2%	13/20 65%	8/15 53.3%	8/34 23.5%	6/11 54.5%	23/34 67.6%	8/14 57.1%	10/11 91%

It should be noted that RAISEonline data also uses a colour-coding system, with green or blue highlights to indicate that a particular measure is significantly above or below the national average. My colour-coding is not linked to this system, though the underlying principle – drawing attention to figures that buck the trend – is the same.

In Example 2 (Table 5.3) the clarifying effect of the shading system is even clearer. FSM students are underperforming in core science and seriously underperforming in BTEC science, but doing averagely in triple science.

A typical problem with taking an individual student approach to data is being faced with too much to look at. A poorly presented, overly data-heavy table makes it difficult to identify trends and general issues, and can be overwhelming for staff who are less confident with data.

Data is only as good as it is useful. Example 3 (Table 5.4) has a simple layout, uses a visual shading system to draw the eye to key data points, and contains a large amount of information on a single page. It has been very useful for most schools that I work with – but I encourage you to adapt the principle to a format that works best for your school.

Table 5.3: Example 2 – drawing more attention to outliers

Year 10 – SUMMARY OF ATTAINMENT / PROGRESS – Met or exceeded target grade			
INCLUSION GROUP	**SCIENCE**		
	Core	**BTEC**	**Triple**
Free school meals	2/12 16.6%	0/8 0%	8/14 57.1%

Using soft data

Mines of soft data

The overall goal with soft data is to identify barriers, on the one hand, and motivations, on the other, for specific students. There are a number of resources for soft data that are often not used to their full potential:

- Teachers
    - When getting feedback from teachers, be specific. Ask about how a student is doing with one particular issue, rather than about their performance in general, as this will be difficult to sum up.
- Parents
    - Look for factors that might limit or attenuate achievement. For example: is a child a young carer? Has she had to live with a grandparent for several months because a parent has been absent?

Table 5.4: Example 3 – clear and concise presentation

Surname	First name	English	Maths	Geog	History	RE	Spanish	ICT	PE GCSE	Business
[name]	[name]			✓			✓	✓		
[name]	[name]	✓	✓					✓		
[name]	[name]									
[name]	[name]	✓	✓		✓			✓		
[name]	[name]									
[name]	[name]	✓			✓					

- Feedback from agencies
  - Look into how agencies are currently communicating what they know with the school. Although the fact that they are outsiders reduces the specificity of their information to some extent, such agencies can be a valuable resource.
- Teaching assistants (TAs)
  - TAs can be a source of the most useful feedback as they often spend the most time with the most vulnerable students. Their feedback may not always be language-specific and accurate but often they perceive what is going on better than all other staff.
  - Use TAs to liaise with parents. Give them the necessary guidance and support to do this and they can be a very useful tool in contacting hard-to-reach parents who find school threatening.
- Students
  - Student-led data is highly important – both in practice and to Ofsted. If your interventions are in part decided because of students' feedback it will demonstrate that you are a listening school.

All of these groups, and TAs especially, will have a large amount of information to pass on and they should not be overlooked or undervalued. Sometimes, however, the level of information can become unwieldy. Try to strike a balance: you want enough information to feel that it is comprehensive and meaningful, but not so much that it becomes cumbersome.

Organising soft data

Much of the information that you collect about a pupil when doing soft data research will seem quite disparate. One pupil, it may transpire, is consistently disruptive in class, lives between the houses of separated parents, and is particularly quiet in science lessons. Rather than just recording these facts, arrange them into a set of categories: 'Behaviour', 'Home Life', 'Involvement in Lessons', alongside 'Attainment', 'Health', 'SEN' and so on.

If you set out with rigorous categories such as these and try to stay within them, it will not only make your data clearer and better organised, but will also increase the ease and efficiency of data-gathering in the first place.

Meaningful data

Ensure that you always record data in a way that is meaningful. Meaningful data is:

- clear
- specific
- measurable.

A good acid test to decide whether or not an item of data fulfils these criteria is to think about whether it could act as a point of specific comparison to future developments.

For example: 'Anna is quiet in class.'

1. This could mean a wide range of things. We assume it refers to Anna's level of involvement, but it could equally mean that she keeps her head down and works hard.
2. If Anna's attitude changed, it wouldn't be particularly helpful to record 'Anna is no longer quiet in class.' Emphasise this slightly more – 'Anna is noisy in class' – and suddenly the assumption is that we are talking about behaviour, not involvement: Anna is noisy and disruptive, but not necessarily more involved in the lesson.
3. Even if we understand intended meaning in both cases, 'quiet' to 'not quiet' is a binary change that doesn't give a great deal of insight into the situation.

Versus: 'Anna never raises her hand, and when called on, doesn't want to answer.'

1. In this case, we know exactly what issue the line is referring to and have some insight into Anna's specific challenges.
2. If Anna becomes more loquacious we could easily note that 'Anna now does raise her hand', or 'if called on, Anna responds.' This would clearly denote a change in the situation. Anyone looking at Anna's record would know exactly what the situation had been, was now, and what had changed.

Tracking soft data – a framework

Essential information is very difficult to sift through. How do you capture precisely what you did for one individual? A lack of careful and clear soft data can make and break tribunal cases, annual reviews and any major pastoral meeting. Table 5.5 introduces the 'one document to save them all', containing the core information about a single student. It is a robust structure that asks for the most essential information and gets to the heart of capturing and tracking soft data.

One example of where this table might work well would be for an FSM student who was predicted As but because of a challenging home situation refused to come to school. Interventions were put in place to bring her back to school and she ended up with Cs. According to the hard data, the school failed this student. However, the soft data demonstrated a tremendous success: the student was clearly not going to sit any exams and only because the school went beyond the call of duty and expertly spent available funds did they manage to help the student attain any grades at all.

A table like Table 5.5 could articulate this story simply. It could also be used as a template for a case study. You don't have to use this for every single student, but it will be helpful for your most challenging students and in the case of issues that affect numerous students that you want to focus in on (e.g. attendance or aspiration).

Table 5.5: Resource 1 – demonstrating the impact of interventions per individual student

STUDENT NAME:		
	IN THE CLASSROOM	
PRESENTING ISSUE	**ACTION**	**IMPACT (last half term)**
Calling out (lack of respect of class rules, teacher authority, inability to self-settle)	**TA** (prompting and supporting understanding under guidance of specialist and in liaison with teachers)	Where a TA is available the student has significantly cut down on calling out. He seems to be getting all the attention he needs from this adult Problems persist: - in classes where no TA is available - with over-reliance on TA
	Seating plan (sat away from Beth, Sana, Aneesh)	Has significantly contributed to a reduction in outbursts
	Differentiation (specifically designed with specialist support)	- When this is given at the beginning of the lesson, the student settles well - When it is provided more than ten mins into the lesson, he has usually already lost interest
	Reward and sanction (monitored daily by Key Worker; liaison with home)	- Lack of consistent application at home - Use of rewards has been well-received
Jumping out of seat (distracting other students and dominating teacher's focus)	**Planned movements** (by both teacher and TA, working with the student)	- In lessons where this has been planned well, no more incidents - About two thirds of lessons remain challenging
	Time-out card (student is encouraged to use it responsibly)	- Student keeps forgetting to use this and needs prompting by the TA - Teachers sceptical about whether he uses it appropriately
No exercise books or equipment (no record of any written work)	TA keeping **folder in school** (also used to review work every day)	- Student now has half a term's work and is very proud of this - Every lesson, he looks back over work he has done and is excited to add new things
	Colour-coded timetable (to enhance student's confidence in reading and managing the plan for the day himself)	- Student has lost this a number of times - This has not been a successful action
	NON-CONTACT TIME	
Etc. (…)		

An important benefit of using this framework is getting your staff and teachers to think about data in a manner that transcends the basic 'result focus' and considers a much more holistic impact on the student. This document can also help you anchor useful information in a manner that avoids the two common extremes: vagueness, e.g. 'so and so can't concentrate', and an excess of information that no one has the time to read.

Finally, the framework could be a useful stage in the process of articulating to parents or teachers that a student has serious pastoral issues and is perhaps even at risk of exclusion.

Various features of this table are worth noting:

- It's divided into sections: 'in the classroom', 'non contact time', etc. These can be adapted to whatever makes most sense to you and to the circumstances of the student. Common options include 'social', 'learning' and 'self-management'.
- The headline action in bold is followed by further information in brackets, so that the key information can be taken in at a glance but relevant details aren't lost.
- The impact section records whether the objective of the action was achieved, or achieved with limitations. This reinforces thinking in terms of long-term impact: what precisely did an intervention achieve, how did it affect the people involved, and what issues remain?
- Information is captured in two to three bullet points. Further detail can be held elsewhere if necessary, but bigger isn't better: writing too much will guarantee that readers either don't read the document at all or don't take in all the information.
- Impact bullet points are written with a view to what the next step could be.

Managing support for disadvantaged students is a whole-school undertaking, but within schools there are distinct levels of planning and impact: school, cohort and individual. Information gets lost all too easily when it comes to dealing with individuals: 'liaison with home' is often recorded, but what is not recorded are things like how that is done, how difficult it transpires to be, what impact it has, timetabling and so on.

There is a danger of losing time and resources on the paperwork, and creating endless documents that will never be read – 50 documents about a single student are unlikely to help them or anyone else. This document helps to map out what is actually important: the impact that interventions have on a pupil's needs. There's no mention whatsoever in it of hard data, but the hard data would be equally meaningless without the document's strict focus on a particular individual. Where relevant, a sentence could be added to capture broader context about the student (e.g. currently living with grandparents). It's also important to construct the document led by both the classroom teacher and the student herself. It should be from and for her, not a forced measure.

The two-bullet-point rule is worth applying here: two bullet points have more significance than 30, because no one will read 30. It may be necessary to have the 30 somewhere, but for the process of tracking and following up on the interventions applied to a single pupil, it is more useful to have a condensed record of the core information.

Key takeaway

Despite the value of soft data, it doesn't do anyone much good to gather pages of unsorted information that no one has the time to read. As far as possible, keep data concise and actionable.

Presenting individual student needs – a framework

Table 5.6 is useful for summarising everything you need to know about, and do for, one student. In-class differentiation by the teacher and support from TAs are most effective when they have clear, specific, recorded objectives. Having these allows a visitor to the classroom, with a table like Table 5.6 in front of them, to quickly check whether interventions are being delivered successfully.

The golden rule for interventions is: consistently less is more. Consistent use of two or three effective techniques has greater impact than the intermittent use of many. This principle is also useful for teaching staff; they can become accustomed to the same clear and easy-to-deliver interventions. Use the 'Action' and 'Impact' columns to help you track how the provisions are being implemented.

Elements to note in Table 5.6 include:

- Not all attainment gap students have SEN, though plenty do. This document details those needs at the top where applicable, to make sure that they aren't overlooked in the planning of interventions.
- All the advice is concise and specific – four short bullet points at most. It's hard to work on much more than that simultaneously.
- In the 'Action' section, detail how you will make your objectives happen: list who will organise them and by what date.
- The impact section allows you to come back to the document in due course to assess your work.

Analysing data

Once you've gathered data about your students you need to make sense of it. Careful analysis, bringing together soft and hard data with insight into the stories that the figures tell indirectly, is essential.

Funding is all too often misspent because data has not been sufficiently probed. For example, grade data may show a number of students seriously underperforming in history.

Table 5.6: Resource 2 – individual student needs analysis

Student: John Smith **DoB**: 01/01/00 **Hours / Allocation**: 15 hours		
SEN / identified need:		
SPECIFIED PROVISION	ACTION	IMPACT
• Weekly speech and language sessions supporting expressive and receptive language. • Structured literacy programme incorporating ICT equipment with audio functions to develop language skills. • Testing for exam concessions.		
SUPPORT/TRAINING REQUIRED FROM EXTERNAL AGENCIES	ACTION	IMPACT
• Speech and language therapist to devise an appropriate programme to be delivered in school. • Speech and language therapist to train a TA to competently deliver speech and language sessions to John. • Ed psych to advise on an appropriate structured literacy programme with ICT audio programmes.		
GUIDANCE FOR TEACHING STAFF	ACTION	IMPACT
• Give definitions with key words to provide pre-learning and over-learning. • Link new learning to areas already covered. • Chunk activities/tasks so they appear manageable. • Chunk instructions to provide small sequential model answers, so that it is clear what success will look like.		
GUIDANCE FOR TEACHING ASSISTANTS	ACTION	IMPACT
• Check that John fully understands what he needs to do in order to complete the work in the lesson. Get him to repeat back instructions to demonstrate engagement. • Read through completed work with John and get him to suggest where improvements could be made. Prompt him if he is unable to see any errors or areas for improvement. • Set tasks for John that are time-bound. Leave him to work independently then return to check his work.		
STUDENT TARGETS	ACTION	IMPACT
• Proof work before declaring that it is finished. Could it be improved in any way? • Write new words in the back of your book, with definitions, so that you know what the words mean. • Sound out new words to yourself so that you become more confident using them. Then practise using them in a sentence.		

The knee-jerk reaction might be extra academic support for those students in the subject. In reality, however, it may be that the grades are the result of a coursework term, and the real issue is that students are struggling with research-based writing, or because they have less access to online resources than their peers. To make the most out of the resources available, every problem needs to be properly understood before the attempt is made to combat it.

You will be in a strong position if you can answer the following three questions:

1. How well do your disadvantaged students do in each subject?
2. If they are doing well, why?
3. If they are struggling, why?

On the second question – as I've mentioned before, whenever I've sat as a witness on permanent exclusion tribunals, there seems to be at least one subject in which the student was doing really well. The school should have asked – at a much earlier stage – 'Why? What are the motivations and the barriers for this student?'

Senior leaders may want to consider the question of student performance in the light of teacher residuals. You may find a trend that shows how certain teachers' lessons work for some cohorts but not for others. Why is this? Is it simply the preference for the subject or are there other factors? In some schools, it has proven to be good practice for successful teachers to share their experiences with the teachers who seem to struggle the most.

The first stage in analysing your data is to pick out basic facts and broad trends. Try to answer the following questions:

1. How are disadvantaged students performing as a group compared to the rest of the school's students?
2. How are they performing compared to official external expectations (e.g. those from RAISEonline/ASP)?
3. How does disadvantaged student performance differ between year groups? E.g. do they do relatively better or worse in sixth form compared to at GCSE level?
4. How does their performance differ between subjects? Are there any subjects where performance is particularly poor?

Once you have answered these questions, start to delve deeper: look into performance between subjects in each year group, at individual classes, and at individual teachers. Pick out trends at each stage.

Table 5.7: Resource 3 – key stage snapshot

KEY STAGE 3 – SUMMARY OF ATTAINMENT / PROGRESS – Met or exceeded target grade									
INCLUSION GROUP	**CORE**		**HUMANITIES**		**MFL**		**BICT**		**ART**
	English	**Maths**	**Geography**	**History**	**Spanish**	**French**	**ICT**	**Business**	**Art**
FSM Year 7	17/29 58.6%	25/29 86.2%	22/29 75.8%	26/29 89.6%	20/28 71.4%	23/28 82.1%	29/29 100%	23/29 79.3%	22/29 75.8%
FSM Year 8	39/49 79.5%	17/49 34.6%	32/49 65.3%	41/49 83.6%	35/49 71.4%	27/47 57.4%	31/49 63.2%	36/49 73.4%	30/49 61.2%
FSM Year 9	17/35 48.5%	8/35 22.8%	15/35 42.8%	16/35 45.7%	27/35 77.1%	20/35 57.1%	10/35 28.5%	10/35 28.5%	12/35 34.3%

The Key Stage 3 snapshot presented in Table 5.7 is taken from a real school and is fairly representative. The broad trend here is from unshaded in year 7, lightly shaded in year 8, to darkly shaded in year 9 (using an adaptation of the RAISEonline colour categories, explained above, where unshaded represents being significantly above expectations, lightly shaded represents being on target and darkly shaded represents being below expectations).

Not every whole key stage viewpoint will be useful. In this example it was. The school didn't realise that there was a trend specifically for its FSM cohort, as it didn't reflect the general results of the key stage.

The school considered the findings with heads of departments, heads of year and individual teachers. They found that the most useful feedback came from parents and the students themselves, who talked about the increasing realisation that school wasn't going to work for them, although they had begun their school career with some enthusiasm. School staff felt relieved that this wasn't related to teaching performance but was much more to do with broader cultural issues. However, this opened a whole new Pandora's box of issues – how were they going to use the school's available funding to address this?

Looking at results across the year group is the most obvious way of measuring peer-related performance. However, you should bear in mind two key challenges:

1. How useful can you make this information for heads of department and individual teachers?
2. What can this information tell you about the real issues – what's the story behind the data?

In this real case, the school concluded that there were three main issues:

a) slightly lower performance in subjects with greater emphasis on working memory (history, Spanish, religious education) and higher in more creative subjects (English, media, art)

b) lack of stretch and challenge across the cohort

c) lack of support for the sciences.

The school needed to explore these issues further. It needed to talk to stakeholders and especially the students themselves. The 'story' behind the data needed more substance. The ideas were all good ones and doubtless would be useful anyway – but were they identifying the real issues and ensuring that the maximum number of FSM students could succeed? This depth of understanding and precision is often the difference between good and outstanding.

Key takeaway

Data is only useful if you interrogate it. What are the trends? How do less-well-off students perform compared to better-off peers, and compared to the national average? Where things are going right, why? Where they're going wrong, what could change?

The more angles from which you approach the data, the more in-depth and useful your understanding of it will be.

Combining hard and soft data

In the data above, progress figures in religious education are very poor compared to other subjects: the figure for students who have met or exceeded their targets is about half of the next-worse performing subject. From just this hard data, immediately spending money on assistance in this area would seem like a sensible decision. However, speaking to the head of department and relevant teachers might suddenly produce a very different picture: perhaps, for example, the current topic is particularly challenging, whereas target figures were set during a much easier topic.

Another example of the importance of such consultation is that of teachers who appear, in hard data, not to be achieving grade-based results for their pupils. Speaking to their head of department, to other teachers who know the class involved, or to any TAs or SENCOs who have been present in the lessons may reveal that this teacher is, in fact, helping their students significantly in a more indirect way, such as in self-confidence or social skills.

How and why?

From these consultations and from collating soft data, schools can move to the next level of detail: the justification behind the trends. If progress in essay-based subjects is generally lower than in numerical ones for example, why is this?

- Are such subjects being badly taught?
- Is there a high proportion of students for whom English (or whatever language the subject is taught in) is a second language?
- Are your disadvantaged students relatively unlikely to access written resources beyond set textbooks, such as articles and websites, ancillary to success in these subjects?
- Most importantly, what does the soft data contribute to your understanding of the results?
- What is going on at home or even in the playground that could contribute to these results?

Having done this analysis, schools should have some substantial answers to the questions posed below:

- How well do your disadvantaged students do in each subject?
- If they are doing well, why?
- If they are struggling, why?

Another way to get everyone on board

I've often encountered schools where a couple of pioneers in the leadership team have gathered huge amounts of data and analysed it every which way – but have neglected to share the fruits of their labour. This makes it basically pointless. It's critical that data and analysis are shared with all relevant staff, from heads of year and department down to individual teachers and assistants. If progress in year 7 is particularly bad, the head of year 7 should be informed and given details of all the relevant hard and soft data. It needn't all be bad news, of course: if a year or department is succeeding, relevant staff should similarly be informed – and their practices looked into, for potential use as a model for sectors in which performance is not as strong.

It is also worth writing up a more general summary of findings for the purpose of sharing it with groups of stakeholders who are less directly involved. Aim to articulate your research so it's succinct and easy to read, without leaving out so much information that it becomes useless. The emphasis should be less on the identification of data and more on making it usable. Clear, concise analysis is the key to this: boil it down to your 'Why?' and 'How?' points (see page 122) and include only the items of data directly needed to support these.

Key takeaway

Data shouldn't be siloed. An easy way of preventing this from happening is to create a general summary of data, both soft and hard, to be shared with all relevant stakeholders.

Once created, your general summary can be tailored to each group with whom it is to be shared. Produce some anonymised information, for example, for parents and other external groups.

Conclusion and actions

Tables 5.8, 5.9 and 5.10 offer a broken-down action timetable for gathering, analysing and presenting attainment gap data in your school.

Hard data

Table 5.8: Action timetable for hard data

Task	Assigned to	Report to	Deadline
Meet with the person in charge of data in your school. Discuss what data is currently held and where and how it's available. Look together at the school's data handling systems. Ensure that you can work them, and find out how the information they contain is usually presented. The school may have a standard format on which your work needs to be based.			
Label everything as you go along, so that it is clear what each item of data is and to what or whom it refers. Make sure that these labels are clear and bold (e.g. increase the font size or colour-code them).			
Set standard formats and stick to them rigorously. It can be easy to slip from storing pupils as 'Jones, Michael' to 'Michael Jones' without thinking about it, but this can really confuse the data when it needs to be sorted or searched.			
Further divide up your hard data to give you a clearer picture of the intersectionality of your cohort. The standard inclusion group labels can be used – SEND, EAL, EMA, LGBT etc. – or you can use any other system of labelling that makes sense in your setting.			
Check that your data is accurate, comprehensive, clearly presented and structured flexibly (see explanation on page 106).			
Check that your data is easy to understand and is labelled so that it is clear what everything is and refers to, and that trends and anomalies are easy to spot.			
Back up your data! And make sure edit protocols are adhered to.			

Soft data

Table 5.9: Action timetable for soft data

Task	Assigned to	Report to	Deadline
Interview the student to understand key factors that impact their learning.			
Record the views of the parent/ guardian (from any of the existing channels of communication).			
Speak with TAs or other in-class support who may be able to give useful feedback.			
Ask for written feedback from any outside agency and keep this on record.			
Ask for bullet points of feedback from the student's teachers that address the key issues raised to date.			
Get the head of year, SENCO or equivalent to condense this large amount of information into a few key bullet points.			
Meet in year group or key stage teams to discuss the accuracy and usefulness of the data.			

Analysing data

Table 5.10: Action timetable for analysing data

Task	Assigned to	Report to	Deadline
Look at key stage data and identify successes and concerns.			
Look at individual student data and identify successes and concerns.			
Identify reasons by discussing trends, recurring issues and influencing factors.			
Identify areas for further investigation through soft data research.			

Task	Assigned to	Report to	Deadline
Consider what this information can tell you about the real issues – what's the story behind the data? Talk to stakeholders and especially to students themselves to check your understanding.			
Consider how useful you can make your information for heads of department and individual teachers.			
Write up specific feedback for heads of department and year. Ask them to create an action plan and to get back to you in the next couple of weeks.			
Write up a more general summary of your findings for sharing with stakeholders who are less directly involved. Aim to articulate your research so that it is succinct and easy to read, without leaving out so much information that it becomes useless.			
Check your understanding by answering these key questions: a. How well do your disadvantaged students do in each subject? b. If they are doing well, why? c. If they are struggling, why? d. How are disadvantaged students performing as a group compared to the rest of the school's students? e. How are they performing compared to official external expectations (e.g. RAISEonline/ASP)? f. How does the performance of disadvantaged students differ between year groups? (E.g. do they do relatively better or worse in sixth form vs at GCSE?) g. How does their performance differ between subjects – are there subjects where performance is particularly poor or particularly good?			

Conclusion

The goal of reviewing your school's data is to understand where, why and how students are succeeding and failing, and to organise and share that information in a way that allows you to get value from it.

In the course of consulting projects, I have occasionally been asked to meet with students from the cohorts we've been looking at. I remember asking one girl, who had a long record of lateness and absence and persistent low attainment, what would motivate her to come to school more regularly. She told me that she loved science. I asked (I think she was about nine) what she meant by that, and with a bit of probing it came out that she loved outdoor activities – specifically gardening. I took this up with the school and they agreed to allow her to garden in a corner of the grounds and give her things to plant as a motivator for successful weeks of attendance. This was a relatively low-cost, high-gain intervention.

I'm always hearing examples of this sort of thing, and it underlies my soft-data-forward approach. For all the statistics on attendance and grades in a school, sometimes the most powerful thing is to speak to a student and ask them what would help.

6 Assessments and interventions

Working out how the funds available to your school will be allocated is the central decision in creating a strategy for narrowing the gap. It isn't simple. There are provisions, such as social skills groups, that we know to work in a broad sense, but it's difficult to pin down precisely why and in what circumstances they are effective.

As is no doubt apparent by this point, a motif of my approach is quality over quantity. Good spending is not about having lots of initiatives, but about having a handful that you know and can prove work really well. Achieving such quality begins in a highly nuanced understanding of the contexts and trends of the cohort of disadvantaged students in your school.

The Education Endowment Foundation (EEF) provides a toolkit (http://educationendowmentfoundation.org.uk/toolkit) that gives comprehensive details, including estimated cost and average impact on progress, of about 30 interventions. Some of these are specific (e.g. performance pay), but most are more general umbrella categories (e.g. after-school programmes, sports participation), representing a number of different types of programme.

Even the specific ones, of course, could be focused and/or run in a wide variety of different ways. Innovation is important, and schools should be open to designing new interventions where relevant.

Ultimately, providing a comprehensive list of the options open to schools is impossible, but I do my best in this chapter, drawing on and adding to the information from the EEF and other sources. Unlike the EEF toolkit, however (which is highly detailed and worth spending some time on in its own right), this chapter offers a sort of 'Intervention Smorgasbord', giving an overview of the huge range of options available.

As you skim through these options, bear in mind the motif of quality over quantity: it is the quality and good management of interventions, not the number, that does the most to narrow the gap.

Deciding where to intervene

As discussed in the previous chapter, the most important step in deciding how to spend your funding is identifying where and how the money will be genuinely helpful by using detailed data. The aim is to meet a specific type of need with an intervention that both fits the issue and makes sense according to your setting.

I've come across a few schools that run highly successful breakfast clubs to motivate students who are regularly late (or who wouldn't otherwise get a morning meal sufficient for them to concentrate through to lunch). But I also spoke to a school a little while ago that had tried this and failed miserably – they simply had no uptake. After speaking with their students, the school found out that, instead, providing something like kick-boxing or karate would get them to school for 8am. They set up such classes with great success.

Different settings emphasise certain aspects of educational leadership. There are no catch-all solutions; only ones that work in certain types of schools because of their specific capacity to manage and closely develop a particular type of intervention. For example, some schools line manage TAs once a week and some spend that time preparing more materials, both of which approaches are valid according to the context.

Expensive isn't necessarily better; as we saw on page 81, peer-to-peer coaching is often a highly effective – and completely free – way to get through to and provide a role model for a disadvantaged student.

Write down all provision needs and how many times they recur in each year group. Often the same type of provisions can be brought together; for example, a social skills group and a social communication class could be delivered by the same moderate learning difficulties specialist, whereas social skills and social time (Breaktime Buddy for example) may be run by different staff altogether but involve similar students. Use Table 6.1 to map out your needs according to group and cohort. This will help you rationalise what the whole-school budget should look like for your disadvantaged students.

Remember to record your process of deciding where to intervene. Inspectors are keen to see that schools have a process whereby they identify needs and work out appropriate responses.

Table 6.1: Frequency of provision need by year group

	Year 2	Year 3	Year 4	Year 5	Year 6
Speech & language					
Lateness					
Reading comprehension					
Etc.					

Interventions galore

The intervention egg

In their 2011 report for the National College for School Leadership, 'System leadership: does school-to-school support close the gap?', Simon Rea, Robert Hill and Leigh Sandals use a simple egg diagram to demonstrate the impact group of different types of intervention. The egg has three layers. The outer section ('eggshell') represents the whole school, the middle section ('egg white') represents underperforming students, and the inner section ('yolk') represents FSM students.

I find this concept helpful, and have divided up my list of interventions into the three groups that Rea, Hill and Sandals define.

Eggshell policies (for all pupils):

- quality teaching and learning, consistent across the school and supported by a strong CPD culture, observation, moderation and coaching
- an engaging and relevant curriculum, personalised to pupil needs
- pupil-level tracking, assessment and monitoring
- quality assessment for learning
- effective reward, behaviour and attendance policies
- high-quality learning environment
- inclusive and positive school culture, underpinned by values and 'moral purpose' that all pupils will achieve
- effective senior leadership team with ambition, vision and high expectations of all staff and pupils.

Egg white policies (for underperforming pupils):

- early intervention and targeted learning interventions
- one-to-one support and other 'catch-up' provision

- rigorous monitoring and evaluation of impact of targeted interventions
- extended services (e.g. breakfast and after-school clubs, including homework and study support) and multi-agency support
- targeted parental engagements, including raising aspirations and developing parenting skills
- in-school dedicated pastoral and wellbeing support and outreach
- developing confidence and self-esteem through pupil voice, empowering student mentors, sport, music or other programmes such as SEAL (Social and Emotional Aspects of Learning).

Yolk policies (for pupil premium students):

- explicit school-level strategies to identify and support disadvantaged pupils through, for example, targeted funding.
- incentives and targeting of extended services and parental support
- subsidising school trips and other learning resources
- additional residential or summer camps (including, in England, the pupil premium summer scheme for students transitioning to secondary education)
- interventions to manage key transitions between stages or between schools
- dedicated senior leadership champion, or lead worker to coordinate support programme.

Timeframe

Work on the basis of a marathon rather than a sprint with your interventions. Aim to create systems that have a long-term effect, improving things within three to five years. Inspectors want to see that you are aware of the issues faced by your disadvantaged students, have thought about and analysed them carefully, and are putting concrete strategies in place. In England, as things currently stand, Ofsted don't even require evidence of actual improvement to the attainment gap, providing you demonstrate that there will be improvements within the next three years.

With this in mind, you can be realistic and a little more laid back about timeframes. It can take a while for new programmes to establish themselves fully and start to have an effect. A TA running a new literacy programme, for example, will take a number of weeks to settle into the role and learn how to do it effectively, so make sure they are given this time.

Simultaneously, though, you need to think often and pragmatically about where your funding is going. A relaxed attitude to interventions, where they're put into place and forgotten about, really should be avoided at all costs. Aim for the comfortable midpoint between the two approaches: medium-term interventions, which are flexible enough to be refreshed or renewed as appropriate.

Key takeaway

Don't expect instant results from interventions. Run them over a reasonable period of time, with periodic review and adjustment.

Quick wins

This said, in every school there are quick wins to be had. These generally come in the form of a small group of students or a very specific problem, tackled with SMART targets over a period of a few weeks.

I created Table 6.2 when I was working with a group of schools on narrowing the attainment gap throughout the local area. I asked each school to pick a handful of students – ten to 20 per cent of the attainment cohort – whose hard data revealed obvious challenges and who faced clear barriers to learning. We then used the table as a format for planning and reviewing targeted interventions.

Table 6.2 brings together all the elements of an effective response to the gap: tailored interventions, personalised differentiation, positive engagement with home, regular review and so on. In an ideal world, schools would take this approach for every disadvantaged student. But not only would this not be sustainable in terms of staff time and management, but such a micro approach could also stop schools seeing the wood for the trees, and systemic issues (e.g. problems with a feeder school or the relationship between teachers and the SEN department) might not get attention.

So this approach is decidedly short-termist, but it's valuable nonetheless. By addressing a few of the most stark student cases, the overall hard data attainment gap of schools in the group narrowed by up to 30 per cent. This had a subtle, more lasting impact: the quick wins created successes to celebrate while medium-term interventions unfolded, and proved to staff and stakeholders (and inspectors) that the schools were working on the attainment gap issue, and that it was one that could ultimately be solved.

Reviewing your spending

Many schools find that their budget slips through their fingers as a result of interventions that are put into place and then not properly managed or reviewed. With every new intervention, book in periodic reviews of hard and soft data to monitor its impact. The

Table 6.2: Quick wins for small groups of students or very specific problems

QUICK WINS				
PUPIL	**Pupil**	Jo	Student 2	Student 3
	Key motivators	• Call time on phone • LEGOLAND®		
NEEDS AND INTERVENTIONS	**General barriers to learning**	• Concentration • Self-esteem • Resilience and willingness to try		
	Support with general barriers	• Staff lead to motivate Jo every morning and remind him of key motivators • Breakout times • Specific teacher praise in every lesson		
	Specific barriers to learning	• *A* • *B*		
	Support with specific barriers	• *X* • *Y*		
	Pre- and over-learning	• Ask Jo to speak to an adult from another class or set about the previous lesson, 3–5 mins between lessons		
TRACKING	**Target**	• **Maths** is yr 3 emerging; needs to be yr 4 emerging to close the gap • **Writing** is 2d, needs to be 4e • **Reading** is 2s, needs to be yr 4 emerging		
	Progress	• **Maths** ... • **Writing** ... • **Reading** ...		
ADMIN	**Staff lead**	KT		
	Weekly call home	Speak to aunt once a week to share progress – Thurs and Fri afternoons preferable		

attitude should be: 'We will do this for *x* amount of time and then review it' – and the timeframe, '*x*', should be agreed on from the outset. If a school told me that all of their interventions were working perfectly, I wouldn't be impressed; I'd be suspicious. It's rarely possible to get it right first time.

If a programme is not succeeding, rationalise:
Is the programme being run well?

If 'no', why not? Does the person running it need more time to get to grips with what they are doing? Could they benefit from support or training, either internal or external (see below)? Would a different staff member do a better job?

Is attendance good?

If 'no', work with TAs, class and form teachers to encourage students to attend.

If the answer to both of the above is 'yes', but a programme is nonetheless failing to achieve results, think about whether you might have misunderstood the root issue, and go back to the data.

If programmes consistently come across poorly in review, cut them, though not before doing a final soft data check. Hard data can often be misleading. Maths support sessions, for example, may not directly be increasing performance, but may be having a positive effect on students' confidence and willingness to engage in lessons (which will eventually have a positive effect on results). Or the sessions may be performing badly overall but really helping two disadvantaged students. If this is the case, try to work out why it works for them specifically: is it particularly suited to their level of attainment or learning style? What principles can be picked out for application to future interventions? If you are still thinking about cutting the intervention, do a value calculation:

$$Value = \frac{cost}{level\ of\ impact}$$

OR

$$Value = \frac{cost}{number\ of\ people\ impacted}$$

Investing in quality

To return to the core message of this chapter, having a few high-quality interventions is preferable by far to having a glut of moderately run programmes working on a scattershot principle – one for every single problem picked up on in the data.

The best way to work towards quality programmes is to spend on training the people who run them. This gives your staff members the skills and confidence to maximise what they achieve for students with the funding they have been allocated. Moreover, it creates a resource that you can use for as long as the member of staff continues to work in your school.

Specialist training an English teacher, for example, to help weaker readers keep up with their class in lessons, is much better than giving those students extra practice sessions after school. While post-school sessions do generally improve reading ages, they also tend to leave students still struggling with what their class is working on. Promoting engagement with the curriculum in class is extremely important: if students are constantly being taken out of lessons for interventions they feel singled out, and in turn might decide that they are stupid, or so hopelessly behind that there's no point trying.

One school I worked with took the approach of getting the classroom teacher to work with their TA, with the support of the SENCO, to develop a short reading comprehension course based on the book the students in question were reading in class (*Of Mice and Men*, I think). When I observed the class, I saw two of the SEN cohort volunteer to answer questions and give their views. The added bonus was that the teacher was in charge of the withdrawal too, as opposed to not knowing where the group was going and what the students were doing in isolation in an SEN room down the corridor.

Key takeaway

Sometimes the best thing to do is not to purchase things but to invest in additional time and support for your staff.

As you work through your intervention strategy, it might well be preferable to decide to spend money on doing fewer interventions to a higher quality, rather than introducing more, especially if your school already has a number of interventions in place. If you do want to introduce more interventions, make sure that these will be appropriate, well structured, carefully thought through and closely managed.

What should impact look like?

Community involvement often produces interesting results. The following examples demonstrate innovative, personalised thinking that came from considering the broader issues surrounding the student and listening carefully to other stakeholders. In each case, the bog-standard approach of setting up yet another additional class wouldn't have addressed the underlying issue and would have had limited impact. Each of the schools that came up with these approaches confidently justified their spending to their Ofsted inspector. They were all found to be outstanding. It is not the specific interventions that we are pointing out here but rather the approach: schools prioritise their understanding of the student and create bespoke interventions that address the real underlying issues.

Examples of innovative, personalised and outstanding spending:

AJ, year 7

Road bike – £250

'I was always late for the first lesson coming across town on the first bus. The first lesson of every day is maths, so I never got the chance to keep up with the work. I fell behind and then my teacher said that the school could lend me a bike to get to school. I leave later and have a dynamo for lights in the winter. I'm calmer when I sit down for the maths lesson, no longer getting stressed about being late.'

Hana, year 6

Hotel for mother – £150

'I had never been on a school trip before, but was really scared about being away from my mum – there's only us two. We were doing castles and I was really interested in going on the trip to Skipton, but knew that I wouldn't sleep and neither would my mum. When I don't get enough sleep I'm useless. When the school paid for my mum to stay at a hotel nearby I saw her before I went to bed.'

John, year 5

Nutritionist – £120

'I was always tired by break time and took loads of sugary drinks to give me energy. Then I couldn't settle in class and my teeth went an orange colour. The lady from the hospital came to talk to me about what I ate all week and I started to keep a diary for what I ate and when I was tired and hyper. For breakfast I have slow energy release bars and I cut out the fizzy stuff on school days; I have cranberry juice instead. I feel less tired than I used to. A lot of the other kids keep a diary like this now.'

Hamid, year 10

Personal advanced mathematics tutor – £1,200

'Both my mum and dad are in the army so we lived all over the world, which was great; I've been to five primary schools and this is my third secondary school. I've been tested loads of times for English and maths; I've always done okay in English, but every maths teacher does it differently, which means that I have gaps and use different methods to the rest of the group. I got moved to one of the lowest groups, which made me upset, as I know I'm good with numbers. The school then decided to let me have a tutor once a week in the evening. She started right at the beginning and showed me how to recognise types of questions on the exam. She thinks that I should now get a grade A next year.'

Angus, year 3

Shoes and clothing – £50

'My dad isn't really around, and I just live with my mum. She can't always afford to buy me nice clothes, as I've got older siblings and often get their things when they don't fit them anymore. My football shoes always wear out quickly, as I play football a lot with my friends. One time, my shoes were full of holes and I came to school in my slippers! Someone in the school went out that morning and bought me a new pair of shoes, and a few days later also got me some football boots and clothes for PE. Another time, the school bought a dress for my older sister to wear to her end-of-school dance.'

Group of year 10 and 11s

Adaptations to the curriculum – £500

A significant number of pupils going into Key Stage 4 options had additional learning and communication needs, being on the spectrum of autism disorder. The school introduced small animal care, accredited by City and Guilds. The school paid towards making the compound safe with fencing and sheltered areas, as well as food towards the upkeep of animals like ducks and chickens, ponies and dogs. Through this work, atypical pupils are able to develop confidence and transferable skills in an alternative curriculum.

A fundamental part of narrowing the gap is developing a personalised approach appropriate to your particular context, so think about what impact is most needed in your school.

Just a note on the first example (the road bike) before I move on. I wrote about it in the press some time ago, and to my horror a school responded by proposing a purchase of 20 bicycles. This completely misses the point of how the bike intervention was identified as relevant.

The student in question was struggling in maths. Instead of immediately putting additional maths support in place, the school looked at the cause more carefully. In fact, the student was always late to first period, which happened to be maths, and so missed vital lesson time. Rather than trying to motivate attendance using rewards or penalties, the school investigated why the student was always late. He kept missing his bus because he was a young carer for two younger siblings. Like all carers, this pupil found getting out of the house in the morning a struggle.

The school understood that there are two big 'nos' that you avoid when meeting the needs of a young carer: 1) don't take away their break times – they really need down time when they are off duty, and the social connections they can make during break are vital, and 2) protect their self-esteem – if you put them into a low set or remedial group they will be likely to feel that they are 'bad' at the subject.

The reason why I herald this as the best case of interventions I have seen is because the school took the opportunity to look beyond what could easily have been the 'standard' response to the problem. They spoke to the student, his parents and the supporting social worker and didn't make assumptions about the best way to respond to the presenting issue of poor performance in maths.

In addition, and equally impressively, the school managed the expectations of the student's peers so that they didn't get jealous and demand a bike for themselves. I think when a school can identify the real issue behind the attainment gap and address that, then they will see outstanding results. I hope this explains how investigating cause and effect and tackling the root issues really inform work to identify effective interventions.

Other creative interventions

At one of our regular team best practice sharing meetings, I asked a handful of Inclusion Expert associates what single intervention, if they had to pick, would have the maximum impact on narrowing the gap in all schools in the country.

There was a resounding agreement among us that if all schools did 'pre-learning' and 'over-learning' we would see a massive closing of the attainment gap. This one action, if done well, enables students from almost the full spectrum of learning issues to gain an advantage in their learning – from those with speech and language issues to dyslexic students, from shy learners to those with attention deficit disorder.

Interestingly, a lot of outstanding schools drill vocabulary. I think this solves a problem without them even necessarily being aware of it. In the UK, a lot of what the GCSE and indeed SATs actually test requires students to have acquired and recall language. Such fundamental learning processes are not picked up in the battery of tests we put children through, such as CATs and reading comprehension. These test comprehension and cognition, but a student with language acquisition and/or recall issues might be able to read excellently or pass a cognitive test with flying colours. I often find that students are easily misdiagnosed. As I've already mentioned on page 69, some children who are supposed to have problems with maths actually have no issues concerning number bonds at all but struggle in picking up the complex language of the subject. Pre-learning and over-learning could be the closest thing to a panacea that I can think of.

No more maths, just take them on holiday

A common attainment problem schools report is engaging small cohorts of boys in maths. The issues are more attitudinal than ability-based (e.g. poor relationships with teachers and continuous low-level disruptive behaviour). One school tackled this problem by funding the maths department to take their identified cohort on a five-day trip to the Lake District for some fun and maths. By the time they had returned, they had bonded with the maths teachers and also caught up some very basic maths that was holding them back. This school sought to heal the heart of the issue as opposed to just dealing with the symptom.

Aspire to aspire

I've mentioned some excellent examples of this type of intervention previously, but to give another example: one school decided to prioritise work experience but they were not going to accept the bog-standard set-up where their students made the coffee and did the photocopying, as they felt that this simply confirmed their own self-limiting aspirations. Instead, they had meetings with individual businesses and asked them to experiment by allowing students to closely shadow senior executives (inviting them to meetings, asking their opinions, listening in to phone calls, and getting a taste of management and senior leadership). This worked out well not just for the students, but also for the businesses, who found it very worthwhile.

Connect the dots

If you meet with stakeholders from your school's postcode and they advise that the key to addressing the gap could be parental engagement, promoting aspiration or developing oracy and confidence, then apply these across the school, not just with individual interventions but throughout the curriculum and in all pastoral aspects of school life.

One school wanted to address vocabulary acquisition beyond the classroom and set up a 'word of the day' in the entrance hall. Class teachers asked their students to come up with new words to share with the class each day. Another school made sure the parents of their most concerning FSM cohort were getting positive feedback about their child once or twice a week in order to promote parental engagement.

I hope these various examples demonstrate that any individual intervention is only as good as the extent to which it addresses the real need. The phenomenon of the gap itself involves a very wide-ranging set of issues; the notion that these can be solved simply with additional literacy or numeracy is ridiculous.

Preparedness for learning

I carried out a narrowing the attainment gap review of Milton Hall Primary School in Southend, where I was shown four innovations that targeted 'preparedness for learning'. The school is surrounded by high-rise social housing, archetypal multi-generational unemployment and so on. Headteacher Debbie Priest identified several issues underlying engagement in learning, such as confidence, aspiration and enthusiasm for school. The first innovation was a disused plane, which they put on the school field. There was a very practical element to this, which is that they needed an additional room and had no money and the plane only cost them four thousand pounds compared with an expensive new building. The staff volunteered their time and skills to deck it out into a room that could be used for up to 15 students. Debbie says, 'these children and their parents have never been on a plane and now, every time they study a new topic, they get on the plane and fly to the volcano or jungle or whatever they are studying.'

Another innovation that fits in well with this imaginary journey around the world is a school-built immersion room, which is a cheap hut next to the playground with a 3D projector facing each wall. The students put on 3D glasses and are surrounded by tropical fish swimming around them or a mountainscape or the New York City skyline. Stepping onto a plane and immersing in amazing vistas doesn't necessarily solve aspiration but it does excite the students and it promotes engagement with the curriculum.

The two other innovations focused on developing confidence and communication skills. The school hired a couple of outstanding drama teachers and got all students involved in productions and plays, and subsequently they have become a LAMDA (London Academy of Music and Dramatic Art) examination centre for their region. Once a year, they put on a 24-hour live TV broadcast entirely run by the students, from the technical studio aspects to script, direction and performance. These things do not narrow the gap per se but they create conditions for maximising engagement and excitement about school.

The most challenging cases

Heads frequently lose a significant part of their time to a small number of challenging cases. These students are often in the cohort of the attainment gap, which collectively suffers from the sheer quantity of time its most challenging members take up: it's common to see 80 per cent of senior leaders' time go on firefighting the same five to ten cases. It's not just time-consuming, it's incredibly emotionally draining – but most staff assume it to be part and parcel of the job. I am here to say, in the words of Ira Gershwin, 'It ain't necessarily so.'

In the course of a recent pupil premium review, I noticed that the school in question had an unusually high level of permanent exclusions: 20 in the last year alone. Apparently this was not so uncommon in the local authority. The powers that be had put together an intervention programme for the local schools, which, when I heard how it had been set up, sounded like hogwash. Their plan was to send in the educational psychologists (ed psychs) to work with five students in each school. Hogwash, right? It wasn't just missing the point but it was a real red flag to me because it underlines the gap in understanding I see between the education psychology service, the SEN leadership in local authorities and the school's real needs on the ground.

This is a big bugbear for many heads but they don't speak out about it because who are they to challenge the experts who swan into schools to cast opinions? Most heads I meet confess they neither like nor 'get' their ed psych. Their chief complaints relate to the amount of time ed psychs spend writing reports; what does end up being written in these reports is nearly always useless and often appears like a copy-and-paste job. (I have met plenty of exceptions, the brilliant ed psychs who we love and are a gift to the schools they work with – but I'd put the figure at one in 200.) There are inherent problems with ed psychs being so outside classroom practice, being trained by fuddy-duddy lecturers who last taught a class back when the Whigs were in government, and so their processes do not seem to be in step with the day-to-day needs of school systems and their staff. I have a master's degree in education psychology, and although I am no ed psych, I speak with some more understanding than the usual annoyed and frustrated outsider to the profession.

Rage aside, the value of thinking about this problem here is that the students we are most concerned about are reliant on the views and support of the ed psychs, and this is one of the flaws and challenges in the system that leads to the phenomenon of school leaders spending quantities of their life embroiled and embattled with the toughest student cases. The obvious hogwash in the plan I mention above is that ed psychs won't solve anything by swanning in to work with a challenging student for a couple of hours per half term then writing a lengthy report. So, what was my solution to their problem? I spoke with Michael Purches, who is the head of my northern team at Inclusion Expert, a former headteacher of a special school for 19 years and a real expert on supporting schools to manage their toughest cases. This is a record of our discussion around this particular case, and lays out some principles of good and bad practice when dealing with the hardest student cases in your school.

Common challenges and frustrations – my top 'if onlys'

1. There is a type of student that most of your teachers despise for making their life a misery. The student is actually lovely when they sit in your office and you chat with them about anything but their teacher or home. They love engaging with you and you think they are bright in their own way. You understand their home life challenges and there is that ancient, tectonic part of you ignited that led you into the profession in the first place: to help the needy and vulnerable in our society. So, they are fine in your office – and something approximating the terminator when in the classroom. This is a common experience. The challenge here is for the leader to bridge their understanding, patience and belief in this student with the staff who seem to 'not get' them.
2. As I have mentioned before, in nearly every case that I've seen as an expert witness in tribunals and court cases about students who were permanently excluded, I have noticed the same unfortunate patterns:
    - **a.** There was a lack of early identification – if only the school had picked the challenges up sooner and planned meaningfully, all could have been prevented.
    - **b.** In every case, there were one or two teachers with whom the student was successful – if only they had shared the good practice with the teachers that struggled.

c. There was a moment in time, a specific occurrence that tipped the balance, and instead of it being treated as a one-off, it became the excuse for the ultimate fall – if only everyone had taken a breath and worked out how to prevent this more extreme, one-off event from happening again.

3. The referral times to support services such as CAMHS are shockingly, woefully inadequate – if only a meaningful support had been available earlier on, we might have been able to prevent this decline.
4. Social services change their key person in this case every three months and you secretly think of them as a nincompoop who simply doesn't act quick enough and doesn't seem to follow up on their agreed actions – if only this child had the same half-decent social worker who could help develop some consistency in their life and drive forward the changes needed.
5. You resent sitting at yet another team-around-the-child table playing pass the buck and blame. You know that everyone is really tick-boxing and you always come away thinking what a waste of time that was – if only there were an acknowledgment by everyone that we all have a role to play here and if we pull together, we could achieve something.
6. You spend dozens of hours in support of an application for SEN funding and when it finally comes you forget to question what the purpose of it was after all because it doesn't seem to make a blind bit of difference – if only the SEN panel process was easier and clearer about what could be gained and the limitations of support.
7. The same teachers who don't seem to 'get' challenging students provoke this child into responding with anger and then you have to deal with the consequences, coaching the student to see their role in this while knowing that the teacher is equally to blame and yet everyone's focus is now on the student – if only the teacher could see that their rude manner provokes the child and is definitely a manifestation of their own frustrations.
8. The student just doesn't seem to help themselves and if they were being assessed for a degree in self-destruction studies, they would be on target for a first – if only they could see what I can see, that this school is their best opportunity and every action they take seems to being throwing it down the drain despite my best efforts.

I doubt there is a head or principal in the country who hasn't encountered most of the above problems. But wait a minute: where's the training to deal with all this stuff? And, why are our school leaders having to take responsibility to mop up the mess of other services and factors way out of their control?

When I spoke to Michael Purches, he recounted a story he had witnessed that very day:

This morning, I went to consult with a primary school. While waiting in the reception area to meet with the headteacher, I met a mum who had been called into the school because her year 6 daughter was being excluded. I was fortunate enough to have a good conversation with this mum. What I took away with me was the despair and anxiety she was feeling about her daughter's behaviour (she is unable to identify a cause or triggers for her deep anger that presents as aggression). We spoke about her daughter's imminent transfer to secondary school – another source of great worry. For this mum, her daughter's future is a bleak one. We all know that the transition from primary school to secondary is a difficult one for children anyway but for this troubled youngster, it is likely to be a huge challenge. After a hand shake and a 'good luck', my heart sank as I too shared mum's concern about her daughter's educational future. BUT, on further reflection I thought about all the secondary schools I do know that are highly inclusive and do a fantastic job in forging positive relationships with troubled youngsters that translate into good outcomes.

Putting this into practice

Of course, the real challenge is getting all the key players in your team to be coordinated, consistent and implementing the clearly outlined plan. This means: whole-staff buy-in, attitude shifts, quality-first teaching and helping teachers to breathe and hit the refresh button with the same students that are causing them grief. You know, the usual lot of incredibly challenging day-to-day things a head needs to tackle alongside the incessant wave of firefighting. All of the usual stuff is the ingredients of managing challenging students too; no surprises there. Here are some very specific actions that you could do, which don't take long and will probably end up saving you time and can support your efforts. None of them will replace the need for good ol' outstanding teaching, but if you can get that up and running as well, these actions will absolutely help:

A. Two reams of paperwork

You need the paperwork for the referrals, for building a case and for ensuring that you have everything tracked in case something happens. Don't fault on this, be thorough and record everything. Get an HLTA or someone in the office to ready your file for as and when you need it. Two tips: use folder dividers so that you can quickly reference which agency has said what and get someone from your pastoral team or your SENCO to write a summary page at the front, which looks like a timeline of incidents, support and impact of that support. Having this ready and in order means this is one less thing to worry about and if you suddenly need to take action, such as exclude or refer and so on, you are ready.

However, this is not going to help your staff; this exercise is for managing the outside agencies. The other type of paperwork you need is exactly the opposite: it is one page; it is bullet-pointed and as succinct as can be. This is 'the one page' all of your staff are going to be on, and an example of how this can be structured is given in Table 6.3.

The trick is to focus on just three specific issues – not all 50 that the student needs. Be specific and limit the challenges to just those that (with some concerted effort) you could

Table 6.3: Summary document for your staff (see Chapter 5, page 118 for a more complete example of this type of document)

Presenting issue	Action	Impact
xyz	*xyz*	*xyz*
xyz	*xyz*	*xyz*

solve. This would then allow you to move on to solving the next level of problems. An example would be starting with helping a student positively settle in the class, because without doing this, you can't work out any of the other things that happen later. Or, it could be a matter of needing the student to not swear at staff, because this is where the line must be drawn for the sake of the other students and once you have this basic behaviour issue addressed, you can move on to other issues. Think of it as 'less is more' – tackling the most fundamental issues. Be brave and think first about what the teachers can do rather than the student, because you can probably bet that the student isn't going to do anything different unless you and your staff do. The actions need to be simple and clear and, most importantly, consistent. The impact measures need to be measured most lessons and you need to review them at the end of each week to ensure that they are beginning to work.

B. Stop looking at the student to change – they are just responding to you and your staff

As I mentioned above, think of the student as a simple mechanism of 'Action–Reaction'. This is not a fundamental truth of nature and is way too simplistic to even remotely be a real truth, but I am advocating that thinking in these terms is a useful exercise. Ask not how you can change the student but, rather, what you (and staff) can do that will initiate change in the student.

'Insisting', 'forceful persuasion' and 'appearing cross' are all strategies that have, until now, failed. Your looks of frustration and upset are only going to fuel the fire; the teacher's annoyance and exclusions from the class will play directly into the student's subconscious hands and ultimate goal. In most cases, staff end up colluding with students who engineer a situation that reinforces their own self-image of not being worthy to sit in this class; being rejected is the game they learnt at home and they are getting you to play it out in your school – their other type of home. Don't play their game; play a different one. You and your staff's actions are the ways of rewriting the rules of the game. Here are two examples to make this more concrete:

1. Instead of calling home to complain about the latest incident, pre-emptively call home to praise the student to their parent/carer for something wonderful they did (do this repeatedly). Your action is changing the game.

2. Instead of the teacher expressing frustration at the student in front of the whole class, the teacher should go over to the student during break to have a gentle chat with them, and tell them how much they like them. They should ask about something they really like (a computer game, football?), express genuine fascination and praise the student for being so interesting and great. Of course, this is counter-intuitive for most teachers. When I first started teaching, I had a student who was making my life a misery. I did this exact exercise (it took every ounce of my untrained acting skills to pull it off) and the dividends were clear in the next lesson.

C. Re-shift the attitudes of staff – their opinions make and break students

A specific example of this could be seen in not choosing students for a class role or responsibility – instead, staff could actually promote student engagement in positive leadership. One of the best examples I tried of this was with a boy in year 8 who was on the verge of permanent exclusion. He was given an opportunity to raise some money for a boy in the community who could not walk and had other significant disabilities, and needed a special chair that would cost £2,000. His idea was to organise some football competitions in the school and get students to pay a little something to enter. He also went around the form rooms and got some students to nag their parents for a donation. After three months, he had raised the money, the chair was bought, he went and gave it to the boy, the local paper was there and the year 8 student was as happy as could be. Aside from the obvious dynamics that contributed to the student feeling wanted, worthy and that he had something positive to give the world, it was the sheer quantity of staff who all went up to him throughout the three months saying how impressed they were with him and what a fantastic job he was doing and so on that made the biggest difference. He was showered with praise but, most importantly, it changed what the teachers thought of him.

D. Successes breed successes

There is a possibility to reduce the student's timetable all the way down in order to hit the refresh button and start again with just a few school-based activities. A starting point as low as simply coming in to do an activity with a TA could be a good first step from which to build one successful step after another. The purpose of doing this is to help the student reimagine school from being a place that is out of control and a consecutive series of failures to one that is built up slowly, each step being understood and clearly accomplished before adding the next and it becoming a place where a sense of achievement happens.

Although this is obviously targeted at changing the perception of the student, it is equally beneficial for staff to see this process happen before them and understand that there is 'control' over the situation. Failures, mistakes and stumbling blocks should be expected to arise, and these can then be tackled in isolation and amid a process that is full of 'well dones' rather than trying to eke out a candle flame of positive achievement in a never-ending thunderstorm of failures.

E. There is always one class

In larger primary settings and in all secondary schools, there is always one teacher or a handful of teachers who seem to have absolutely no problems whatsoever with the student. Of course, they are an outstanding teacher who knows their craft exceptionally well and don't see this student as troublesome. They rely on that good ol' outstanding teaching, which is replete with personalised, differentiated and intelligently adapted learning delivered in firm but very positive language. They, more than any ed psych or specialist or CAMHS expert, are your source for your other teachers.

In cases I have seen in a legal setting as an expert witness, there were always one or two teachers in the school who taught the student as if they were any other. It begs the question why on earth those teachers weren't used to help support the other struggling teachers? The obvious answer, I hear you muttering to yourself under your breath, is because teachers *X*, *Y* and *Z* are super stressed, don't have a great attitude towards children and they simply don't differentiate – which is why they wouldn't get anything from the successful teachers anyway. I hear you. But you see, we end up pathologising the student for the failings of the teacher, which is at best morally dubious and certainly a breach of professional teaching standards.

F. 'Us' not 'me'

Since I had undertaken a variety of training and work experience in psychology prior to entering teaching, I took it for granted that when you deal with a challenging case, you get support from a peer. Every profession allied to education gets this and the institution is called 'supervision', which is not to be mistranslated as 'let's oversee your work' but instead 'get this off your chest'. It is human nature to be affected by the trauma you bear witness to and I think most people know that keeping things bottled up in the old English tradition doesn't do anyone any good. Yet, years of school leadership can take their toll and the teaching profession does nothing to recognise the drip-drip effect of exposure to massively painful circumstances of vulnerable children on stress and, ultimately, mental health.

I have met way too many super stressed-out school leaders who are burdened with the personal stories of children in distress. The topic of trauma management in schools frankly requires its own set of books and training, and is way beyond the brief mention here. However, there are two foundational aspects to be aware of:

1. Psychological trauma is contagious and can spread through a staffroom.
2. Stressed and emotionally challenged people are not in a position to manage the emotional pain of others in a healthy way.

The elegant solution is simply to work as a group. This makes sense particularly in larger settings, which can benefit from a range of personalities and experiences around the table. Simply talking in terms of what 'we' are going to do and what do 'we' know removes the burden from any one individual. This group is best made up of those who know the students in different contexts, including TAs, SENCOs, teachers, counsellors, social workers and ed psych. See if you can get someone from CAMHS to join in too (...good luck! Although I do know of cases where this did happen, including my own school). Meet at the same time each week, bring tea and biscuits and make it a sacrosanct meeting that is respected and enjoyed. Each of your staff members should be encouraged to talk about your top ten most challenging students and how you are all struggling and working together. This can turn the burden into a valuable and even enjoyable experience.

G. Learn what behaviours mean

The most common behaviours that staff misinterpret are either autistic spectrum, attachment or hyperactivity. Yes, there are lots more behaviours you need to be savvy about, but you can bet that pretty much every state school in the country has students that present with these behaviours, and in their top ten most challenging students, you will find these issues. You need to understand these behaviours and make sure your staff do too.

Don't think that running out of a classroom is unique to one specific student in your school and wonder what on earth is going on for them. This is not an uncommon occurrence with students experiencing attachment difficulties. You are not the first school to tackle this problem and there are many simple and successful strategies you can put in place.

It's difficult to persuade highly educated and experienced school leaders that their level of knowledge of child psychology and behaviours is inadequate and ignorant. It's not going to be a popular sentence that last one, I know, but please be reassured that I don't blame you or indeed anyone. I don't blame full stop. You are simply not given enough guidance, support or training about these matters. Let's face it, you can become a headteacher, and a darn good one at that, without knowing how attachment trauma plays out – why should you know this? It wasn't part of your QTS or NPQH or any point of study for that matter. And yet, you have to deal with this on a daily basis. My argument isn't with you; it's with the position you have been landed with. Please spend time and money on CPD around these issues, as it will ultimately save you that time and money many times over. Take this as my encouragement to question your level of nuanced and sophisticated understanding of children's behavioural language and how to respond.

H. Be creative, be brave

Whatever you do, don't seek off-the-shelf solutions. I promise you, they don't work – if they did, you would have heard it by now. Similarly, don't wait around for whichever service to eventually see the student for 45 minutes and hope that it is going to do something when it won't. Don't try to make up for a lack of good solid teaching when the experience of turbulent and badly managed classrooms has real damaging effects and cannot be solved by a time-out card so the poor student can manage their resulting anger and frustration.

A simple question of motivations and barriers can result in some insightful ideas, which can result in your own in-house solutions. A boy I met in a school in Clacton, who lived in the poorest area in the country, told me he loved gardening – and it transpired that his housing estate didn't have any greenery. We worked out that the school would reward him with seeds, a trowel and an area of the field to grow some things. It was linked to SMART targets, including attendance, preparedness for learning and classroom engagement, but at the cheap cost of the motivating reward and the eagerness of the student for this, they found ways past some of the barriers. The student ended up going to horticultural college as opposed to drifting into the inevitable NEET status. Please don't misread me and go off and start a vegetable patch outside your entrance hall – the point is that it was bespoke and that the more bespoke your solutions are, the more likely they are to work.

This is the point at which Michael and I tried to answer the not-so-simple question: 'What do we know about the schools that are successful in managing really challenging students?' Here are some of the answers we came up with:

1. First and foremost, they 'get' troubled young people. They appreciate that such young people 'are distinguished by their regrettable ability to elicit from others exactly the opposite of what they really need' (Tobin, 1991).
2. They work hard at working *with* parents and families. Michael could tell in an instant that the mum he met the day we spoke really wants to work with a school to find some answers and solutions.
3. Teachers reinforce consequences for the things young people get right, as well as when they get it wrong. They help young people understand their responsibilities, make the right decisions and do not blame others.
4. Their feedback is specific (e.g. 'You made the right choice there by walking away from that situation'; 'I like the way you asked me for help with that first task in the lesson earlier', etc.). This also helps decision-making.
5. Staff don't let troubled young people push their buttons – they maintain control and don't 'lose it'. They maintain professional responses rather than emotional ones.
6. Teachers use 'time in' rather than 'time out'. Banishing young people may only compound any sense of worthlessness. Imagine how being sent away might affect someone who has already been rejected and abandoned numerous times in their life. The message of keeping them close is that whilst their action is unacceptable, they are not.

7. During a crisis time, staff remind students of when things went well to give them a broader perspective of the situation.
8. Staff help young people express their emotions, so they don't have to rely on negative 'acting out' behaviour.
9. Staff carefully watch and listen to the young people. By doing this, schools can predict 'flash points' and prevent them.
10. Young people are prepared for change and transitions. This reduces stress and anxiety.
11. Lessons are suitably differentiated so that learning is matched to needs, interests and aspirations.
12. Teachers provide choices to young people. This is not, of course, whether to complete the task or not, but to offer a choice of tasks or ways of doing things.
13. Teachers develop and use peer support networks. This benefits all young people with regard to personal development.
14. Above all, schools that are successful with the most troubled young people are great at building relationships with them. Students are treated respectfully and are championed.

Final thoughts

I'm the first person to admit that this isn't easy and if you say you don't struggle with the most challenging students or take it to heart or get affected sometimes, then I don't believe you. It's one of the defining aspects of your school leadership role that makes you worthy of some genuine praise and applause.

With this in mind, I want to end with two additional points:

- Think about bringing someone in from the outside to help you see where things are going well and where you need support. It is difficult to get perspective on your relationships and with anything that takes up your internal emotional space, let alone such significant amounts of time. This could be your ed psych, or someone from a local specialist school.
- Be guided by one key question, which you need to ask yourself, your colleagues and agencies: 'Is this student a danger to themselves or others?' When you meet with social services and especially CAMHS, ask this question and record the answer because this is the basis of your decision about whether to keep the student in your school or not. This is not just your last resort and vital evidence you may need for exiting a student out of the mainstream, but your legal duty to your staff and students. Don't use this nuclear option without fully exploring positive behaviour management and techniques for de-escalating challenging scenarios.

Good management: guidance and examples

As we have seen in this chapter, the management of interventions is much more important than the number of programmes the school provides. More than this, the quality of the management of an intervention could easily be more important than the specific substance of the programme. An excellently managed literacy programme, for example, could have positive effects on classroom participation, self-confidence, social skills and so on, well beyond the specific ability it targets. Its strong management would also ensure that teachers gained valuable skills for helping future disadvantaged students, and that a team of staff members became actively involved in the wider issue.

A prime example is the approach taken by one college in West London. Rather than just asking the school librarian to run a reading programme, a senior leader, the head of English, several heads of year and some TAs together devised and quality-controlled a programme tailored to their students and local area. This quickly developed into a flagship cross-school literacy scheme focusing on encouraging parents to read to their children. Money was invested for reading prizes and assemblies were held to get students involved. All of this required only marginally more investment than a librarian-run programme, but its strong management got staff and other stakeholders involved, generating a much greater impact.

Key takeaway

Often, the best interventions are those that involve a range of people. The greater the number of people involved, the greater the skillset at the disposal of the programme's manager.

Always assign a coordinator to a programme, and give them someone (you, a head of year or department, or a senior leader) to report back to. When you review interventions, focus as much on their overall management as on the running of individual sessions. Work out criteria for measuring good management, and encourage staff to fulfil them. For example:

- Do all the staff involved in the programme know exactly what they should be doing?
- Have they been given a strong set of resources for planning the content of sessions?
- Are all the relevant stakeholders (parents, SENCOs, community workers if relevant) informed about and, if possible, involved in the programme?

Case study: assistant RE teacher

An assistant teacher in the religious education (RE) department is the coordinator of a lunchtime session for attainment gap students on GCSE exam essay writing. She runs the sessions herself, but meets at the beginning and end of each half term with the head of years 10 and 11 to report on how individual students are performing. She also meets with the heads of the RE, English and history departments to discuss what features exam essays should include. In the early stages of the programme, she met regularly with study skills advisers in the SEN department to discuss how best to run each session. This is an example of good practice in involving as many people as possible in an intervention.

Conclusion and actions

Tables 6.4 and 6.5 offer a basic action timetable and self-evaluation questions for managing your school's intervention strategy.

Table 6.4: Action timetable

Task	Assigned to	Report to	Deadline
Establish entry and exit criteria for all interventions.			
Plan and schedule reminders to measure impact every half term on average, and to update records accordingly.			
Include soft data in records (e.g. 'increased participation').			
Adjust interventions according to impact.			
Monitor carefully when new staff take over interventions.			
Produce an annual intervention report for staff, inspectors and stakeholders.			

Conclusion

As I have said often in this chapter, interventions have to be tailored to their context. The examples in the preceding pages demonstrate creative thinking and good management,

Table 6.5: Self-evaluation questions

Reflective question	Actions taken (where relevant)	Key lessons	Impact
How did you choose your interventions?			
Is there clarity in the school about the chosen interventions?			
Are all stakeholders kept up to date about your strategy?			

but you're the best judge of what has a chance of working in your school. There are, nonetheless, a few general principles that can be stated about interventions. I'll list them here by way of summary:

1. Interventions should be targeted at specific issues identified through comprehensive and well-analysed data.
2. Interventions should never act as sticking plasters for poor teaching. They should be aids to good teaching.
3. Training teachers to help disadvantaged students within lessons is always preferable to giving students additional support outside of lessons.
4. Keep an eye on your finances and ensure that strategy is guided by how much money you've got available. There's not necessarily any need to be tight-fisted, but try to make sure that the amount spent on an intervention is proportional to the extent of its impact and the number of people impacted.
5. Always return to interventions once they are in place and measure their impact against baselines of performance. If they aren't working, review them.
6. Finally, and most importantly, think in terms of whole-school development. The danger is that work on the attainment gap ends up taking place down some managerial side road, quietly and ineffectively, so that money vanishes into a school's overall budget and barely helps the pupils it is spent on. For interventions to be effective, the issue needs to be a talking point, something that all staff members are aware of and that is prioritised on meeting agendas and in informal discussions. Everyone, from governors to senior management, teachers, TAs and parents, needs to be involved; your aim should be to galvanise the whole school in changing collective attitudes and approaches. If this is done well, support for disadvantaged students will improve well beyond the apparent limits of available funding.

7 Demonstrating impact

The previous chapter looked at the process of choosing and implementing gap-narrowing interventions from a variety of angles. But there's one part of the process I feel deserves a chapter of its own: the need for schools to make spending decisions in a way that is rigorously accountable. Not many school leaders are trained in accountancy, yet a key proviso of school funding in the UK, and in most countries with publicly funded education systems, is that all spending is transparent and closely tracked. But in what format? How much information is necessary? How can schools record both the most detailed spending data and their context and rationale for budget assignment?

There are three aspects to demonstrating the impact of your school's work on the attainment gap:

1. Fulfilling formal accountability criteria: presenting data on your website, creating a folder of information for inspectors, and so on.
2. Making sure all staff and stakeholders are engaged and kept updated.
3. Ensuring this becomes an ongoing cycle and not just a one-off. Addressing the attainment gap is a process, not a project that can be easily completed and tidied away. The advantage of this approach is that it sets you up to be judged on the dynamism of your system rather than just your results.

This chapter aims to address these issues and more. There is a proposed financial spreadsheet and guidance on how you can build your own. I also cover other (more fun!) ways of communicating your achievements.

Telling the right people in the right way

It is neither unreasonable nor unusual to have to justify what you do with a pot of money, especially in the public sector. If taxpayers' money is to be used in a certain way, it seems fair to qualify and defend this decision. How will it be used? What is the return on investment?

Such questions are neither complex nor esoteric, but can appear irrelevant and perhaps even foreign for school leaders when making pedagogic decisions.

Many heads have told me that inclusion costs significant amounts of time and money, and I believe for us to become truly inclusive in our classrooms we have to address this attitude. When conducting narrowing the gap or SEN reviews, my associates and I frequently find that schools are haemorrhaging resources on inappropriate and low-value outcomes.

We ask the same three questions every time:

- What issue did you identify?
- What action did you take?
- What impact did it have?

More often than not, we find there is an inadequate measure of impact of interventions and nearly always a lack of strategic thinking about how to maximise the impact. No one wants to challenge why you spent £500 on this provision or £1,000 on that rather than adopting a cheaper approach. Rather, justifying your spending is simply making sure that the decisions you make around money to achieve certain goals with your FSM or SEN cohort are sensible and considered. In short, it has nothing really to do with the cash, but everything to do with how well you can demonstrate your thinking.

Communicating success

There are a variety of stakeholders who need to look at the same data but from different perspectives. This belies the need to continuously celebrate your successes and to draw upon a variety of formats to do so.

There are two easy forms of demonstrating success, which actually go the furthest but are the least drawn upon by schools. First is the local media, which loves the occasional heart-warming story. The intervention I mentioned in the previous chapter on page 139, for instance, where a school took a group of students who were disengaged with maths to the Lake District for a week of fresh air, exercise, seeing the world and fun maths, is a perfect example of a local-media-friendly story. (Sadly, the school in question missed the opportunity.)

The second most commonly missed easy opportunity for schools to communicate their success is on a board in their entrance hall, which tells of all the innovative ways the school has spent their funds. Obviously, this needs to be done anonymously and carefully, but as I have said, a hallmark of outstanding schools is that they tend to quite literally write their successes all over the school, and highlight everything from trips to provisions, clubs and the achievements of their alumni.

A two-stage process

Justifying your spending is a two-stage process: before (while considering what interventions to apply) and after (when evaluating what happened).

Before: focus on the outcome before choosing your provisions. As we've already seen, a common mistake is to misread the underlying issue and to attempt to solve a by-product. If an identified cohort is not engaging with their English lessons, before setting them up with, say, a computer-based booster programme, think about whether this will really have an impact on their engagement with classroom learning. The root issue may not be simple lack of literacy skills.

After: manage your and others' expectations. Even the best provisions will not ensure 100 per cent success. I have encountered excellent provisions where the sought impact was not achieved, despite the efforts and resources spent by the school to include them. If you can demonstrate your effort and your thinking, you should not be held responsible for an unfortunate lack of a positive outcome. This is not true from a whole-school perspective but is very much the case when working with individuals.

Whole school versus individual

When I work with schools, they have to be up to scratch on two levels to convince me that they have spent their money well: whole school and individual. The obvious approach to demonstrating your work with individuals is through case studies, although the key ingredients are easy to miss, especially when you can so easily get bogged down in the complexities of a case. Similarly, on a macro level, it is easy to generalise and miss out on substance. This brings me back to the three golden questions that should structure all articulations of a school's strategy:

- What issue did you identify?
- What action did you take?
- What impact did it have?

This formula is true on both a whole-school and an individual level. For example, student A presents with five issues, you take action with three provisions, and the impact is *X*, *Y* and *Z*.

See the box below for a real-life example.

Example

Student

Presenting issue: Difficulty in language acquisition (20 per cent of new words).
Action: Pre- and over-learning sessions.
Cost: Four 30-minute TA sessions per week, reinforced at home = £*xy*.
Impact: Acquired 75 per cent of the previous term's new curriculum words.

Whole school

Presenting issue: 85 students present difficulty in language acquisition.
Action: Purchase two days per week of speech and language support to train teachers and TAs for a term in pre- and over-learning.
Cost: 24 sessions with a speech and language therapist = £*yx*.
Impact: 17 staff and 12 TAs confidently use pre- and over-learning with a good understanding.

Though these examples are from different perspectives, they employ the same formula. You do not have to rigidly stick to this format, but something similar will demonstrate how you are aligning your provision decisions with the identified needs.

Making sure that all staff and stakeholders are engaged and kept updated

This is covered at length in Chapter 4 and revisited subsequently. To reiterate those discussions in the form of some key takeaways:

- The first step in demonstrating the impact is being clear about what the make-up of your cohort is, and the specific challenges that it faces in your local area. Convene a stakeholder meeting and invite representatives from social services, police, youth work, parents and parent support groups, and even local government. Ask attendees about the key factors that inhibit progress and how to build aspiration within your student community.
- Consider preparing four or five case studies to share with stakeholders, to demonstrate how you tackled different types of issues. Not all of the cases have to end in success. It is your thinking, effort and measure that make all the difference.
- It is okay to use soft data to demonstrate your impact. The vast majority of progress cannot be ascertained by the crude measure of a grade or a percentage point.

Getting the details right

The devil really is in the detail: if you haven't accurately identified the issues, you can't hope to address the real gaps. I have come across too many schools that are confident about their provision, but whose assessment procedures are in fact flawed on closer inspection. Usually this is due to a lack of clear entry and exit criteria for interventions and robust assessments of students' needs.

To get beyond the myopic attitude of hard-data-based judgements, a quality justification of approach and systems has to be found within the soft data, based on how engagement, positivity and esteem are affected by each intervention.

Getting comfortable with the financials

Though I emphasise soft data, it's obviously also important to engage with the facts and figures, particularly financial information. Schools sometimes tell me that getting to grips with their finances has been one of the most eye-opening aspects of a review, giving them a new perspective on the energy and focus attributed to perceived and real challenges. In addition, teachers are often surprised to learn that there's a disproportionately huge amount of funding allocated to one type of intervention and hardly any to another, where both were equal in their minds.

Money and time aren't the best measures of outcome. Parity between students must be in appropriate outcomes, not in the money or time spent on them. A student with substantial physical impairment, for example, will obviously require greater financial resources. All students have different needs, and so the only correct measure of value is whether or not something is working. All this said, expensive, bought-in interventions are usually not as effective, or at least not any more effective, than cheap and cheerful homegrown versions. Expensive computer-based literacy programmes are a particular bugbear of mine.

More data work

Breaking down your school's spending in a clear, straightforward way will ensure that you will always know exactly how the funds are being spent. Done well, it can enable you to track spending down to a pupil-by-pupil level of detail. You will be able to monitor spending in specific areas, such as literacy or numeracy, or on specific classes and year groups.

Key takeaway

Close financial tracking will help ensure that there is no wasteful spending, and that no pupils are accidentally being overlooked.

In order for you to record your spending effectively, you will have to analyse it and break it down into its separate components. Although this may seem like a mammoth task at first, it is a brilliant opportunity to think through your school's use of the funding in close detail. It will provide an insight into the possibilities and limits of the amount of funding that you have, as well as allowing you to plan out future spending in a careful and informed way.

Presenting data clearly is essential. There are two destinations for useful data: the back office (to help you and your staff manage your resources) and the front office (website, inspectors, governors, etc.).

Data is only as good as its usefulness, and in some regards, the most important aspect of your data is less the final result but rather the framework that will allow you to analyse your results; your results will continuously change and require adjustment. Your best way of accessing the information is to have it all in one place where it can be seen at a glance and sorted according to individuals, cohorts and interventions.

Figures 7.1 and 7.2 show an exemplar spreadsheet that demonstrates how well-organised data can enable you to track your spending in close detail (down to £50 segments) without losing focus on the bigger picture. Key design features are explained in the bullet points below:

- Individual pupils are listed down the left of the sheet, divided into year groups (Figure 7.1, 1).
- Categories of intervention (literacy, numeracy, study skills, organisation, etc.) are listed along the top of the sheet (2), subdivided into specific interventions (e.g. one-on-one reading, homework club; 3).

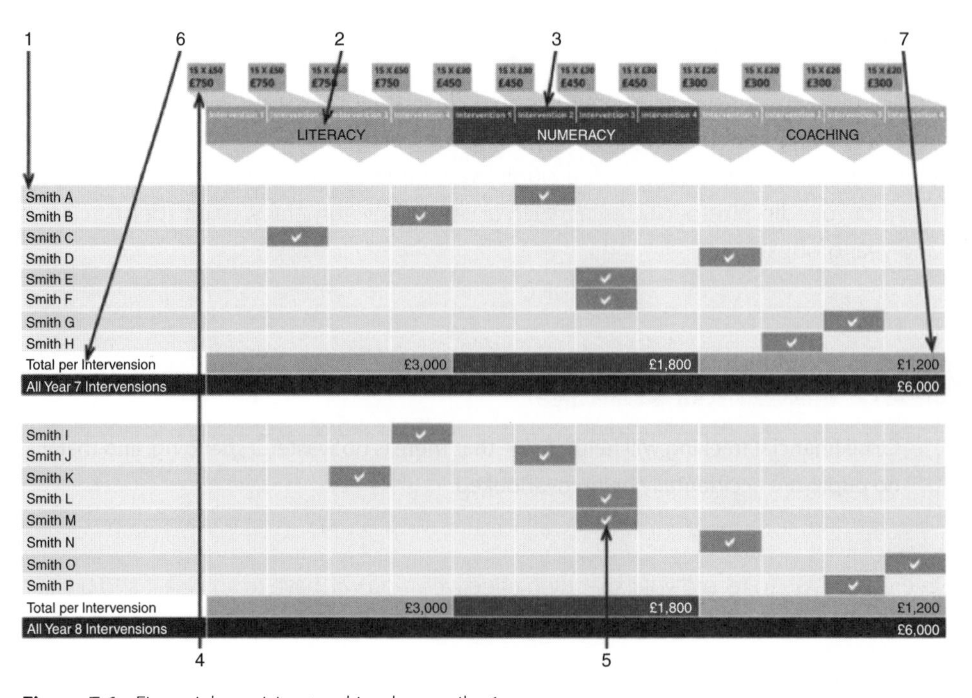

Figure 7.1: Financial provision tracking by pupil – 1

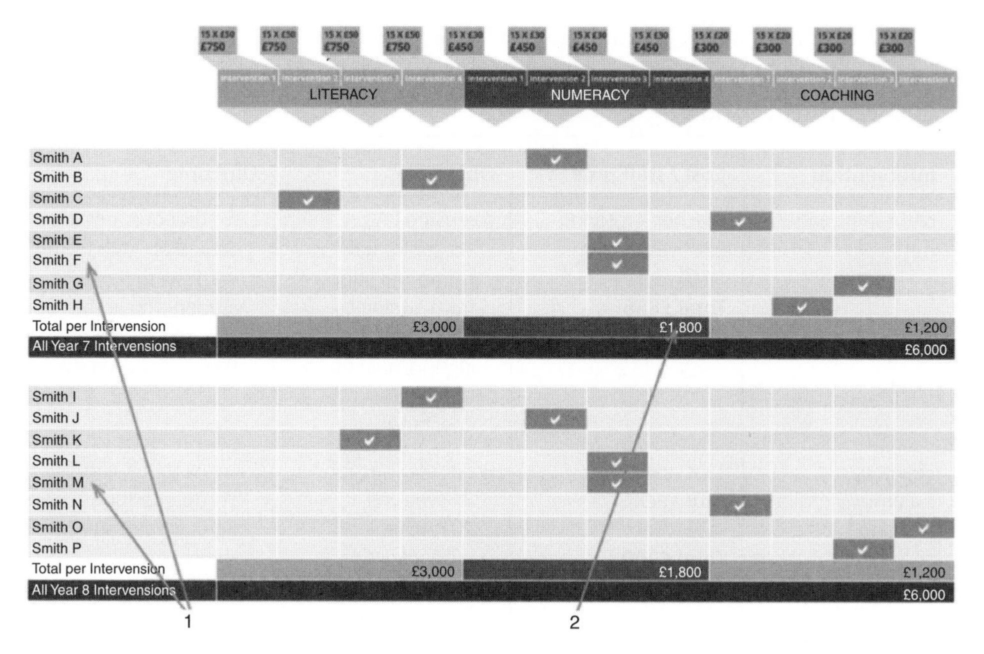

Figure 7.2: Financial provision tracking by pupil – 2

- Once the cost of each intervention has been added (4), users can simply tick which pupils are in receipt of which interventions (5) and the sheet will automatically calculate total spend per category (6) and per year group (7).
- All year groups are listed together on the same sheet, but clearly delineated using colour or shading and spacing. This means that a user can quickly take in the spending on attainment gap pupils individually, in a single year, and in the school as a whole. If interventions differ greatly between year groups, separate sheets for lower school, middle school and sixth form could add clarity (Figure 7.2, 1).
- Running totals allow users to play around with different interventions and map out how their finances can be put to use most efficiently (2).

The big question, especially in relation to accountability, is: 'What did you spend your money on?' But this can be difficult to articulate precisely. It is often a sign of a good spending policy if small amounts of money have gone on a wide range of highly specific interventions, but this makes representing the spending even more difficult. You can use a table like Table 7.1 to show what you spent your money on and briefly explain why by giving a snapshot overview.

Points to note:

- The 'Intervention' column contains a full list of the school's interventions. The value in this is to create a concise record that is easy to process and review. As such, there's no need to record every variation of each intervention. Group things together. Where money has been spent in highly individual ways ('a bike to get AJ to school on time'; 'a home printer for Johanna'), for example, these could be grouped under 'Individual interventions'.

Table 7.1: Financial provision tracking by provision

COST PER INTERVENTION			
Intervention	**Cost / staff time**	**Objective**	**Outcome**
LAC mentoring	Teacher *X* tutoring £22/week @39 weeks **Total £858**	To ensure LAC student is gaining maximum support from all staff by coordinating, liaising, helping organise and coaching	LAC student issues are picked up and dealt with swiftly. LAC students have the maximum support the school can offer
Reading comprehension group	TA *X* session £10/week @20 weeks **Total £200**	Pre-school sessions 3x/week for 20 mins to raise reading comprehension levels above 11	Increase in reading comprehension age over the age 11 threshold
Homework club	TA *X* session £10/week @20 weeks **Total £200**	After-school sessions to enable students to focus on successful engagement with homework	Students' homework marks have consistently increased over two terms

- The 'Objective' column contains a concise description of the entry criteria for the intervention.
- The 'Outcome' column offers a similarly concise description of progress made. Where possible this should be hard data, or at least measurable soft data.

Use Table 7.2 to articulate everything the school does for a quantifiable number of students – and how well the school does it. This is useful for governors, inspectors, mentioning on the school website, and so on. This table doesn't capture everything but it gives a useful, positive snapshot. All the principles set out previously also apply here: concision, a substantial but useful amount of data, and no overkill (nothing that would come at the expense of overall concision). A document like this can also help staff think in terms of impact. They can see that the interventions they run are being recorded, articulated and appreciated, and it is clear that their contribution fits into a larger strategy. The table also encourages using soft data over hard: not just exam results but broader schemes, such as clubs and buddy support.

Table 7.2: Provision impact tracking

Intervention	Group size	Impact	Graduated
Literacy			
Reading scheme	34	Half made good progress	17
Literacy intervention	47	Only about 40% graduated but two thirds made significant progress	20
Literacy skills	10	All graduated	10
Phonics	13	Mixed results – worked very well for half the group	6
Numeracy			
Numeracy scheme	26	Progress all round, excellent progress for half the group	13
Maths tutoring	8	All graduated	8
Pre- and over-learning	40	Strong results – only five students failed to graduate, and there were mitigating circumstances for two of these	35
After-school maths club	20	Good graduation rate, although late pickup proved problematic for some parents	14
Social inclusion			
Breaktime club	52	Feedback very positive so far	Ongoing
Buddy support	110	Results unclear so far	Ongoing
Social intervention club	8	Seems to be working well so far	Ongoing
Social games club	17	All graduated – and really enjoyed	17
Social skills	16	Excellent results	15

Points to note:

- As in the 'Financial provision tracking by pupil' sheets, subdivide your interventions into general categories. This may reveal useful trends about relative performance of interventions in different academic and social areas.
- 'Group size' refers to the number of students who met the entry criteria and were included in the intervention.

- 'Impact' contains a very basic description of the overall effect of the intervention. Unlike 'Graduated', this information is not quantifiable.
- 'Graduated' refers to the number of students who met the exit criteria of the intervention.

Table 7.3 can be used before the intervention starts *and* to measure its impact afterwards. This could also be part of a regular review – a process that is important but shouldn't be overdone. Having reviews too regularly doesn't give the intervention time to establish itself and develop. Having too few is obviously detrimental, and amongst other things creates an atmosphere in which standards are more likely to slip. On average, once per half term is a good benchmark.

Points to note:

- Entry criteria ('Who is it for?') will need to be adjusted to specific settings (cohort, individuals) depending on the intervention. It sets out what the intervention is trying to achieve in hard data terms and defines its remit (e.g. 'slower readers').
- 'Details' should contain a maximum of three sentences – don't get lost in nuance.
- 'What does success look like?', i.e. exit criteria, should echo the measurables and language of the entry criteria.
- 'Impact' merges soft and hard data. Hard data in this case would be specific reading ages with reference to the entry and exit criteria of the intervention. This isn't captured, but the information here is important and useful nonetheless, and typically might not be recorded (apart from in the kind of lengthy write-up that almost no one ever reads).

Table 7.3: Provision tracking – before and after

WHO IS IT FOR?
Students below the reading comprehension age of 11
DETAILS
Pre-school sessions three times a week for 20 minutes. Coach will check understanding and prompt with comprehension questions throughout. Student expected to read two pages a day at home and write a review of the book at the end.
WHAT DOES SUCCESS LOOK LIKE?
Students attain reading comprehension age 11
IMPACT
17 of the 36 year 9 students who took part (47%) graduated 31 students (86%) improved reading age by the end of spring term 35 students (97%) grew in confidence reading in front of others

Finally, consider including a link for users to request fully detailed information (as far as this is possible in accordance with data protection regulations). This demonstrates that you have worked hard compiling information and strategising on the issue, and intend its spending to be as transparent as possible.

Building your own tracking and monitoring system

The following steps offer simple guidance on building a tracking and monitoring system for your school:

1. Gather a list of the pupils in each year who receive additional funding for the purposes of narrowing the gap. Input this list as the left-hand column of the spreadsheet. Make sure that at this stage you also know: – the total number of pupils in receipt of the subsidy; – the total amount of money your school receives.
2. Breaking up pupils into year groups will make the table clearer. It will also allow you to extract more specific data from it. Consider using different colours, lines or blank rows to make the years more easily distinguishable.
3. Find or make a list of each different intervention your budget is being spent on, and the amount that is being spent on it. These will go along the top row of the sheet. This may well range from very large interventions (e.g. an extra staff member) to much smaller ones (e.g. provision of free textbooks or peer-run reading sessions). Record them all; although this may take time, having a list of every single intervention will give you the broadest picture of your school's spending. Make sure you also know at this stage: – the total cost of each intervention; – the number of pupils each intervention is intended to apply to (for example, a homework club may only be aimed at lower-school pupils, whilst university application support would only be applicable to students in sixth form).
4. Divide these interventions into categories, such as 'Numeracy', 'Literacy', 'Study Skills'. Some provisions, such as staff members, may be hard to pigeonhole into a single area, but it isn't a problem to use on very broad categories (such as 'one-on-one support') if necessary. Note these categories on the sheet in whichever way you feel will be clearest. Consider colour-coding or using an extra row to write in categories underneath a few specific interventions.
5. Next to every intervention listed at the top of your table, add the total amount being spent on it.
6. You will then be able to divide up your spending into highly specific blocks by calculating how much is being spent per pupil on each intervention. The calculation

is as follows: $\frac{\textit{total cost of intervention}}{\textit{total number of pupils receiving it}}$ For example: Blossom Hill School offers an hour of one-on-one numeracy sessions to all of its 35 FSM pupils. The total cost is £525. $\frac{£525}{35} = £15$ so the total amount spent per pupil on the intervention is £15. The school also offers one-on-one assistance with essay-based homework to all FSM students in year 9 and above. This accounts for 23 pupils in total. The number of hours that a pupil may use is unlimited, but last year 56 staff hours were required in total, at a cost of £12 per hour. This means that the total per pupil is: $\frac{(56 * £12)}{23} = £29.22$ These figures can then be recorded alongside the total cost of each intervention. A good model for this is: '£ x pupils = total', where '£' is the amount allotted per pupil for each intervention. 'Pupils' is the total number of pupils receiving that intervention. 'Total' is the total amount spent on the intervention overall.

7. At the bottom of each column, include a formula to calculate a 'total spent' per intervention.

8. Use conditional formatting (www.wikihow.com/Apply-Conditional-Formatting-in-Excel) to write a formula that works as follows: if a box is ticked in the column of a particular intervention, add the amount allotted per pupil for that intervention to the total. The column headed 'Intervention 2' in 'Financial provision tracking by pupil – 1' (see Figure 7.1), shows how this works in practice.

Design features

Have a look at the examples above for suggestions of how to make it easier to extract information from your spreadsheet.

Conditional formatting is one great way to add clarity. Consider creating a conditional rule that turns boxes from white to a more visible colour when they are ticked. This will make it very clear on first glance that a box has been selected. Conditional formatting could also be used to automatically reject any data that seems to be outside of reasonable boundaries.

For example, if the total spent on a single intervention was supposedly exceeding the school's overall spending, an error would obviously have occurred. Conditional formatting can be applied so that any such cells were automatically flagged up in red.

Statutory requirements

In regard to the pupil premium grant in England, the government believes that headteachers and school leaders are held accountable for the decisions they make through:

1. the tables that show the performance of disadvantaged pupils compared with their peers
2. the Ofsted inspection framework, under which inspectors focus on the attainment of pupil groups, and in particular those who attract the pupil premium
3. the reports for parents that schools have to publish online.

I think this works well as a general framework for demonstrating a school's work on the attainment gap, and so I have elaborated on each point below.

1. Performance tables

Two sources of external data are relevant: the performance tables, which show end-of-key-stage data, and the RAISEonline/ASP data, which provides the 'value-added' information, showing how well students have done relative to expectation. Year-group data (without individual names) from these sources should be included on the school's website. For your own clarity in tracking interventions, however, you should also have access to half-termly performance data. This doesn't necessarily have to go on the school website, but it could; it is useful to inspectors and other interested outsiders.

What your external performance tables actually *reveal* – improvement or the lack of it – is, of course, the topic of this book. The positive view to take, then, is that they will effectively take care of themselves, providing that funds are used effectively, responsibly and all the rest. In our experience of inspections into schools' attainment gap strategies, it isn't actually necessary that performance tables show evidence of immediate or past improvement; they just need to be able to prove that there *will be* league table improvements within the next three or so years.

2. Ofsted

In the UK, Ofsted place an increasing emphasis on schools' performance in driving up standards among disadvantaged students. According to *SecEd*, 'It is very unlikely that a school will be judged to be outstanding for achievement (which would also make an overall outstanding judgement unlikely) if disadvantaged pupils are not found to be making sufficient progress.' (*SecEd*, 2013)

Ofsted, in essence, want to make sure of the following:

- you know who your disadvantaged students are
- you have a plan for spending funding on them effectively
- you regularly evaluate whether or not the plan is working.

If you have followed through the steps suggested by the book up to this point, your school should have no problem with any of these requirements. However, one way of making absolutely sure that you have such information to hand and in a format that is easily accessible is to compile an inspection folder.

This should include:

- summary paragraphs from your conversations with stakeholders (Chapter 4, page 85)
- consolidated data from your hard and soft data research (Chapter 5, page 106)
- a write-up of your analysis of this data (Chapter 5, page 117)
- your intervention framework (Chapter 7, page 163)
- the minutes of meetings in which the funding has been discussed; if these are numerous, and particularly if there are minutes from senior management and governor meetings included, making them available to inspectors can be a big plus; it proves beyond doubt that the attainment gap is high up on your school's agenda
- case studies and impact reports for individual students and/or interventions, ideally covering two or three students
- a write-up of what you and the school have learnt through this course; this is another powerful way to demonstrate that your school cares about the issue
- miscellaneous: one or two other relevant documents detailing work that has been done on the issue; completed action timetables, for example, are a good way to demonstrate strong organisation and management of a team that is working together on the issue.

3. School website

There's no mandatory format for information on school websites. According to the Department for Education in England, in relation to the pupil premium grant, school websites should at least contain:

- the school's funding allocation for the year
- details of how the school intends to spend the allocation
- how the school spent the previous year's allocation
- the impact of this spending on attainment for the pupils to whom the funding was allocated. (Department for Education, 2014b)

Websites can include much more than this, though. Providing, obviously, that it is in line with data protection regulations, the more detail the better. The following list suggests information you could include and the order to arrange it in:

1. **Hard data on the attainment gap in your school**: number of students, comparisons to regional and national averages, etc.

2. **The nature of impoverishment in your school setting**: what the key factors of the gap are. This shows that you don't work in a bubble and recognise that the attainment gap is both a whole-school and, in a sense, a whole-area issue.
3. **Summary of your local community stakeholders' meeting**: to demonstrate that you listened to your stakeholders and that you are responding to meet the needs of your students.
4. **Summary of your governors' meeting about the attainment gap**: this shows good governance and leadership.
5. **Celebrations**: highlight individual cases (anonymously), interventions and approaches you have taken that have had outstanding results.
6. **Parental engagement**: explain how fundamental home–school liaison is to you and what you do to promote engagement of all parents – especially those where there is an attainment gap.
7. **Hard data showing where both the gaps and the successes are**, drawn from whole-school and out-of-school data (e.g. RAISEonline/ASP): highlight the key challenges and account for your approach to date and why you may or may not have been successful. Be brave and honest.
8. Bring together the first five steps into a **summary** that narrates the specific challenges in your area, the data, your approach until now and the lessons you have learned that will guide your approach in the future.
9. **Examples of individual students** (anonymise names!): mention their barriers, motivators and your plan to meet their needs (an example of how to present this information is given in Table 7.4).
10. **A list of identified needs**: what your actions and interventions are to meet those needs, how much those interventions cost and their expected and actual impact (an example of how to present this is given in Table 7.5).
11. **Intervention reports** that bring together both hard and soft data (an example of how to present this is given in Table 7.6).

Schools are encouraged to publish this information on their website because it is meant to be read. Make sure that it is easy to find, concise, and in a format that is easy to understand. This increases awareness of the issue and shows that it is something the school cares about, which will not only look good to parents and inspectors, but also motivate staff and stakeholders to continue their hard work.

Table 7.4: Examples of individual students

Student	Their top 3 presenting needs to make progress in the curriculum	2–3 simple ideas to help them access the curriculum	What are their motivators?	How you can use their motivators to help incentivise their progress
A.	• *X* • *Y* • *Z*	Arrive on time	Loves football club 'X'	If arrive on time for half term then will buy them a football ticket
B.	• Runs out of class • *Y* • *Z*	Appropriate differentiation Reduce timetable	Passionate about climbing	If doesn't run out of reduced timetable of classes then will be rewarded with a Go Ape ticket

Table 7.5: A list of identified needs

Identified issue	Action	Expected impact	Actual impact	Cost
Language acquisition	Pre- and over-learning	Higher engagement in the curriculum	To be measured after 4 weeks	£1,000 (staff training)

Table 7.6: Intervention report

DATE:	INTERVENTION TITLE:	STAFF:	RELATES to SCHOOL IMPROVEMENT PLAN:
ENTRY CRITERIA			
DESCRIPTION			
EXIT CRITERIA			
HARD DATA MEASURE OF IMPACT			
SOFT DATA MEASURE OF IMPACT			
STUDENT VOICE			

Conclusion and actions

The steps outlined in Table 7.7 are easy-to-implement ideas that are designed to help you in your demonstration of impact.

Table 7.7: Action timetable

CONTEXTUALISE Demonstrate that you really know your students and your approach makes sense for your school.			
Task	**Assigned to**	**Report to**	**Deadline**
Convene a stakeholder meeting and invite representatives from social services, police, youth work, parents and parent support groups and even your local MP. Ask them about the key factors that inhibit progress and how to build aspiration within the community of your students. It is possible that this will end up being a tick-box exercise, but some of the best narrowing-the-gap strategies I have come across have resulted from such meetings.			
Put a summary of the minutes of this meeting in the relevant section of your website. When inspectors pay you a visit be sure to always begin your discussion of your disadvantaged cohort with: 'Our community is unique and our stakeholders have helped us understand that they face issues *X*, *Y* and *Z*. As a result we have taken the following actions...'			
PERSONALISE Demonstrate that you have a bespoke approach to narrowing the gap.			
Along with the broader data, include a number of exemplar documents that give a much more precise level of detail. These provide not only a more specific, but also often a more accessible insight into one or two of the interventions that the school is using. This allows readers to engage with specific programmes and targets, and to see the students that these are benefiting (or, equally importantly, not benefiting). Such documents also demonstrate the level of care in the micro-management of the whole project.			
This information can be given to your team, to senior management, governors, and even posted on the school website, providing individual names are removed. Also, prepare four to five case studies demonstrating how you tackled different types of issues. Not all of the cases have to end in success – it is your thinking, effort and measure that make all the difference.			

THE RULE OF THREE Issue, solution and measure			
All major research into narrowing the gap, as well as basic common sense, tells us that the myopic view of RAISEonline/ ASP or whole-school data will simply not tell the story adequately enough. If that is all you show inspectors when they come knocking at your door, then it will be difficult for them to get a picture of whether you fully grasp the issues. So it's critical that soft data is included too. There is a basic formula that succinctly captures progress in soft data terms, using three columns: 1. the presenting issue 2. the action you took 3. the impact of your action. All key pastoral and inclusion documents and forms are based on this simple formula, from a Pastoral Support Plan to an EHCP.			
MARKETISE It's not just what you do but who you tell.			
Encourage your school to celebrate its achievements with the attainment gap. Keep parents and other external stakeholders in the loop: mention the issue in newsletters and emails, and perhaps even link the relevant section of the school website in your email signature. Post information and positive results on boards in the school. Preface the information on your website by saying that the issue is a high priority for the school.			
Beyond the information necessary to fulfil statutory requirements, consider including a list of your interventions, and mention that these are in regular review, as well as some success stories if you can anonymise them appropriately. (Similarly, as discussed, it is good practice to produce a report on the issue for submission to your governors.)			

Conclusion

Ultimately, there are three aspects to demonstrating the impact of your school's work on the attainment gap. The first is fulfilling formal accountability criteria where relevant (presenting data on your website, creating a folder of information for inspection, and so on). The second is the broader, but equally important, process of making sure that all staff and stakeholders are engaged and kept updated. The third and most important aspect is ensuring that all of this becomes a cycle, not a one-off. Narrowing the gap isn't a project that can be easily completed and tidied away. This may sound exhausting but there's a silver lining: seeing the attainment gap as a process allows you (and your stakeholders) to judge yourself on the dynamism of your system, not just your results, however good or bad they might be.

PART 3

Reviewing your work

8 How to conduct an attainment review

This final chapter provides instructions for carrying out an attainment review. I wanted to close the book with these instructions for various reasons. Firstly, they offer a convenient way of recapitulating the advice set out in previous chapters, but from the fresh perspective of an external reviewer or assessor. Secondly, schools with a particularly bad attainment gap are often encouraged, especially in England, to commission an external review. Clearly I have a bit of a vested interest in giving such advice, but there are many advantages to doing so: in my experience, both as a school leader and as a consultant, outsiders are more perceptive and less blinkered when it comes to identifying the factors holding a school back; the same logic obviously applies to almost any organisation.

With this said, every school is different, and the issues peculiar to each need careful attention. External reviews are all too often authoritarian and judgemental, and this has fostered some justified scepticism among school leaders with regard to experts who periodically swan in, at great expense, to tell them what they are doing wrong.

Schools could, if they choose, use the instructions in this chapter as a guide to reviewing themselves. I don't necessarily recommend this, but if a school has had a particularly bad experience with external reviews in the past, then this might be an option worth considering. Alternatively, schools could give the instructions to an external consultant and ask her to structure her report around the framework described.

Far from revealing trade secrets, I think it's extremely important that schools understand the sort of things that consultants might look at in the course of a review. A common frustration I hear from school leaders is that consultants helicopter away without properly upskilling and supporting staff, leaving behind an improvement plan that no one remembers quite how to implement. I have always understood the name of my firm, Inclusion Expert, to refer not to us but to the client: we provide training and support, and you become the expert about inclusion issues in your particular setting.

Protocol and etiquette

When conducting an attainment review, the first thing you should do is meet with the school head (or principal) and go through the following broad checklist points. Use this initial step to demonstrate that you respect the school and the headteacher's leadership and want to honour any specific circumstance that needs to be approached uniquely. This will demonstrate that you are listening, open and flexible to the school's needs. Something I have found in visiting many schools is the fear factor that can sometimes come from having been over-inspected by local or national authorities and the walls that come up as a result of wanting to protect themselves from being exposed. Any support visit will be crippled by this understandable self-limitation and so it should be the first port of call of any visitor to a school – or, for that matter, any organisation – to demonstrate respect, consideration and empathy.

1. Why has this review been commissioned?

Has it been externally imposed on the school? Has it been requested by someone other than the person you will be spending the day with?

In one school I visited, the deputy principal had been asked to work with me on the review. She had applied for the role of principal a few months earlier and it went to an external candidate who had now requested the review. I managed to work out eventually that as far as she was concerned, this was his way of getting evidence to show that she wasn't a good school leader and that my review information was to be used as a tool against her as an individual in some intriguing leadership struggle. She was obviously closed and uncooperative, and told me plenty of information that in no way matched the evidence. This is one example of many varieties of political scenarios you can walk into when you visit lots of schools. Know that your day will be as successful as the person you are working with allows it to be. In this circumstance, I had to insist on meeting with other staff privately as well as the school principal. I made my position clear about how I was there to try to solve a narrowing-the-gap problem and my views could not be solicited on this staff member in this way, because she was so nervous that any exchange with her was not helpful or meaningful.

2. What is the background of the school that has led to this point?

This simple question could tell you everything you need to know. You are looking to work out why there's an attainment gap. The school principal should be able to tell you.

As important as what they say is what they don't say. Look for obvious but commonly recurring themes such as:

- Is there a lack of soft data?
- What is the level of differentiation and personalised learning?
- Is the gap monitored carefully enough?
- Think about what they say they have tried and why this hasn't worked – how have they adjusted and developed their approach?
- Are they flexible and adaptable to trying new things?
- How well do they know their individual students' barriers and motivations?

3. What is the background of the people I am meeting today?

I do find the discussion with a senior leader who has a head-of-department and 'teaching and learning' background different from those with more of a pastoral or SEN background. Their understanding and areas of understanding are obviously more advanced in some aspects than others. Knowing what they know gives you a good standing to harness, as well as a door to open to aspects of the gap in which they simply won't have experience or sufficient knowledge.

In a recent review, I found the deputy principal of the school knew a lot about outstanding classroom teaching and relatively little about what vulnerable children management and pastoral systems really require. Inevitably, we ended up focusing quite a bit on the pastoral aspects that she didn't know.

4. Is there anything I should know about that indirectly informs the gap (such as HR or leadership issues)?

At this point, you are looking for any issues to do with staff turnover or problems within specific departments.

In a recent school visit, I found the school was headed for a perfect storm: the head of maths was off on long-term sickness leave, two teachers had handed in their notice and one was about to go on maternity leave. There was one maths teacher left who was newly qualified and of very variable standards. The issue of having an entire maths department who are new or temporary to meet a significant gap in maths attainment was necessary to know about and address.

You can look for any details about governors and the senior leadership teams and how effective they are.

5. Don't mention the war

I have visited a number of schools where a catastrophic tragic incident has occurred in the recent past – the death of a student or, in one case, the serious assault of a teacher by one of his pupils. Slightly lower on the scale of seriousness, but still extremely difficult, are the handful of schools I have visited where 'mismanagement' of funds has led to a court case that has made the press. Such problems require sensitivity. Bring them up very carefully, and only when it is critical to the issue at hand.

There may be staff who don't want to be observed or met for personal reasons. You may be introduced to staff who are going through disciplinary procedures and you may be told about this to help you understand the context of your conversation. It would, of course, be wholly inappropriate to mention anything.

Community and school

As has been discussed throughout this book, each school serves a community. Ask school staff to tell you about this community:

- How big, where and what do we know about the specifics of impoverishment?
- How well does the school know and interact with its community?
- Have school staff done home visits?
- What relationships does the school have with outside agencies – specifically social workers, GPs, MPs, etc.?

Help the school to identify and make a note of the key factors that inform the gap in their community. The purpose of this is twofold:

1. To identify any uniqueness, key themes or specific issues pertaining to the poverty in their specific community.
2. To orient the school leader to thinking about their community and realise the depth of the sociological issue.

One school I reviewed suggested that although the index of impoverishment was unemployment, their community was comprised of many farm hands who were paid the minimum wage and were equally impoverished, sometimes more so, than those relying on state benefits. We explored how identifying the specific FSM cohort was insufficient to meet the real needs of the school. I encouraged the school to capture this narrative in their pupil premium report on their website and justify their approach.

In a similar vein, small coastal town schools that have experienced unemployment due to the decimation of the local fishing industry do not have the same issues as inner-city schools struggling with gang violence. Every school should be encouraged to think of their situation as unique, and consequently, their approach should be individualised.

Action

The school should convene a community stakeholders' meeting with key people to explore the real issues in more depth. Invite representatives from a broad spectrum of services including social workers, police, GPs, local government and so on. Even if they don't come to the school, they should still contribute some bullet points over an email. Put the summary of that meeting on the website – this is your starting and end point for the bespoke approach to narrowing the gap in this school.

Related to this is the role of the governors and their input. Convene a special governors' meeting to update them about this review and the findings of the local stakeholders, and to provide them with details such as in Chapters 1 to 3 of this book. Encourage the governors to think about how they, as community representatives, can really support the school through a process of change. They need to come up with some specific questions they can ask that will support staff in implementing their plan of action. Put the summary of this meeting on the website, thus demonstrating outstanding governance.

The temperature of the school

'Taking the temperature of the school' is an exercise I carry out with senior leadership teams as part of an attainment review. It generally makes for a fascinating discussion. The purpose is to consider the major factors that could contribute to narrowing the gap in a particular setting. It is fairly obvious that any one of the key points in Figure 8.1 could exacerbate the gap if not addressed. For example, your school may promote the most amazing aspiration but if this is not coupled with excellent differentiated and personalised learning, then it will only go so far. The exercise asks senior leaders if they agree about these key areas and, most importantly, if they can identify a strategy to get the school where it needs to be.

You should discuss with the school the generic issues we know impact the gap in order to take the temperature of the school. Do not assume that their self-evaluation is necessarily accurate or has been moderated with another, equivalent setting.

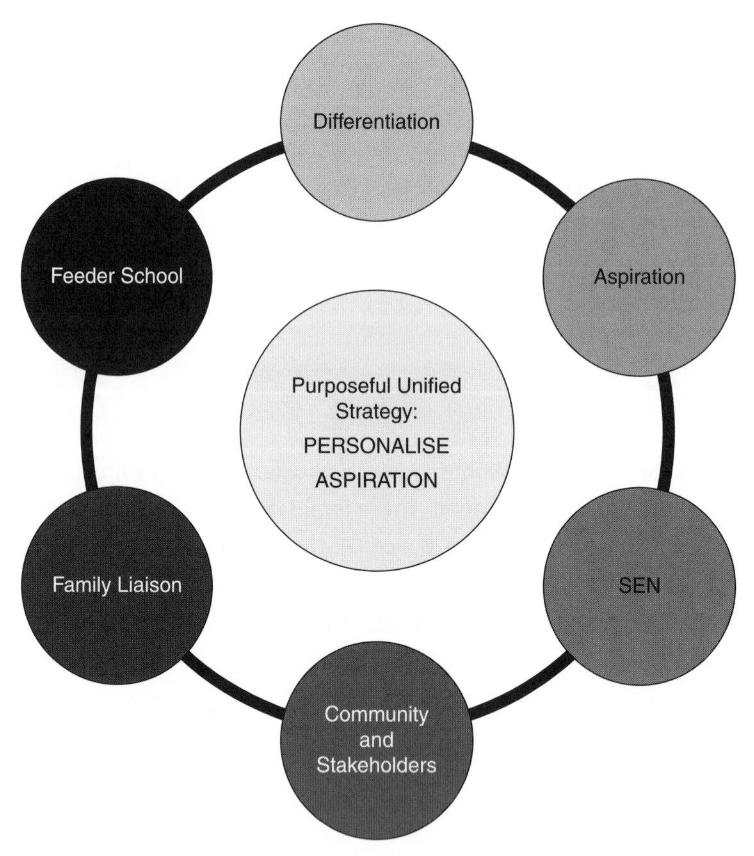

Figure 8.1: Taking the temperature of a school – major factors that could contribute to an attainment gap

In a school that had told me their 'differentiation' was eight or nine out of ten, it ended up being more like a three by the end of the day, and the main focus of the implementation plan. They had standard differentiation sheets in every subject, which were of course useless for personalising each lesson to meet the needs of individual students. Self-perception is usually not deception but simple lack of experience or ability to see the wood for the trees. The taking of the temperature of the school then is not just for you to get to grips with the key issues, but to help you get to know how this school leader thinks.

Taking the temperature

In order to take the temperature of the school, first ask senior leaders to self-evaluate out of ten (ten being as outstanding as you could possibly be) according to these key areas:

- home engagement /10
- aspiration /10
- SEN /10
- differentiation /10

- other schools* /10
- stakeholders* /10
- a unified, clearly articulated strategy bringing together these individual efforts /10.

***Note:** 'Stakeholders' usually refers to anyone who impacts the school or could contribute and these include GPs, MPs, social services, police, CAMHS and parents. 'Other schools' may refer to feeders, trusts and academies but, most importantly, other schools that serve the same community as your school.

You should then discuss the scores with the senior leadership team of the school and any other stakeholders. Map out:

1. the impact of not being 10/10 in any one of the areas on your FSM cohort progress
2. your plan of action to get to 10/10.

This process can lead you in a number of different directions, so be open to the process of discovery. It is more important to see where the school ends up by opening this can of worms rather than simply fulfilling this task because it is on your to-do list. In one school, we got sidetracked talking about the mental health of some of the parents and how the school leadership is impacted by challenging home lives. This point was slightly adjunct to the above task but it opened a vitally important door that was central to narrowing the gap in that school. This exercise, along with my whole approach, is not meant to be a dogma, but a process from which you can be flexible – tailoring rather than inventing, and adapting rather than box-ticking.

The students

This chapter began with the community and whole-school issues, and the next stage of an attainment review is to understand the background and specific issues in the student body. Firstly, ask about how many students are on the impoverishment register (eligible to receive pupil premium) and then what percentage they make up of the school and, of this cohort, how many are not meeting their expected attainment. The next obvious questions have to do with the basic information around how this cohort breaks up into subcategories.

Identifying groups within the attainment gap cohort

You should ask about the overlap between the attainment gap cohort and:

- gifted students
- special needs (you can assume there should be a significant overlap and, if there isn't, interrogate this further – for example, this could reveal a lack of SEN identification or simply an unusual group or any other issues)

- child protection, mental health and vulnerable status (again, this is a common overlap and in some areas, this will be significantly high. This will tell you that you need to explore the quality and measures of impact of pastoral support)
- EAL, ethnic minority attainment and any specific cultural issues
- attendance and lateness factors.

These hard data statistics should indicate a pattern of a group or groups of students within the attainment gap that you can focus in on. If it doesn't, then this was a worthy exercise to go through with the school anyway to reflect on the groupings of traditional issues and how they spread across the school.

It is quite common to find an overlap where there is an attainment gap of students who have both SEN and child protection issues, resulting in issues like lateness and attendance. Schools often talk about certain ethnic minority students all performing in a certain way – I have often heard schools say, 'We have many students from Poland and they are very studious.' Be careful not to accept sweeping statements and assumptions; we are on the hunt for meaningful data and it is important to veer away from both positive and negative discrimination.

Feeder settings

Something schools often neglect to work out is where they are inheriting their gap from. Remember that the gap emerges at the age of two and so by the time it reaches the setting under review, it may well have passed through an entire school phase. Ask the following core questions:

- Where do your students come from?
- Which feeder EYFS setting?
- Which primary school?
- What did the feeder setting do about the attainment gap?
- What worked for them and what didn't?

Discuss what we know about the feeder schools. Remember – the gap grows and gets more deeply rooted the older the student gets. We need to trace any gap to its source. The relationship with feeder schools can vary from being acrimonious to deeply entrenched; this point has to end in action that is going to work for the feeder school and the school under review. There's no point in convening a meeting between the two settings and getting them to commission a review when there isn't a chance anything would happen in reality. This has to be carefully managed.

Example

One EYFS school was convinced their work was outstanding and yet when the children arrived in primary school, their baseline tests demonstrated poor performance. The EYFS thought the primary school wasn't doing well at all. For the primary headteacher to chat this through with the EYFS head was going to be difficult. The approach they came to was a 'community-wide' narrowing-the-gap project, which involved an element of EYFS, with the review bankrolled by the primary school. The EYFS head was not going to refuse to be part of the solution of this wider project, and it took the sting out of the personal relationship between the primary and EYFS heads. The EYFS review revealed a host of problems that Ofsted had not picked up, including a lack of moderation and questioning of their results. The solution didn't lie entirely with the EYFS setting but it played an important part.

Individual students

Ask to see details about some random individual students. Try to see a variety of years, issues and challenges but make sure these are from the cohort where there is a gap. Look at the hard data – you should be able to get a clear picture of how the school tracks and measures its individual students. Is the data useful? Have they captured meaningful progress information? Next, ask for the students' stories: background, home life, barriers to learning and motivations. Consider how well the school knows this information, whether it is recorded and tracked and whether they need to find out more. I always ask staff to go and have a brief chat with a couple of random students and find out their motivators and barriers. This helps them work out a specific plan for them and they realise that they can easily do this for all of their gap students.

Think about the following:

- When the school presents real-life stories, do they echo what the hard data is saying? Do they lead you to think that there are other issues here?
- How prevalent are parental mental health issues? Or barriers such as transport, lack of motivation or specific issues in aspiration?
- What has the school learnt from this process of focusing on individuals? Would this be a useful exercise to do with all students? Could they put this in a plan and make an arrangement to send you some details and you can follow up with them?

Case studies

In a similar vein, ask to look at case studies. A case study doesn't have to be a perfect example of pedagogy that was executed outstandingly. I always used to present tough cases that had varying degrees of success but clearly demonstrated my understanding, approach and capacity to adapt when things didn't go to plan.

Ask yourself whether the case studies include too much information that doesn't clearly depict the specific barriers, simple actions and their impact. This is very often the case. Case studies are a way for the school to demonstrate impact and show its approach. If it can't do this in one page, then most stakeholders such as governors and outside inspectors will find it too long and lose the thread. Like everything, keep it simple and accessible. A one-pager (see Chapter 6, page 145) would suffice, with a line or two about the student background followed by an additional quote from the student themselves.

Child protection, lateness and absence

By this point in the review, it is most common for the themes of child protection, lateness and absence to have emerged, and so consider the following points, remembering that this is an issue that needs its own separate investigation and planning if necessary:

- Check that child protection is managed effectively and legally. If not, recommend an urgent review, and make it clear that the school must do this as a basic legal requirement and can be shut down immediately if this isn't in place. This is more rare than common and you are not expected to be an expert to work out if they have the basic procedures in place. Ask the school how they do their training and who their appointed officer is, and perhaps what they do with their procedures and files. This is not meant to be an extensive investigation but it should be enough to know whether it warrants further work.
- Consider how home management impacts the students and whether there are any shared cohort-level issues that need to be invested in, such as a counsellor.

One school had paid for a play therapist to work with their students who were victims of terrible home lives and this made a lot of sense, especially when I asked what the impact was; the school leader said, 'Well, one of the students went from 50 per cent attendance to 85 per cent attendance in one term.' One could be worried that 85 per cent is still below the national expected standard but if presented as a result of the intervention, and then perhaps as a case study, this would highlight one of the outstanding achievements of the school. This is a clear example of why a school needs to present a narrative and clearly harness soft data; otherwise many varied successes like this will get missed.

Ask the following questions:

- How well does the school know about the causes of both lateness and absence and what is their record of improvement? Again, this has to be dealt with as a separate issue if it is chronic. Explore the value of the current attempts to solve these issues and it should tell you quite a few things.
- Who leads, and how, on pastoral challenges? How well equipped and skilled are the staff to tackle whole-school management issues?
- What has worked and why? Would it work to do more of this?

Sign-up

In England, the issue of sign-up is important because if parents or guardians don't register their children for FSM, the school will miss out on funding that could add up to tens of thousands of pounds. This problem collides with a much bigger issue around hard-to-reach parents (see Chapter 4, page 81 for a fuller discussion). Many schools I have come across have used the incentive of a prize, gift, raffle ticket or free uniforms for anyone eligible who signs up. In a recent chat with a village school headteacher, she told me that parents don't sign up for fear of everyone else finding out – we explored more secretive ways that the school could go about this process.

Special educational needs (SEN)

The issues around SEN and vulnerable student management all emerge here if they haven't already cropped up in the previous exercises. It is at this point you can think about the leadership and management structures and some of the factors that may be limiting the school as described in Chapters 2 and 3. Is SEN coordinated by the same person who is looking at the attainment gap? Do they have the requisite skills and job description to carry out these functions? How well does the 'back office' of SEN communicate with the teachers? How effective is the advice to teachers?

Pause

Think about what you have learnt so far about the attainment gap in this school:

- **How well is the students' hard data identified and cross-sectioned?**
- **How well is the soft data gathered?**
- **Do the issues identified when finding out about the community match the specific case studies?**
- **How does this picture lead us to an understanding of intervention planning?**

By now, as a result of general exploration, you may have come across some broad-stroke issues that need to be addressed and, for this, I would suggest referring to Chapter 3. Consider:

- Are there staff that the school currently relies upon to deliver aspects of intervention planning that are simply not up for the task? If so, this needs to be carefully handled and dealt with.
- Are the related issues of SEN or other cohort groups harbouring a hornets' nest of problems, which, if not addressed, will thwart any meaningful attempts to execute this plan?
- What tracking and planning systems are in place? Are they sufficient to handle a more advanced, more sophisticated approach to soft data gathering and tracking?

Communication that impacts the classroom

Assuming that the gap will significantly be impacted by the capacity of classroom teachers to both understand and adapt to the needs of individual students, then we need to look at two issues as a priority:

1. What advice is given to classroom teachers about individual students?
2. What is the quality of advice to teachers like?

Two questions that I ask can be a helpful way into this topic. Ask the senior leader you are working with:

'If I have just joined the faculty in your school as a classroom teacher, how will I find out the key information about students? Where is it stored? Can you show me?'

And

'How many clicks of the mouse would it take me to locate computer-based information about students?'

I find that this is usually very revealing. Many schools store information for teachers as part of larger school programs (such as SIMS), which can be quite prohibiting because of the lack of easy access. I like to do what I describe as a 'clicks exercise', which counts the number of clicks of the cursor until you have the information available. In many schools, this comes out as 12 clicks, which is too time-consuming and unreasonable for already stretched teachers. They should not have to spend this much time laboriously wading through screens simply to pick up information. The information should be accessible from the desktop of every teacher and should take one or two clicks maximum.

A classic mistake to look out for is providing teachers with pages and pages of information per student. As a general rule across all inclusion problems, less is more and the golden rule is consistency. With this in mind, suggest the school sticks to providing three bullet points of advice for teachers per student that crucially all staff should implement. When I first started teaching, I was given five to six pages per student and there were 35 students out of the 200 per week I was teaching. I will hold my hands up and say that of course I didn't read that information and most of it was completely irrelevant anyway. Keep the goal in mind – to get teachers on board, make their lives easy and maximise consistency. One other point: by advising teachers to implement something that can be spotted at a glance when someone pops into the class, all senior leaders can join together in ensuring they are implemented. A good example could be: 'provide printed instructions to accompany the verbal instructions' – this is something that can be seen just by glancing at the desk. Something like 'be encouraging to Jack and make him feel welcome in your classroom' will, at best, get a varied result and most likely half of the teachers will not be doing it, which of course misses out on anything approximating consistency.

You may decide that the school does not have a strong capacity to work through meaningful advice to teachers and this is something that should be prioritised as a form of consultancy support for another day. The attainment gap is much more to do with good teaching and learning than most people realise. I would go as far as to say that schools should prioritise teaching and learning before calling in someone to conduct a review, as it will inevitably be among the resultant recommendations. The skill of differentiation and personalising learning to meet the needs of all students in the classroom is perhaps not as well trained for at the point of entry into the teaching profession and so it is not surprising that where there is an attainment gap, there is often a teaching and learning issue as well.

Interventions and deployment of resources

Coupled with the issues surrounding classroom practice is how SEN students are identified early enough and how they are supported. Are they constantly being removed and provided for outside of the mainstream class or are they included along with their peers but adapted for well? How does the school know? How do they measure and track the impact of whatever extras they provide for students?

How are the SEN students identified? What is the school's process and how do they catch mid-year (mid-phase) entry students or students who don't speak sufficient English? Related to these issues are how the transition from the previous school is managed and what sort of information transfers.

Look at the range of assessments and consider what they will actually tell you about a student. Very often, schools will be able to harness details about cognition through standardised tests, which are commonly used in England (e.g. CATs), and reading tests. However, these will not give the school sufficient understanding about either comprehension or speech and language acquisition and recall. When schools say that they have a battery of tests that they are satisfied with then it is worth interrogating this a bit, as well as how they plan against the results.

One school I went to shocked me by having more assessment procedures than I had ever seen in a school before. They seemed to have acquired every available assessment package out there and yet I realised their understanding of their students was limited. Why? Because the assessments were removed from the classroom setting, and any real and meaningful data is more about progress than starting points – how the assessment is reviewed against. It is also about how the data is used in the planning. A single school leader knowing a lengthy report full of assessment results is meaningless unless it is used by all classroom teachers to adapt their planning to meet the students' needs.

The process of the pre-assessment (baseline) followed by the post-assessment (progress measure) is at the heart of all intervention planning (see Chapter 6 for more). Look at all of the interventions the school may be carrying out for any of its gap students and consider the following questions:

1. Is there a clear and measurable baseline assessment or entry criteria?
2. Is there an exit criteria, which mirrors the entry criteria, to measure against no more than six weeks later?
3. Are any significant details being measured in each session if necessary?
4. If the interventions are not going well, are they reviewed not just for their capacity to meet the specific needs of the students but also for how they are set up, staffed and managed?
5. How can senior leaders or external stakeholders such as governors find out what interventions the school offers and how well they do?

Spending and accounting

Logically, this is the point at which you would consider how the school manages the finances, although it would be a rare thing to find a school that doesn't mention it in the first half an hour of the day. Schools are obsessed with this issue for fear that the public accounting of their spending will expose their vulnerabilities and demonstrate more to the world about their mismanagement rather than accurate and proper planning. I find myself needing to reassure schools that financial accountability is peculiar to England and is only there to make sure schools are not spending their additional allocation on fixing the roof instead of supporting vulnerable students – although you perhaps could argue Maslow's hierarchy of needs in this specific example. (This is a famous motivational theory in psychology, which states five tiers of human need. Basic needs like food and warmth come before psychological needs like achieving one's potential.)

I haven't yet met anyone who is both trained in advanced financial management and accounting and a specialist in pedagogic interventions. Such a bogeyman doesn't exist and no one is going to question why you spent £500 on this but £5,000 on that. Accounting only really becomes a problem when the school has spent significant quantities of money on staffing, and this issue has to be handled carefully. Additional allocation is not meant to be spent on staffing, but there are ways of articulating anything – especially if it makes sense for the school.

One school had a shortage of maths teachers in the local area because they were in a fairly remote part of the country. They used some top-up money to attract a very experienced head of maths who ended up leading their department to attainment victory. This is sensible staffing, which can be easily justified to stakeholders. It is also measurable – not necessarily in the short term or in hard data, but there are ample soft data results you can draw on to show value for money.

Look at the written details that already exist about:

- How the school is spending additional funds to meet the needs of the gap.
- What evidence there is to demonstrate that this works. What rationalisation exists to promote the value of the intervention?

Table 8.1 is a useful tracker for schools because it helps reorient their thinking from 'action and cost' to 'identified need and impact'.

It is important to reiterate to schools that it would be irregular if every single action they took resulted in a high impact immediately. Assume that real impact can emerge over the course of at least a year (as long as the interventions are being scrutinised along the way to make sure they are on target) and that every school will try things that they thought would make sense but didn't work out how they had planned – isn't this the same for all organisations of every sort?

Table 8.1: Interventions tracker focusing on identified needs and impact

Identified issue	Action	Cost (£)	Expected impact	Real impact

Report writing

I am not a fan of extensive reports with long phrases and opinions. I don't know who is. It is a tradition though that visiting experts will leave behind an extensive essay about the school. I don't buy in to this. If it is not useful or saying anything the school doesn't already know, it is a waste of space and paper. I favour a co-authoring approach where a representative from the school and I both write a report together. I usually stick with the same format for each school unless they request otherwise. The features include:

1. A brief summary of key priority findings, for example:
   - DM (senior leader I had worked with) has gathered all the right data and is asking all the right questions. The next steps are to take the detail up a level of sophistication and ensure there is effective advice to teachers and a plan per student that is being reviewed twice per half term.
   - 'Hard data rich'; need to harness soft data.
   - SEN is not coordinated with pupil premium and appears to be ineffective for SEN K students (students with SEN concerns who may gain some support in schools but who remain below the need for a formal EHCP). This needs to be brought under one person at SLT and an external SEN Review should happen ASAP.
   - Self-evaluation of key contributing factors to narrowing the gap:

Aspiration	7/10
Home engagement	5/10
Differentiation	4/10
SEN	5/10
Feeder schools	4/10
Stakeholders	6/10

   - Easy wins: regularly call home with positive news; identify and speak with individuals where the gap is present and work out how to overcome specific barriers and use bespoke motivators.
   - The long-term plan has to be to engage the feeder schools in narrowing the gap from EYFS and Key Stage 1, work together to rethink the transition and unify identification and information management systems (e.g. same provision map, advice to teachers and 360 etc.)
2. A table such as Table 8.2 (see page 194), which clearly articulates what the issue is, what needs to be done, who will do this and when, what success looks like and (where appropriate) what the follow up will be.
3. A group of template resources and tables like those found throughout this book so the school is fully prepared to start populating them.
4. With some schools, it is also necessary to give a shorter-term view, which can be titled accordingly (e.g. 'the next two months'), with a very detailed account of the key actions to be taken each week. This is usually for a school where the senior leader or another staff member will potentially be unable to deliver the plan, and this will be a help to either them or their line manager, who will use it as evidence for their lack of action.

5. Whatever you write, make sure that it is understood or articulated in a language that the school will understand. Check every point and ask if the relevant staff would like to rephrase anything in a different way.
6. Bear in mind that implementation is key. Who cares about your plan if the school isn't going to implement it? Your reputation as a consultant or helper will be diminished if you go into the school, do all this work and nothing happens as a result. So be mindful of the implementation, especially in the write-up stage. Ask yourself if they are really going to be able to do this. How do you know or, more importantly, how will they know?

Table 8.2 is an example template report. It won't make sense for every school and needs to be tailored, but the construction can be useful for schools when they think about the identified issue and what the impact of a specific action could be.

Tables 8.3 and 8.4 demonstrate how an example school adapted the above plan to best fit their setting. Notice the split between a short- and long-term plan. The implementation plan is detailed with names and dates. The longer-term plan, conversely, outlines broad, gap-contributing issues the school wants to work on over an extended period of time.

The challenge when conducting a pupil premium review

Michael Purches, who (as I mentioned in Chapter 6) heads up the Inclusion Expert team in the north of England, says the following to potential new attainment gap consultants, and it is equally applicable to all school leaders attempting to review the attainment gap:

'The key challenge when carrying out a pupil premium review of a school is to cut through the complexity of the school's organisation to identify the important and underlying issues.'

A pupil premium review has to get under the skin of the whole school and it can be likened to lifting the bonnet of a car. If one merely looks at the attainment gap and the list of things that the school is spending its funding on, no one benefits. Reviews should do far more than that.

As a reviewer, it is important to be mindful of the bigger picture and have a number of key indicators to guide the conversations and inform questions:

- How well does the school know its pupils, their families and the wider community? Are approaches to narrowing the gap genuinely matched to the needs, interests and aspirations of the pupils?
- What is happening in the classrooms? Are lessons appropriately differentiated within the context of quality-first teaching? Do teachers take responsibility for all vulnerable pupils including those with SEN?

Table 8.2: Exemplar report

Identified issue	Action	Who?	When?	What does success look like?	Follow-up
Pre- and over-learning across the school.	Focus on strengths of key teachers and utilise these to support and develop weaker staff. Identified through gaps in hard data, learning walks, observations, stakeholder feedback (soft data). All students where progress gap is evident. Pre-learning – understanding of vocab for forthcoming learning. Teachers to encourage and target/motivate student in class. Over-learning – revisit vocab of pre-learning.			Better deployment of support staff. Students better prepared for learning. Promotes independent learning. Quality-first teaching improves. Measure through soft data from expert (SENCO) and feedback from teachers. Evidence in learning schemes. 360 degree feedback.	Support every 2 weeks after first implementation and review every 6 weeks.
A. Implement provision map. B. Create more detailed overview of pupil premium expenditure: how much does each intervention cost per pupil?	Appoint admin role to oversee implementation. Trial throughout summer term with one or two year groups. Have specific costings per pupil for each intervention to help create costed provision maps for each pupil.			Breakdown of costs per pupil so as to have clearer understanding of where and how pupil premium funding is being used.	Review interventions every 6 weeks against whole-school progress data.
Aspiration development – look at ways to develop higher aspirations in pupil premium pupils: whole-school, prior school, broader than school, community-owned, pervasive, persistent, insistent.	Look for every opportunity within the curriculum to develop inspiration and build aspiration. Start immediately in year 7.			List of ideas for discussion. More in-depth understanding of issues and how to tackle them.	Include aspiration talks when meeting with pupil premium pupils.
Clearly identify pupil premium budget and spend.	Identify need/action/impact in a tracker. (See page 191 for an example.)			Expenditure compared to impact.	Annual feedback to all staff on impact.

1 pager	(See page 145 for an example.)				
Establish clear teacher accountability if they do not implement the advice to teachers.					
Upskill staff with language and communication issues.					
Re-establish the TA role.	Commission a TA audit.				
Every teacher coaches Take 2 students.				Identification of barriers to learning: • motivation • punctuality/ attendance • engagement in learning • aspirations • progress.	
Build governors' confidence around pupil premium e.g. write a guide for pupil premium – put an outline of this on website for them and other stakeholders to read.	Governors to read the guide. Arrange for pupil premium review and plan to be discussed at next governors' meeting. Prep governors with Ofsted prep questions.			All governors have read guide and are aware of responsibilities. Pupil premium is an item on next governors' meeting agenda. Governors fully briefed and able to answer Ofsted questions: - What are the issues? - What are you doing about them? - What is the impact?	EDITED minutes of governors' meeting on website, demonstrating active involvement of governors. Governors' next steps that arose from meeting.
Use the website to promote the unique setting of the school and how you engage with the community.	Representatives of governors, parents, police, religious leaders, primary feeder schools, MP, social services, early intervention team, GP, EWO, etc. engage with the school to develop a robust system that enables pupil premium students to engage with their learning. Discuss barriers to individualising.			List of ideas for discussion. More in-depth understanding of issues and how to tackle them. Improved local understanding of the pupils, the unique context of the school and how they can support the learning of the children.	Discuss at SLT for implementation. Evidence of stakeholder involvement on website.

Use the overview of the characteristics of pupil premium – are there any overlapping features? What do our pupil premium pupils look like?	Review data and identify groups and individuals to speak to about their individual barriers to learning.			Anonymise summary table on website – use to help contextualise school. Raise awareness of all staff and ensure they have an understanding that everybody is on the journey.	Update accordingly (at least September for new cohort). Part of all hard/soft data produced. All staff to understand and address the needs of all their pupils.
Understand the barriers to learning for pupil premium pupils and put in place support to help overcome these issues.	Meetings with pupil premium pupils and profiles created that can be shared with teaching staff.			Pupil premium profiles outlining aspirations, barriers to learning and ways forward. Put snippets and quotes on website = pupil voice.	Regular review to check barriers and make adjustments to support and interventions.
	Looking at both the hard and soft data.			Highly targeted plan, which is hard- and soft-data-based and engages all school community.	Review plan and take action accordingly – end of summer term.
	Analysis and discussion of findings with all staff.				
	Robust action based on data.				
Evidence meetings with pupil premium pupils to better understand what would help improve their attendance, punctuality and overall engagement.	Meeting and notes to show ideas as to what would make a difference for these pupils.			School using a range of incentives that have a positive impact on attendance, punctuality and engagement.	Annual review to update relevance. Anonymised feedback on website.
	Put on website.			Celebrating the focus on key welfare issues and that you are aware of them and doing something about them.	Review strategies end of first year.
Produce case studies from a range of vulnerability e.g. pupil premium, attendance & welfare, SEN.	Ensure soft data supports the time, spend, outcomes (whether successful or not)		Termly	6 case studies from each area of inclusion show support and impact. One-pager.	Termly review.
Be able to readily access pupil premium information that is concise and relevant that you can use to make a difference.	Collate all pupil premium information into one file. Print out website page.			File in place. All staff familiar with contents.	Updated termly.

Create a whole-school overview of the interventions.				Publish on website.	Update annually.
				Interventions report every term.	6-week view.
Every intervention has entry/exit criteria and measure of impact. Compare intervention list to the needs of the actual pupil cohort.	Include both soft data and hard data impact criteria. Match intervention list to pupil needs, add interventions that target actual need.			Interventions listed with expected outcomes for each intervention. Impact can be RAG rated to show whether intervention had desired effect.	Update annually.
Personalise learning: ensure differentiation and in-class strategies are outstanding.	Connect to SEN review. Regular and ongoing CPD for all staff on meeting needs in the classroom.			Reflective and outstanding practice around the school that enables pupils to achieve the outcomes you know they are capable of.	Continue to ask questions: 1. What impact am I having? 2. What learning is happening because of me? 3. Am I making a difference? 4. Do the pupils really need me here? 5. What happens if I'm not here? 6. Am I promoting independence? 7. Am I using my initiative? 8. Am I flexible in approach? 9. What do I need for my CPD?
Continue to update website – make it work for you.	1. Nature of community 2. Governors' meetings 3. Stakeholders' views 4. Successes so far 5. Aspirations across every aspect of the school 6. Current data including breakdown of types of pupil premium pupil.				
Restructure inclusion: SENCO class facing	Prioritise: • improving teaching and learning • SEN learning walks • feedback.				

Table 8.3: Exemplar short-term plan

September-ready actions	Implement when?	Planning notes: who/how/what support you need? How to measure impact?
Provision map		
Advice to teachers		
Support for teachers in meeting the advice		
Regular pop-ins to classes to ensure advice is being delivered		
Professional standards and accountability for not delivering advice		
'One-pager' for all key students		
Clear measures of impact on the one-pagers – happening every other week		
360 for all key students		
Differentiation coaching, standards and support process		
Website ready		
Regular home visits by all staff		
Regular calls home about positive news		
Behavioural issues initially looked at from a teaching and learning perspective		
Most challenging students need outside support prior to permanent exclusion – a day of 5 student reviews, planning and training		
Preparing teachers for managing more complex behaviour – trial the video library as a starting point; can also use the provision map as a method of communicating outstanding practices		
Identify 50 students to focus on		

September-ready actions	Implement when?	Planning notes: who/how/what support you need? How to measure impact?
For each of the 50 students, identify and plan: - motivation (reward) - support to overcome barriers - advice to teachers - one-pager - 360 - regular contact home with praise for attainment - 15 teacher-coaches who should visit the students' homes and meet with the students every other day around SMART targets - regular support for teachers in personalising for them - scrutinising progress every other week - scrutinising classroom engagement through pop-ins every few days - pre-empting problems with classroom engagement (such as moving classes, seating, addressing barriers to learning, etc.) - swift intervention when problems arise with teachers		

Table 8.4: Exemplar long-term plan

Plan	When?	Detail
Work with the key pupil premium feeder schools to narrow the attainment gap		
Develop an ethos of classroom teacher responsibility for all SEN and pupil premium progress		
Develop detailed and meaningful 3–18 plans for vulnerable students		
Develop an approach to outstanding SEN, looked after children, pupil premium and vulnerable students across the local education authority		
Etc.		

- Is the school identifying pupil needs properly and making sure that interventions are the right ones? Are they tracked so that the school can make value for money judgements?
- How does the school demonstrate impact and how do they share the information with all stakeholders?

In many ways, pupil premium reviews show how effective the leadership and management of the school is. However, it is important to ask yourself whether there is clarity about the issues the school has identified, what they did about them and the impact this had. This sounds simple but too often this clarity isn't there. In the better schools:

- There is a senior leader in the school who has responsibility for all things to do with vulnerable pupils and inclusion. This avoids the 'silo' effect and makes sure that coherent and consistent approaches are in place.
- Governors have a clear understanding of the issues and can articulate what the school is doing for disadvantaged pupils and how effective it is.
- There is high engagement of parents and families and they too can articulate what is working for their child.
- For secondary schools, there is early work with their feeder primaries in order to narrow the gap. This is about catching things early and developing approaches to address barriers to learning. Some secondary schools inherit a gap so why not try to do something about it early?
- There is a lot of work with pupils and their families to develop their aspirations and raise expectations about furthering their education and removing glass ceilings with regard to careers.
- School systems allow needs to be easily identified, interventions to be tracked and expenditure monitored closely to ensure accountability and make sure everyone is accepting of their responsibilities.

There is a quote that says 'one of the measures of a civilised society is how well it looks after the most vulnerable members of its society.' Similarly, pupil premium reviews should view a school by how well it looks after its most vulnerable pupils.

Conclusion

One final case study

The number of schools that have not been able to make even a dent in their attainment gap since the inception of the pupil premium funding is quite staggering. But I have also seen success in a myriad of forms. In this concluding case study, I aim to capture what I believe to be a winning formula for narrowing the gap in a school that could be applied in most settings.

I have chosen one particular case study of a primary school where we followed that formula to the letter and within six months we had halved the attainment gap. We then went on to apply these approaches in a number of schools in the local area with significant success. Here, with the kind permission of the school in question, is that story:

Sarah Conant, executive headteacher of the Diocese of Ely Multi-Academy Trust, stepped in to temporarily take over a primary school that had been left with a serious attainment gap for one year. Sarah is an inspirational headteacher willing to take on challenging schools.

She explained, 'We had received a letter from the Department for Education highlighting the key issues. They wanted us to act quickly: financial spending was not specified well enough, monitoring of pupil premium spending was ad hoc, interventions were not assessed for impact, and governors didn't understand the importance of the pupil premium and the targeted funding required. No one had looked at the attainment gap cohorts to look at their real needs. In addition, the school was faced with a brand new senior leadership, issues with teaching, and data that was very much in the red.'

I've structured Sarah's responses to these issues as five key takeaways.

Lesson 1: the gap can be narrowed even from a difficult starting point

Sarah commissioned an attainment gap review, which concurred with her concerns. Sarah wanted the review to identify barriers to progress and articulate the steps needed to close the gap. Although the review was carried out in one day, half of it was spent co-authoring a very detailed and robust implementation plan, which mapped out:

- areas for development
- what success will look like

- specific action points matched against each success criterion
- an identification of who would implement them and by when
- next steps.

The implementation plan stretched to 30-plus points and covered everything from how the school liaises with parents to governance, assessment and interventions, hard and soft data capture, and even liaison with other schools and outside agencies.

The gap doesn't exist in just one area of a school's work; it is a broad socio-economic phenomenon and schools need to sharpen every faculty across a broad range of understanding and skills. But – it can be done from even the toughest of starting points.

Lesson 2: a review and action plan is only as successful as it is specific, relevant and authored by the school

A common assumption that schools make is: 'Let's bring in an external consultant who does pupil premium reviews regularly and let them fix the issue for us.'

However, the situation isn't as simple as bringing in a plumber to mend a pipe; narrowing the gap is a whole-school issue and must be owned by the school. The best ideas will be generated from within, and what works in one school in one region won't necessarily help in another.

The reasons why reviews fail are a lack of breadth, a lack of depth and an insufficient understanding of the specific local setting. Of course, expertise is needed – but it must facilitate the involvement of staff and the incorporation of their own expertise.

In the case of the work in Ely, key challenges included gaining a greater understanding of issues and building relationships. Urgent concerns for the school included:

- The need for nuanced identification of student needs, including soft data factors such as preparedness for learning, engagement and confidence.
- The need to reach out to families and ensure staff know the families, inspire community aspiration and manage expectations.
- The need to tackle a significant mobility issue with a high percentage of mid-phase entry.
- Lack of teacher training in personalised learning and differentiation.
- The need for a SEND (special educational needs and disability) review and focus.

The identified barriers to progress were both typical of many schools and at the same time very specific to this particular setting in their subtlety.

Lesson 3: an environment that fosters parental engagement and promotes aspiration

After the review, when the issues had been explored, Sarah reflected, 'I think it's about trying to understand where the parents are coming from both literally and in their thought processes. You need to target them as much as their children.'

Getting to know the families of students can make a significant difference in narrowing the gap. Not only can a school in this way gain a closer understanding of the major social and economic factors at work in the community, but by bringing parents 'on side', you will also have a greater impact than hiring a few more TAs ever could. The school took swift action across a range of areas. Key among these was the importance of a nuanced identification of student needs, including soft data factors. To achieve this, the school's strategy included a free breakfast club, which doubled as a help and support club, including homework and reading, with teachers present.

Also, they developed a whole-school focus on oracy to boost student confidence, including poetry reading, and an emphasis on performance and performing all kinds of reading. As explained above, reaching out and ensuring the staff knew the families, inspired community aspiration and managed expectations was vital. Some of the actions included:

- Significantly increasing knowledge of families.
- Building community aspiration and offering opportunities for informality, openness, expressing 'you are welcome', 'you belong', etc.
- Emphasising cross-curricular support of students through music and other activities – don't just focus on spelling, punctuation and grammar, and numeracy.
- Inspiring parents through publicised good news stories, such as stories in the local press noting achievements in art and sport.
- Putting up an 'Aspirations Board' in the foyer.
- Inviting parents for coffee and cake at numeracy and literacy participation events – parents aren't invited to a 'talk', but to a combination of activities, food and socialising.
- Making family engagement the focal point of key school events, such as a picnic at sports day.
- Increasing formal forums for parental voice.

After a few weeks of concerted efforts, particularly aimed at hard-to-reach parents, the parents started engaging in a different way towards the school; parents could choose their own pace of increased engagement and how they wanted to get involved. This eventually grew into a fresh interest in their child's education and other opportunities the school could offer.

Lesson 4: successful implementation of a pupil premium plan goes hand-in-hand with management of staff

You cannot separate out the pupil premium plan from staff management. Implementation of a new plan will involve a process of evolution for staff, not just at the beginning stages but throughout the whole journey.

All heads have to find their particular balance between playing the encourager and yielding a stick with their staff. Certainly in Sarah's school, she found that the staff responded well to understanding clearly what the real issues were and what the plan entailed.

A fleeting meeting with a short summary of the plan in a few points would have been inadequate – instead there was a strong emphasis on clear communication, high expectations set for all staff, and clear consequences for not getting on board.

Sarah recalled, 'Initially, there was simply a lack of clarity on what the attainment gap meant from the majority of staff. Staff came to realise that it is a constant evaluation and re-evaluation of what their students need. Emphasising soft data gave them a much better insight into these children's lives.

'For example, focusing on getting students in early rather than on absence has improved their interaction with school. Additional training for staff reinforced the need to be specific about support and impact, and provided the skills to meet the needs in the classroom.'

The lack of teacher training in personalised learning and differentiation, as well as TA training, was a key barrier to narrowing the gap. Wendy Knott, an expert in differentiation training, worked with staff in Ely in small groups of four, over four one-day sessions. The end result was a shift in thinking and action of the staff.

Assume that your teachers and TAs are nowhere near where they could be in their ability to personalise learning and adapt the curriculum to really drive student engagement. Also assume that student engagement in the curriculum is the responsibility of the classroom teacher, once you have provided sufficient training for them.

Lesson 5: know your students

It is an obvious statement to make, but the obvious is the thing that schools often miss. It is a brave school that invests the time to dig deep into the real issues. Both Sarah Conant and Nathan Atkinson (whose school I mentioned in Chapter 2, page 33) agree that headteachers need to feel that they have permission to address the real issues that get in the way of student engagement and preparedness for learning.

It can be counter-intuitive to think you can improve outcomes in ways that seemingly have nothing to do with the curriculum. However, I have seen in multiple schools that creative answers to challenges in academic performance are often more powerful than traditional interventions such as extra tuition.

Your staff may not have the full picture of a student's needs – does a particular student require additional maths or language acquisition support, or just a stronger relationship with their maths teacher?

Staff need to have the means to capture what is really going on with their pupils. This process must then lead to a discussion about how to best meet those needs.

Sarah also commissioned an in-depth SEND review, which provided a similar level of breadth and depth to the pupil premium review. The overlaps between these two cohorts are clear nationally and very often – but not always – in individual schools. The provisions for SEND students required careful unpicking to ensure maximum impact from minimum input.

Conclusion: two students, two paths, your path

Let me end by reflecting back to where we began – imagining our two students, identical twins, who are separated at birth and adopted into different homes. The first child, Jane, is adopted into an average middle-class family. She grows up in financial and personal stability. I hope you now see the lack of the most useful detail in my description. I hope you think back to this opening and say, 'Wait a minute, but what of her aspirations, motivators, barriers? What of her narrative and what soft data can we glean to inform how to make her learning journey equally bespoke to her?'

We imagined the second child, Samantha, is adopted into a slightly lower-income family that rapidly runs into difficulties. Her adoptive father loses his job, her parents divorce and matters are made worse when her mother's drinking becomes problematic and a series of abusive boyfriends appear on the scene. Samantha begins to use drugs at a relatively young age and comes to the attention of social services. Eventually her situation becomes so bad that she is taken into care. I hope you now think about key factors such as early identification and reaching out to parents to support them as part of the community-facing school approach. I hope, after having read this book, you think ten steps ahead with Samantha and consider early intervention before things spiral out of control.

There are a myriad of things to now go off and 'do'. The biggest of all, however, lies in the attitude shifts, in seeing young people as people rather than student data on a page, in reinventing your own aspirations for these students and believing in them – because there is no way they can do it without you. This is less about doing and more about understanding.

With that last paragraph in mind, I believe the attainment gap is not a mystery or too complicated and is not as stubborn as everyone makes out. It is largely a matter of seeing it differently. I hope in this book I have given school leaders a way of accessing that new perspective.

Glossary

CATs: The Cognitive Abilities Test is an assessment of various reasoning skills. It is designed to offer a standardised measure of cognitive ability, testing students beyond the restraints of their first language or previous curriculum-based learning.

Child and Adolescent Mental Health Service (CAMHS): The UK National Health Service services for children and young people with behavioural, emotional and mental health difficulties.

Comprehensive schools: Publicly funded UK secondary schools (i.e. for students aged 11–18) that do not select students on the basis of ability.

Early years foundation stage (EYFS): The standards for the learning and care of children in the UK from birth to the age of five.

Education, Health and Care Plan (EHCP): A document, created collaboratively with schools, the local authority and medical and other relevant services, that sets out the education, health and social care needs of a child or young person and how they will be met.

Free school meals (FSM): Students in England or Wales are entitled to free school meals if they or their parents or guardians meet one of a number of criteria implying economic disadvantage (such as state welfare payments). The free meals are only given if parents sign up for them. The **pupil premium** grant is automatically awarded to students who qualify for free school meals.

GCSEs: The General Certificate of Secondary Education is a UK subject-specific qualification. Students usually sit GCSE exams for six to 12 subjects at around the age of 16.

Gifted and talented: Students who have the potential to develop significantly beyond what would typically be expected for children of their age.

Grammar schools: Publicly funded UK secondary schools that select students on the basis of an exam taken at age 11.

Higher level teaching assistants (HLTAs): Teaching assistants with additional qualifications that allow them to teach classes independently, cover planned teacher absences and take on other additional responsibilities.

Income Deprivation Affecting Children Index (IDACI): An index of deprivation used in the UK, measuring the proportion of children under the age of 16 in a given area living in households defined as low income.

Index of Multiple Deprivation: A study of deprived areas in English local councils, covering seven areas of deprivation:

- income
- employment
- health deprivation and disability
- education skills and training

- barriers to housing and services
- crime
- living environment.

Key stages: In England, Wales and Northern Ireland, the curriculum is divided into four fixed stages. Students are required to sit standardised tests at the end of each stage.

Looked after children (LAC): A child is 'looked after' if they are in the care of a local authority, rather than parents or guardians, for more than 24 hours.

Multi-academy trusts (MATs): A top-level organisational entity that coordinates collaboration and standards of teaching and governance for a number of schools, typically all located in the same area.

Ofsted: The Office for Standards in Education, Children's Services and Skills is a UK government department responsible for inspecting educational institutions in the country, including all public and some private schools, childcare, adoption and fostering agencies.

Programme for International Student Assessment (PISA): A worldwide study by the OECD of the performance of 15-year-old school pupils in maths, science and reading. It was first carried out in 2000 and has been repeated every three years since.

Pupil premium: An additional per-eligible-pupil grant for publicly funded schools in England, designed to raise the attainment of disadvantaged pupils. Schools can spend the funding however they wish, but must demonstrate that it is helping the students it is intended to serve.

RAISEonline: Reporting and Analysis for Improvement through school Self-Evaluation, or RAISEonline, is an online database that provides core hard data on a school-by-school basis. It was replaced by Analyse School Performance (ASP) in 2017.

SENCO: The special educational needs coordinator is a member of staff responsible for managing a school's programme of support for its **SEN** cohort.

SEND Code of Practice: A UK Government code of practice for providers of education and support. In force since September 2014, it sets out guidance on the support of individuals with special educational needs and disabilities from birth until they leave education.

Special educational needs (SEN): Specific learning problems or disabilities that make it harder for a child to learn than a typical child of the same age without SEN.

Teachers' Standards: The minimum level of practice for trainees and teachers to obtain qualified teacher status in the UK.

Teaching school alliance: A group of schools and other partners allied around a 'teaching school', which will typically have been given a high rating on inspection. The teaching school provides support and training to the other schools in the alliance.

Virtual Heads: An individual in charge of a **Virtual School**. All local authorities in England are required to have a Virtual School Head.

Virtual Schools: An additional resource run by local councils to support everyone involved in the education of **looked after children**. It offers additional resources and initiatives but does not replace mainstream provision.

References

Alexander, K. L., Entwisle, D. R. and Olson, L. S. (2007), 'Lasting consequences of the summer learning gap', *American Sociological Review*, 72, (2), 167–180.

Allingham, S. (2015), *Transitions in the Early Years: A practical guide to supporting children between early years settings and into Key Stage 1*. London: Practical Pre-School Books.

Araujo, M. C., Carneiro, P., Cruz-Aguayo, Y. and Schady, N. (2016), 'Teacher quality and learning outcomes in kindergarten', *The Quarterly Journal of Economics*, 131, (3), 1415–1453.

Bercow, J. (2008), 'The Bercow Report: a review of services for children and young people (0–19) with speech, language and communication needs', https://webarchive.nationalarchives.gov.uk/20130321005340/http://www.education.gov.uk/publications/standard/publicationdetail/page1/DCSF-00632-2008

Bobbitt, P. (2008), *Terror and Consent: The Wars for the Twenty-first Century*. New York, NY: A. A. Knopf.

Cesarini, D., Lindqvist, E., Ostling, R. and Wallace, B. (2016), 'Wealth, health, and child development: evidence from administrative data on Swedish lottery players', *The Quarterly Journal of Economics*, 131, (2), 687–738.

Chamberlain, G. E. (2013), 'Predictive effects of teachers and schools on test scores, college attendance, and earnings', *PNAS*, 110, (43), 17176–17182.

Dee, T. S. (2004), 'Teachers, race, and student achievement in a randomized experiment', *Review of Economics and Statistics*, 86, (1), 195–210.

De Fraja, G., Oliveira, T. and Zanchi, L. (2010), 'Must try harder: evaluating the role of effort in educational attainment', *The Review of Economics and Statistics*, 92, (3), 577–597.

Department for Children, Schools and Families (2009), 'Deprivation and education: the evidence on pupils in England Foundation Stage to Key Stage 4', http://dera.ioe.ac.uk/9431/1/DCSF-RTP-09-01.pdf

Department for Education (2011), 'A profile of pupil absence in England', https://www.gov.uk/government/uploads/system/uploads/attachment_data/file/183445/DFE-RR171.pdf

Department for Education (2014a), 'Statistical first release outcomes for children looked after by local authorities in England as at 31 March 2014', https://www.gov.uk/government/uploads/system/uploads/attachment_data/file/384781/Outcomes_SFR49_2014_Text.pdf

Department for Education (2014b), 'What maintained schools must publish online', https://www.gov.uk/guidance/what-maintained-schools-must-publish-online

Department for Education (2015), 'Statistical first release GCSE and equivalent attainment by pupil characteristics, 2013 to 2014 (Revised)', https://www.gov.uk/government/uploads/system/uploads/attachment_data/file/399005/SFR06_2015_Text.pdf

Department for Education (2016a), 'Children looked after in England (including adoption) year ending 31 March 2016', https://www.gov.uk/government/uploads/system/uploads/attachment_data/file/556331/SFR41_2016_Text.pdf

Department for Education (2016b), 'Outcomes for children looked after by local authorities in England, 31 March 2015', https://www.gov.uk/government/statistics/outcomes-for-children-looked-after-by-las-31-march-2015

Department for Education (2017a), 'Outcomes for children looked after by local authorities in England, 31 March 2016', https://www.gov.uk/government/uploads/system/uploads/attachment_data/file/602087/SFR12_2017_Text.pdf

Department for Education (2017b), 'Statutory framework for the early years foundation stage', https://www.foundationyears.org.uk/files/2017/03/EYFS_STATUTORY_FRAMEWORK_2017.pdf

Freeman, A. (2013), *Help Me Understand ADHD*. Self-published.

Hallam, S. and Parsons, S. (2013), 'Prevalence of streaming in UK primary schools: evidence from the millennium cohort study', *British Educational Research Journal*, 39, (3), 514–544.

Hart, B. and Risley, T. R. (1995), *Meaningful Differences in the Everyday Experience of Young American Children*. Baltimore, MD: Brookes Publishing.

Hoxby, C. M. (2000), 'Peer effects in the classroom: learning from gender and race variation', *NBER Working Paper*, (7867), 64, www.nber.org/papers/w7867

Jensen, A. R. (1980), *Bias in Mental Testing*. New York, NY: Free.

Jerrim, J. (2016), 'The 10 key findings from PISA 2015', *Education Datalab*, https://educationdatalab.org.uk/2016/12/the-10-key-findings-from-pisa-2015/

Jerrim, J. and Shure, M. (2016), 'Achievement of 15-year-olds in England: PISA 2015 national report', Department for Education, http://dera.ioe.ac.uk/27761/1/PISA-2015_England_Report.pdf

Johnson, W., Deary, I. J. and Carothers, A. (2008), 'Sex differences in variability in general intelligence: a new look at the old question', *Perspectives on Psychological Science*, 3, (6), 518–531.

Kirby, P. (2016), 'Shadow schooling: private tuition and social mobility in the UK', *The Sutton Trust*, www.suttontrust.com/wp-content/uploads/2016/09/Shadow-Schooling-formatted-report_FINAL.pdf

Lamb, B. (2009), 'Lamb inquiry: special educational needs and parental confidence', http://dera.ioe.ac.uk/9042/1/Lamb%20Inquiry%20Review%20of%20SEN%20and%20Disability%20Information.pdf

Mcinerney, L. (2016), 'Ofsted's focus on white pupils hides ethnic minority under-achievement', *Schools Week*, http://schoolsweek.co.uk/focus-on-white-pupils-hides-ethnic-minority-under-achievement/

NAHT (2016), 'NAHT 2016 recruitment survey results released', www.naht.org.uk/welcome/news-and-media/key-topics/pay-and-conditions/naht-2016-recruitment-survey-results-released/

National College for School Leadership (2011), 'System leadership: does school-to-school support close the gap?', http://dera.ioe.ac.uk/13217/

Noftle, E. E. and Robins, R. W. (2007), 'Personality predictors of academic outcomes: big five correlates of GPA and SAT scores', *Journal of Personality and Social Psychology*, 93, (1), 116–130.

Ofsted (2015), 'Early years', https://www.gov.uk/government/publications/ofsted-early-years-report-2015

Ofsted (2016), 'School inspection handbook', https://www.gov.uk/government/uploads/system/uploads/attachment_data/file/553942/School_inspection_handbook-section_5.pdf

O'Higgins, A., Sebba, J. and Luke, N. (2015), 'What is the relationship between being in care and the educational outcomes of children? An international systematic review', *Rees Centre*

Research in Fostering and Education, University of Oxford, http://reescentre.education.ox.ac.uk/wordpress/wp-content/uploads/2015/09/ReesCentreReview_EducationalOutcomes.pdf

Rijsdijk, F. V., Vernon, P. A. and Boomsma, D. I. (2002), 'Application of hierarchical genetic models to raven and WAIS subtests: a Dutch twin study, *Behavior Genetics*, 32, 199–210.

Rose, J. (2006), 'Independent review of the teaching of early reading', http://webarchive.nationalarchives.gov.uk/20100603160056/http://www.standards.dcsf.gov.uk/phonics/rosereview/

SecEd (2013), 'Guide to: Ofsted and the pupil premium', http://www.sec-ed.co.uk/best-practice/guide-to-ofsted-and-the-pupil-premium/

Shakeshaft, N. G., Trzaskowski, M., McMillan, A., Rimfeld, K., Krapohl, E., Haworth, C. M. A., Dale, P. S. and Plomin, R. (2013), 'Strong genetic influence on a UK nationwide test of educational achievement at the end of compulsory education at age 16', *PLoS ONE*, 8, (12), https://doi.org/10.1371/journal.pone.0080341

Shelter (2006), 'Chance of a lifetime: the impact of bad housing on children's lives', https://england.shelter.org.uk/__data/assets/pdf_file/0007/66364/Lifechancereport.pdf

Stevens, J. (2013), 'Army of teaching assistants faces the axe as Education department attempts to save some of the £4billion they cost each year', *Daily Mail*, www.dailymail.co.uk/news/article-2334853/Army-teaching-assistants-faces-axe-Education-department-attempts-save-4billion-cost-year.html

Strand, S. (2015), 'Ethnicity, deprivation and educational achievement at age 16 in England: trends over time', Department for Education, https://www.researchgate.net/publication/288787221_Strand_S_2015_Ethnicity_deprivation_and_educational_achievement_at_age_16_in_England_Trends_over_time_DFE_Research_Report_439B_London_Department_for_Education

Sutton Trust (2010), 'Poorer children twice as likely to start school with behaviour problems', https://www.suttontrust.com/newsarchive/poorer-children-twice-likely-start-school-behaviour-problems/

Tobin, L. (1991), *What Do You Do with a Child Like This?* Duluth, MN: Whole Person Associates.

UCAS (2014), 'Looked after children and care leavers: raising aspirations to higher education', https://www.ucas.com/file/4996/download?token=YI9B1Wwh

Index

Page numbers referring to figures and tables are given in *italics*.